THE EARLY GROWTH OF THE EUROPEAN ECONOMY

WORLD ECONOMIC HISTORY
GENERAL EDITOR CHARLES WILSON

THE RISE OF THE ATLANTIC ECONOMIES
Ralph Davis

ECONOMICS AND EMPIRE 1830–1914
D. K. Fieldhouse

INTRODUCTION TO THE SOURCES OF EUROPEAN
ECONOMIC HISTORY, 1500–1800
Charles Wilson and Geoffrey Parker, editors

The Early Growth of the European Economy

WARRIORS AND PEASANTS FROM THE SEVENTH TO THE TWELFTH CENTURY

GEORGES DUBY

TRANSLATED BY HOWARD B. CLARKE

CORNELL UNIVERSITY PRESS
ITHACA, NEW YORK

First published 1974 by Cornell University Press.
First printing, Cornell Paperbacks, 1978.

International Standard Book Number 0–8014–0814–8 (cloth)
International Standard Book Number 0–8014–9169–X (paperback)
Library of Congress Catalog Card Number 73–16955
Printed in the United States of America

Contents

Maps

Figures

Foreword

This remarkable study of the early Middle Ages needs no elaborate introduction. M. Duby is his own best expositor and the French edition of this book has already received, in France, the award of the Paul Valéry Prize. A few brief comments may nevertheless be in place.

Some readers accustomed to modern economic history written in quantitative, even econometric style, may be surprised to find few figures or statistics, and little overt theoretical argument. M. Duby says much about the importance of princely gifts, ecclesiastical magnificence, funeral hoards, propitiatory and sacrificial offerings – in fact, all the ostentatious luxury of the early Middle Ages which contrasts so sharply with the widespread poverty that beggars the imagination of our age – the pilgrimages, the famines, even the cannibalism, and the economics of continual war and plunder.

This would have surprised the early pioneers of economic history less than it may surprise some readers of our generation. Archdeacon Cunningham's *Growth of English Industry and Commerce* is replete with references to the work of contemporary anthropologists on India, China, Russia and other primitive societies. M. Duby has returned to a renewed, more refined and infinitely more sophisticated use of such methods. It has been a mark of some recent economic history that it has sometimes tried to impose contemporary models on historical situations to which they are in reality quite irrelevant. M. Duby eschews such methods.

For the period of M. Duby's book few figures or quantities are in any case available. But where he uses the techniques of the economist or the anthropologist, he remains true to his own craft – the craft of the historian who relates everything back to the people of his period. Their way of life, experiences, religion, feelings, needs, are as basic to an understanding of their economic behaviour as their economic behaviour is basic to an understanding of their way of life. Thus trade, or industry, or money, can only be understood as functions inseparable from war or politics or religion. In the Middle Ages, as in the Ancient World, economic institutions were rarely able to function independently. Only gradually, in the course of the six centuries described by M. Duby, did economic activities and functions free themselves and become superimposed upon the non-economic. This is a rich, complex and subtle study. The qualities already recognized in the country of its origin will not escape the readers of this translation.

C.W.

Preface

This book makes no claim to be a definitive economic history. It is simply an exploratory venture, a sequence of reflections upon a long course of development, the uncertain and complex progress of which I have tried to discern and elucidate. Inadequate source materials and the uneven pursuit of historical research explain the large part played by hypotheses in a compilation of this kind. But in putting them forward my prime concern has been to stimulate questions and comments, the most critical of which are also likely to be the most fruitful. What is certain on the other hand is that to cover a geographical area as vast and diverse as Europe then was, and over such a long period of time, it was better to base my observations on ground that felt firmest. To be specific, the history with which I am most familiar is that of the countryside, especially the French countryside. I mention this so that the reader may be less surprised at the particular examples, outlook, and omissions that he will find in this work.

Beaurecueil, September 1969

Part One
Foundations

(SEVENTH AND EIGHTH CENTURIES)

At the end of the sixth century Europe was a profoundly uncivilized place. The 'Europe' with which we shall be dealing in this book comprises the area where Latin Christianity gradually spread until the late twelfth century. With the settlement of the Lombards in Italy and the Basques' descent upon Aquitaine, the era of great folk migrations in the West had almost drawn to a close. But because of this barbarism, early medieval Europe has proved extremely baffling to historians. In regions where writing had been widely practised not so long before, its use was now being lost. Elsewhere it was making headway very slowly. The records that have come down to us are therefore extremely rare. The most informative sources are protohistoric, the kind yielded by archaeological research. Yet this documentary material is itself defective: physical remains of civilization are for the most part insecurely dated; they are moreover exposed to the risk of chance discovery, and their scattered, fragmentary distribution makes any general interpretation a hazardous business. Let us emphasize from the start the narrow confines of historical knowledge and the enormously wide field that has to be left open to conjecture. Further, economic historians are without doubt more deprived than any others. For them there is an almost total lack of figures, of quantitative information to permit calculations and measurements. In any attempt to investigate those symptoms of growth which gradually caused this exceedingly primitive culture to emerge from barbarism between the seventh and twelfth centuries, we must above all refrain from misapplying models based on the modern economy. It now appears that pioneers of medieval economic history were often drawn unwittingly into overestimating, for example, the importance of trade and money. The most essential and probably the most formidable task is to define what really were the foundations and driving forces of this primitive civilization's economy. As aids towards such a definition, reflections of contemporary economists seem less useful than observations by ethnologists on the underdeveloped societies of our own times.

Amid this widespread cultural depression, however, there were certainly variations. On her southern boundaries Latin Christendom was brought face to face with areas that were appreciably more advanced than herself. In regions dominated by Byzantium, and soon by Islam, there survived an economic system inherited from ancient Rome, with cities living off the surrounding countryside, everyday use of money, merchants, and workshops producing splendid objects for the rich. Europe was never separated by impassable frontiers from these zones of prosperity which constantly fascinated and influenced her. On the other hand, two kinds of cultural deficiency confronted one another within Europe herself. One can be identified with the Germano–Slav sphere, the 'barbarian world' (*barbaria*) as the Romans used to call it. This was youthful, immature, had increasing access to superior forms of civilization and was the scene of sustained growth. The other sphere, on the contrary, was one of decay. Here survivals of Roman colonization were reaching the final stages of delapidation. The various elements of a once complex and flourishing organization – coins, roads, centuriation, big country estates, towns – had not entirely disappeared. Some would one day prove capable of renewed life but, for the time being, they were fading away. Between these two faces, the one turned towards the north and east, the other towards the Mediterranean, sprawled an area along the shores of the English Channel, in the Paris basin, in Burgundy, Alamannia and Bavaria, where contacts between the youthful forces of barbarism and the remnants of Rome were made more actively than elsewhere. This was where encounters and interactions were taking place, many of them fruitful. It is important not to lose sight of this geographical diversity; it was fundamental and in large measure governed the early stages of European economic growth.

I Productive Forces

I THE NATURAL WORLD

Throughout the length of the period covered by this book the level of material civilization remained so low that the main point of economic life is to be found in the struggle that man had to wage against natural forces day by day in order to survive. The fight was arduous, for he wielded ineffectual weapons and the power of nature overawed him. The prime concern of the historian must be to measure this power and consequently to try to reconstruct the appearance of the natural environment. The task is not easy. It requires a minute inquiry conducted in the field, in search of vestiges of the ancient landscape which place- and field-names, the road system, property boundaries and vegetation pattern still preserve in the countryside. This inquiry is far from being completed; in many parts of Europe it has hardly yet begun. Because of this the picture remains blurred.

In western Europe the steppe pushes forward with an advanced post in Pannonia in the middle Danube basin. Possibly it intrudes even farther, here and there, as far as some of the loamy tablelands of the Paris basin. Nevertheless, it was forest growth that climatic conditions generally favoured. During the period with which we are concerned, the forest seems to have held sway over the whole natural landscape. At the beginning of the ninth century the landed possessions of the abbey of St Germain-des-Prés just outside Paris lay in a region where agricultural endeavour had probably made greater progress than anywhere else, yet woodland still covered two-fifths of the estate. Down to the end of the twelfth century the proximity of a vast forest reserve was reflected in all aspects of civilization. Its mark may be traced alike in the themes of courtly romance and in the forms invented by Gothic sculptors. For the people of those times the tree was the most striking manifestation of the plant world.

Two observations are called for. On the one hand soils are extremely varied in this part of the world. Their suitability often changes appreciably over very short distances. Peasant wisdom has always contrasted 'warm' with 'cold' lands; that is to say light, easily drained soils through which air circulates and which can be more readily worked, with heavy, sticky and impervious ones resisting the plough. On valley sides or plateau lands vast areas were available where the forest cover was less intractable and where man experienced less difficulty in modifying plant life to suit his dietary needs. In the seventh century the European forest seems to have been dotted with innumerable clearings. Some were recent and small, like those providing the first monks of St Bavon of Ghent with food. Others were more ample, as where fields and scrubland had intermingled for centuries on the loamy plateaux of Picardy. On the other hand it should be noted that round the edges of the Mediterranean summer drought, heavy rains, more pronounced variations in relief, and the forces of erosion tearing earth from the sides of valleys and piling up infertile deposits lower down, all made the forest vulnerable. It was at risk from fires lit by farmers and herdsmen, slow to recover and swift to decay, ultimately, into bush country. In these southern climes the struggle for subsistence production had to be waged less against trees than against water. The problem was to control the latter in order to protect soil on hillsides, drain marshes in flat country and make up for the excessive dryness of the summers by means of irrigation.

It is clear then that climatic variations had a decisive part to play. The degree of resistance offered by the great forests, the consistency of the soil, and the success or failure of man as he strove to extend the arable area were dependent upon temperature, but even more upon humidity and the seasonal distribution of rainfall. Today it is no longer possible to suppose that Europe's climate remained stable during historical times. The historian of an economy as backward as that of the early Middle Ages cannot therefore leave out of account fluctuations which, though slight, nevertheless modified the conditions of the struggle between man and nature. The difficulty is to date them and to assess their magnitude, for medieval texts supply hardly any worth-while information on this subject.

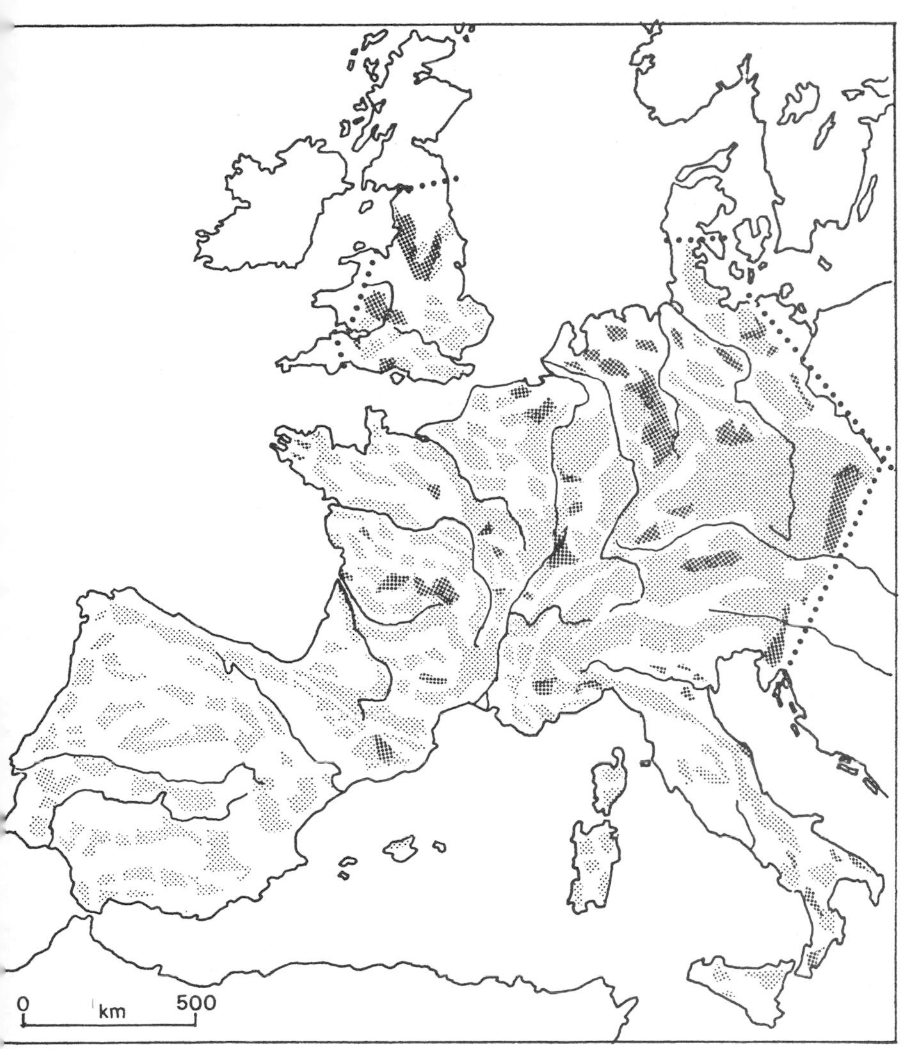

Main areas of forest

Forested areas whose boundaries and density are uncertain

.... Limits of investigation

Map 1 Early Medieval Forests

It is true that chroniclers of those times habitually paid great attention to atmospheric phenomena: as the years went by, they recorded severe cold spells and floods alongside those other calamities with which Divine wrath smote mankind. But their observations are altogether subjective, imprecise and irregular. For this type of research we need a continuous series of measurable data. These can be sought from dendrochronology – the examination of tree-trunks whose annual concentric rings represent, by variations in their thicknesses, the greater or lesser vitality of the plant, in other words, its reactions to climatic influences. But European species of tree do not live sufficiently long to provide evidence applicable to the early Middle Ages. Thus, for the medievalist, the most useful data on Europe remain those derived from the study of the advance and retreat of Alpine glaciers. The peat bog of Fernau in the Tirol, situated close by an ice-front, has been covered over with ice again and again during the course of history. The accumulation of vegetable matter was interrupted at such times so that in cross-sections through the peat beds of sand of different thicknesses can now be detected, interspersed between layers of decomposed plants, which correspond to advances of the glacier. It is therefore possible to build up a chronology, if only an approximate one, of the glacial ebb and flow, that is of climatic fluctuations, since movements of the glacier were directly governed by variations in temperature and precipitation. It would seem then that the Alps experienced an initial glacial advance during the Middle Ages which can be fixed roughly between the beginning of the fifth and the middle of the eighth century. This phase was followed by a prolonged retreat until about 1150, which appears to have been markedly more pronounced than is the case in the twentieth century. This leads us to suppose that western Europe enjoyed a milder climate than today during the corresponding period. Certainly it was less damp and there is a noticeable absence of hygrophile mosses in the soil of peat bogs. Then, from the middle of the twelfth century, the glaciers moved forward rapidly once more. In this period the Aletsch Glacier covered over an entire forest of conifers, whose fossilized trunks have been brought to light by the present retreat. This second phase of activity drew to a close about 1300–50. It must be set in relation to a lowering of the mean temperature (though in fact a slight one, estimated by experts at less than 1° C.) and to an increase in rainfall, traces of which have been discovered elsewhere. On the site of one Provençal village some natural caves were abandoned towards the middle of the thirteenth century because of serious water seepage, probably caused by a worsening of the summer rains and inferior drying resulting from the general cooling down.

Data derived from the study of Alpine glaciers can be collated with factors supported by witnesses of another kind and in other localities. It is risky to postulate any direct relation between climatic fluctuations and invasions by the sea, recently shown to have

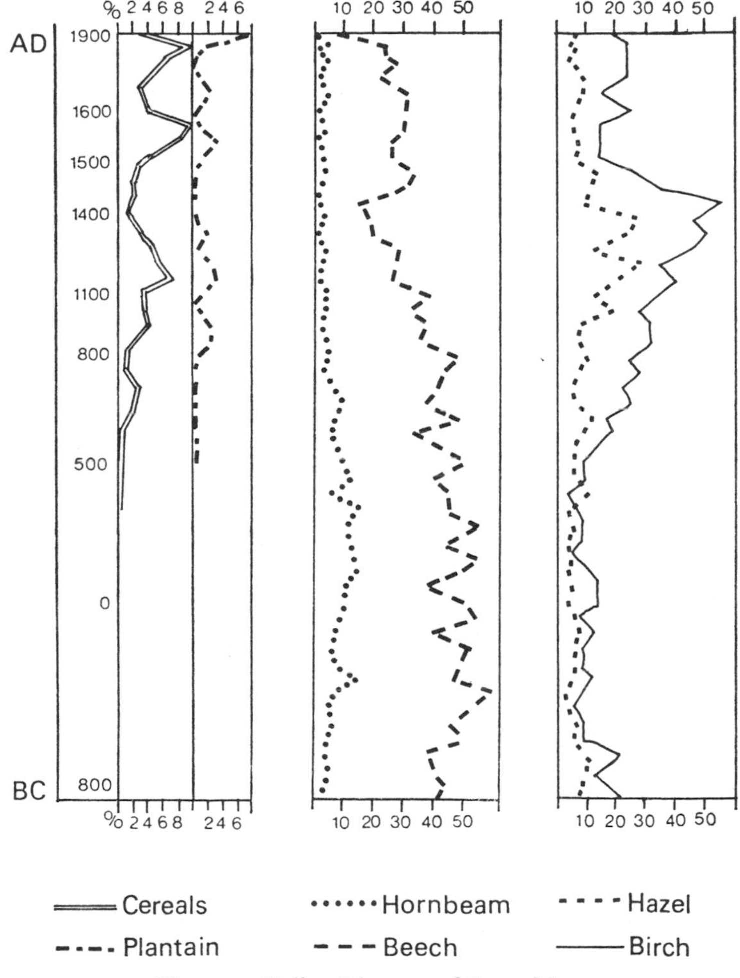

Figure 1 Pollen Diagram of Rotcs Moor

submerged human settlements on the Flemish coast shortly after the year 1000. On the other hand, there do exist some interesting coincidences between the alternate advance and retreat of glaciers and changes in the vegetation cover suggested by the examination of pollen grains preserved in peat bogs. The study of these plant remains enables us to construct a chronology, again very approximate, of the extension and contraction of virgin forest in the vicinity of accumulations of peat. One of the first pollen diagrams ever made shows a progressive retreat of the forest on the plateaux of central Germany between the seventh and the middle of the eleventh century, followed by a slow reconquest of lost ground by trees during the thirteenth and fourteenth centuries. Quite recently, investigations carried out in the Ardennes have brought to light in the same way three successive advances by the beech tree, separated by phases of retreat. These advances are placed round about the years 200, 700 and 1200 respectively and confirm glaciological observations with regard to long-term fluctuations in Europe's climate. Lacking in precision though they are, these signs do point in the same direction and permit us to build up a hypothesis: a relatively dry, warm climate prevailed in western Europe between the eighth and the second half of the twelfth century, in the early stages of a period of economic growth which we shall see was essentially agricultural.

It would be rash to assert that this is not so much a question of mere coincidence as one of close correlation between these two phenomena. The effects of climatic factors on human activity are by no means so simple. Furthermore, the variation was in any case a small one, too small for the rise in temperature and reduction in rainfall to bring about any changes of species in the vegetation cover. Yet even if the increase in mean annual temperature remained at less than 1° C, as may be conjectured in the most tentative of hypotheses, it cannot have been without repercussions on the suitability of soils under cultivation, given the agricultural techniques of this period. This variation corresponds roughly to the difference observable in France nowadays between the climate of Dunkirk and Rennes, for instance, or Belfort and Lyons.

Everything favours the belief that this rise was accompanied by relatively drier conditions, and therein lies the essential point. Research based on English documents dating from a slightly later period than that covered by this book has shown that in those parts of Europe subject to Atlantic influences, cereal harvests were hardly affected by temperature variations. But they were better in so far as the summer and autumn were drier, and tended to be spoiled by too much rain, especially when the excess rainfall came along during the autumn.[1] This information offered by the still very new history of climate cannot be ignored. To all appearances, weather conditions in western Europe, which at the beginning of the seventh century was still enveloped in the hostile environment of a lengthy period of cold and damp, eventually became more favourable, little by little, to working the land and to subsistence production. Northerly regions in particular benefited from this slight improvement. In the Mediterranean area on the other hand greater dryness probably made the forest cover even more precarious and consequently the soil more vulnerable to the destructive effects of erosion.

II POPULATION

Any attempt to describe the human population as it existed at the outset of the period we are studying comes up against almost insurmountable obstacles. Written documents provide virtually no evidence. The first censuses capable of being used by the demographer appear only at the beginning of the ninth century, in surveys of large Carolingian estates. They all come from restricted areas where the use of writing for administrative purposes was by then widespread, that is from lands situated between the Loire and the Rhine on the one hand and from northern Italy on the other. Moreover, they relate only to tiny patches of settlement. Archaeology might provide information greater in quantity and less unevenly distributed in space, yet up to the present day such investigation remains very limited. It has brought to light traces of settlement but to interpret these demographically is a highly delicate operation. From the study of graves and the human remains they contain, it is possible to extract a little information regarding the sex, age and sometimes the biological constitution of the dead, and on this basis we can venture to construct mortality tables. Even so, the contents of an entire cemetery must be recorded in order to ascertain that all the inhabitants of the place were buried there and that segregation according to social status and ethnic grouping has

[1] J. Z. Titow, 'Evidence of weather in the account rolls of the bishopric of Winchester, 1209–1350', *Economic History Review*, 2nd series, xii (1959–60), pp. 360–407.

not occurred; and to define the period during which the graveyard was in use. Graves can be dated, in a rough-and-ready fashion, when they contain grave-goods; but the progress of Christianity and changes which this brought about in the cult of the dead caused all the dating evidence gradually to disappear.

There are also many technical problems which are not easy to solve and which severely restrict the import of the archaeological finds. Extremely hypothetical, too, are the results of investigations that attempt to delineate areas of human occupation in remote periods by examining the landscape, soils and remains of plants. In short, every demographic conjecture relating to this period rests upon flimsy foundations.

The general impression is that the seventh century came at the end of a prolonged downward phase in the history of European population, which no doubt was not unrelated to climatic fluctuations. The Roman world was probably affected by a tendency for population to fall from the second century of the Christian era onwards. This slow decline seems to have been speeded up suddenly in the sixth century by the outbreak of a plague epidemic. According to the Byzantine historian, Procopius, the most reliable witness of this disaster, the disease spread through Italy and Spain in 543–6, ravaging a great part of Gaul and reaching as far as the banks of the upper and middle Rhine. We know from the description given by Gregory of Tours that this disease was bubonic plague, that it followed upon catastrophic floods, and that it struck at the whole population and especially children, causing instant death. As after the second attack of the same scourge, to which Europe was subjected in the middle of the fourteenth century, the disease remained endemic for over fifty years, breaking out here and there in deadly thrusts. Documents report fresh attacks of this kind in 563 in Auvergne, in 570 in northern Italy, Gaul and Spain, in 580 in southern Gaul. In 592 the plague was raging in Tours and Nantes, and was prevalent in Italy and Provence between 587 and 618. Yet no numerical data exists to give the slightest clue to its effects on the death rate. In Italy these effects were combined with those of war and the Lombard invasion. And investigations by archaeologists reveal a noticeable retreat of settlement that was not limited to those areas which documents tell us were stricken by the plague epidemic. They have pinpointed in particular a distinct shrinkage of human occupation in Germany, both in the south-west and along the North Sea coast. To take an example, the site of Mahndorf, south-east of Bremen, was occupied by eighty peasants between AD 250 and 500; from 500 to 700 the population was at most about twenty; while the coastal fringe, which was inhabited around 400, seems thereafter to have been totally deserted.

Some general estimates of Europe's population in the sixth century have been tentatively put forward: a density per square kilometre of 5·5 in Gaul, 2·0 in England (corresponding to a population of less than half a million) and 2·2 in Germany, where the arable did not cover more than 3·5 to 4 per cent of the total area, even in the most densely settled regions. The sole interest of these estimates is to show how scarce human beings were in Europe at the start of the period of economic growth we are about to examine. Those forest-clad lands were virtually empty. Also their inhabitants seem to have suffered from malnutrition: bones and teeth recovered from graves reveal the effects of serious dietary deficiencies. They explain the population's vulnerability to attacks by disease. Unidentified epidemics were still being reported from England in 664, Italy about 680, the Narbonnaise in 694. A counter-attack by the plague occurred in 742–3. Depopulation and abandonment of land overtaken by marsh allowed malaria to secure a firm foothold in the Mediterranean plains. In this human void, space was plentiful. What constituted the real basis of wealth at that time was not ownership of land but power over men, however wretched their condition, and over their rudimentary equipment.

III TOOLS

We know virtually nothing of early medieval tools, which are unquestionably less familiar than those of Neolithic peasants. The few records that have survived do not tell us anything about them. They do provide names, but these are Latin ones awkwardly transposing popular speech, obsolete, and ill-suited to express everyday usage. How can we make out the object, its shape, the materials from which it was made and how efficient it was from these names? What can we learn from words like *aratrum* or *carruca*, which are mentioned from time to time in all-too-laconic written documents attempting to describe the work of the fields during these centuries? These two terms, doubtless interchangeable, merely indicate an instrument drawn by a team and used for ploughing. The first was preferred by better-read scribes because it came from the classical vocabulary; the second translated popular speech more literally.

Carruca would imply at the very most that this device was provided with wheels, but there is no gloss to enable us to ascertain the action of its share or whether it was made more effective by the attachment of a mould-board: that is, whether the ploughman had at his disposal a real plough which was capable of displacing and aerating the soil thoroughly, or only a simple swing-plough, whose symmetrical share could just about open up a furrow but not turn over the sod. Archaeological finds have provided almost nothing which might shed light on the history of peasant technology for this period. Not much can be expected from iconography; in any case the material is scarce and there is no way of telling whether a particular artist was concerned to reproduce contemporary life as it actually appeared or whether, inspired by ancient or exotic workshop models, his work was purely symbolic and devoid of any attempt at realism. Lack of precise data relating to peasant equipment is especially irksome, for how can we form any notion of productive forces if nothing is known about the tools?

Amid such profound uncertainty, we are forced to have recourse to later documents which the rebirth of writing, stimulated by Carolingian administration, brought forth at the very end of the eighth century. Let us make clear straight away that these writings are exclusively concerned with the most extensive and efficiently managed estates, the pace-setters of agricultural technique. Officials charged with taking stock of these big farms were instructed to list the tools available in each manorial centre, especially metal ones because they were more valuable. Here is one of these accounts, preserved in a manuscript from the first third of the ninth century and dealing with the large royal manor of Annapes, on the borders of Flanders and Artois:

> Tools (*utensilia*): two copper basins, two drinking vessels, two copper cauldrons and another of iron, one pan, one pot-hook, one andiron, one lamp, two axes, one adze, two augers, one hatchet, one scraper, one plane, one chisel, two scythes, two sickles and two iron-tipped shovels. There are plenty of wooden tools.[1]

From this passage the following facts stand out clearly: the objects carefully listed on account of their value were primarily cooking or hearth utensils and, in addition, a few tools for woodworking; on this enormous farm, where nearly two hundred cattle were being

[1] *Monumenta Germaniae Historica, Legum*, section II, *Capitularia Regum Francorum*, vol. i, part 1 (Hanover 1883), p. 254.

raised, the only metal implements used for agriculture were intended either for cutting grass or corn, or for turning the soil by hand – in particular, no ploughing apparatus is mentioned. The lord had only a tiny number of metal implements presumably because workers on the land would mainly come from outside, bringing their own tools with them.

The amount of iron in agricultural equipment, then, seems to have been extremely limited and the scarcity of this metal is confirmed by other records. The Salic Law, of which the earliest Latin version dates from 507–11 and which was successively enlarged and altered in the course of the seventh and eighth centuries, punished the theft of a knife with a heavy fine. And the capitulary, *De Villis*, the famous guide issued *c.* 800 for the use of managers of royal properties, bade them draw up the list of ironsmiths (*ministeriales ferrarii*) with care. At the time of their visit to Annapes the surveyors noted that there was none on this manor. At the great abbey of Corbie in Picardy, whose internal economy is familiar enough from statutes laid down by Abbot Adalard in 822, there was a single workshop for which iron would be purchased regularly and where all the equipment of the various outlying manors would be brought for repair. It was not there that ploughs used in the abbey's kitchen-garden were made: provided by the peasants, these were fashioned and mended with their own hands and therefore, it would seem, without recourse to the use of metal. Thus the impression is given that on the huge farms described in manuscripts of the Carolingian period (with the possible exception of those written in Lombardy, which mention smiths more often, and refer occasionally to tenants bound to hand over iron shares for swing-ploughs as rent) the plough, the basic tool for cereal cultivation, was included among the wooden implements neglected by compilers of inventories, who were content to record that there were 'plenty' of them (*ad ministrandum sufficienter*). Since the plough was not assembled by a specialist, but on the peasant's homestead, it would have had a ploughshare made wholly of wood hardened by fire or at best covered with a thin sheath of metal, and would have been incapable of use in stiff soils, even when the plough was very heavy, provided with wheels and drawn by six or eight oxen. It could not even turn over light soils thoroughly enough to provide an active stimulus for the replacement of their fertility content. It must have seemed a derisory weapon when brought face to face with the strength of the natural vegetation.

On the other hand it is uncertain whether the labour force of the great estates described in ninth-century surveys was as well equipped as farmers in more backward areas. Nearly all these farms belonged to monks, lettered men fascinated by the classical models of Roman agriculture and striving to apply its practices to the exploitation of their own lands. Because Roman civilization was a predominantly Mediterranean one, because the Mediterranean is poor in metals, because arable soils there are thin, and because ploughing did not involve turning over the soil but merely breaking its upper crust and destroying the weeds, the Romans had scarcely concerned themselves with improving ploughing techniques. By the beginning of our era, the Latins had discovered to their surprise that 'barbarians' (*barbari*) were using agricultural equipment less rudimentary than their own, yet they did not attempt to adopt it themselves. A few signs from the early Middle Ages point towards a certain technical superiority in less 'civilized' regions than the Ile de France. The study of Slav languages, for instance, suggests that the real plough, as distinct from the simple swing-plough, was sufficiently widespread in central Europe to have acquired a special name before the Hungarian invasions divided the southern from the northern Slavs in the tenth century. In Moravia and the Low Countries, archaeologists have found iron objects that might be the shares of swing-ploughs. In the ninth century the poet, Ermoldus Nigellus, mentions these iron ploughshares with reference to Austrasia, the most barbarous province in Gaul. An illustration in a tenth-century English manuscript shows a ploughing instrument fitted with a mould-board in action. And even if in his *Colloquy* (the Latin version of which is preserved in a manuscript of *c.* 1000) the Anglo-Saxon, Ælfric Grammaticus, allows the woodworker (*lignarius*) to say 'I make the tools', the author attributes a prominent role to the smith in constructing the plough, which owes its most robust fittings and the best part of its strength to the metalworker. These scattered clues should not be ignored. They suggest that during the second half of the first millennium AD, under cover of the total darkness obscuring the history of techniques, the iron-working peoples of primitive Germania may have been extending the use of this metal in agricultural technology.

Nevertheless, we should keep in view the overall picture of a poorly equipped agrarian society forced to tackle the natural environment virtually bare-handed in order to satisfy its basic requirements. The very scattered aspect presented by seventh-century settlement was as much due to this technological backwardness as to population decline. Lands under continuous cultivation were rare and strictly confined to soils that were least unyielding to peasant effort. Men would draw part of their sustenance from these fields, but only part. By gathering wild fruits, fishing or hunting (the net, trap and sundry devices for capturing animals long continued to serve as weapons of prime importance in the struggle men waged for survival) as well as by the intensive practice of animal husbandry, they could find supplementary food supplies in marshland, rivers, tracts of waste and the forest.

IV THE LANDSCAPE

The appearance of the landscape reflects not only population density and type of equipment but also the system of cultivation, which in turn depends upon the traditional diet. For we should be wrong in thinking that a human society feeds on what the surrounding land is best suited to produce. Society is a prisoner of practices passed on from generation to generation and altered only with difficulty. Consequently it endeavours to overcome the limitations of soil and climate in order to procure at all costs foodstuffs that its customs and rites ordain. The historian has to investigate these to begin with when seeking to describe agricultural practices in the past.

It could be said that the encounter and progressive fusion of Roman and Germanic cultures that took place in western Europe during the very early Middle Ages constituted, amongst other things, a collision between strikingly different dietary traditions. We may recall the disgust evinced by the Gallo–Roman, Sidonius Apollinaris, at the manner in which the barbarians whom he had to endure as neighbours used to eat food cooked in butter and onions. These cultures also represented two ways of exploiting natural resources, and two types of landscape coming into contact during the seventh and eighth centuries. The one was Roman and in process of decay, the other Germanic and in process of improvement, while each was gradually merging with the other.

For this period there are a few records that tell us about the dietary customs bequeathed by Rome. We know, for instance, that paupers maintained in the almshouses of Lucca in 765 were receiving every day one loaf, two measures of wine and a dish of legumes cooked in fat and oil. The most reliable clues are provided by chapters thirty-nine and forty of the rule drawn up by St Benedict of Nursia for monastic communities in central Italy during the first half of the sixth century. These precepts regulated the number of meals, what sort of commodities should be eaten, and lastly the size of rations for the various intervals of the liturgical calendar. Briefly, St Benedict's rule prescribes the serving in the refectory of dishes consisting of 'herbs', 'roots' and legumes, just as in the early days of monasticism. It adds substantial amounts of bread and wine to these foods, which were eaten either raw or cooked and which therefore seemed to be little more than a complement, the accompaniment of the bread (*companagium*). Needless to say, we are here dealing with a very special diet, composed for men practising abstinence and especially forbidding the consumption of quadrupeds' meat, save in cases of physical infirmity. As far as we can see, and because this very prohibition is presented as a severe and eminently salutary privation, the normal diet in this area would have allowed a place for meat-eating. We have to bear in mind however that St Benedict and the masters from whom he drew his inspiration, moved by a spirit of moderation, had scarcely deviated from the customs obtaining in the rural society of their own day when laying down regulations of this kind. In the direct line from Roman tradition, this Mediterranean world expected from the land first and foremost bread-stuffs and wine, then beans and peas, 'herbs and roots' grown in the garden, and lastly oil.

Such a method of subsistence had to be incorporated for its own sake into the way of life that Roman colonization had implanted long before in the neighbourhood of towns as far off as Britain and the banks of the Rhine, and which the Germans wanted to adopt because in their eyes it characterized the civilized élite. By virtue of the prestige they derived from being associated with classical civilization, these dietary practices had been held up as a model. The eating of bread and drinking of wine – those two 'kinds' which the chief Christian rites set forth as the very symbols of human sustenance – were regarded throughout the West as basic signs of cultural advancement, and were diffused far and wide in the seventh century. The foundation in the wild regions of the north and east of new monastic communities, whose members were bound by precise rules to subsist like Italian peasants contemporary with St Benedict of Nursia, constituted one of the driving forces behind the spread of these traditions. Their adoption, however, meant either importing certain commodities – the monks of Corbie procured in the Provençal port of Fos oil brought by sea from still farther afield – or it meant putting into operation an appropriate system of cultivation based on cereal production and viticulture. Principles and prescriptions for such a system were to be found in the writings of Latin agronomists, venerated for the same reasons as other remnants of classical literature, and like them recopied in monastic scriptoria. The oldest surviving manuscript of the *gromatici* comes from the Italian abbey of Bóbbio and dates from the seventh century.

Although in a large part of western Europe the climate was ill-suited to corn-growing and still less to viticulture (mainly because of its excessive dampness), both made sweeping advances, and it is tempting to believe that slow changes in temperature and rainfall favoured the process. Members of the aristocracy, particularly the bishops, who played a vital part in maintaining the superior forms of ancient civilization, planted vineyards close by their residences and encouraged the extension of tillage. Gradually the typical Mediterranean landscape, whose main feature was the permanent field, spread northwards and established itself in the barbarian world.

This landscape had initially been arranged to suit the needs of farming in open country, which in Mediterranean lands demanded collective organization to regulate fresh-water supplies. In the provinces most closely subject to Rome this organization had evolved within the orthogonal, rigid state framework of centuriation, of which aerial photography reveals clear traces even now beneath present-day field patterns in North Africa, Italy and the lower Rhône valley. Vast areas given over to the cultivation of cereals and to plantations of vines and olive-trees were divided up into large, compact units, square in shape. In regions farther away from the Mediterranean, the laying out of fields and vineyards had been done in a more and more haphazard fashion, on the increasingly rare and dispersed sites that looked suitable for arranging as agricultural clearings, around isolated *villae*. In this system corn production was based on two-course rotation of crops: ground that had borne a harvest one year was left to rest during the succeeding one. Only a few legumes were sown on the fallow. Arrangements of this kind, along with the presence of the vine, would imply a distinct separation of tillage from animal husbandry; the *ager* stood out clearly from the *saltus*, or area set aside for animals. Let us take as an example Auvergne, that island of Roman culture preserved in the heart of Gaul. A few scattered references in the work of Gregory of Tours, who came from there, give us a fleeting glimpse of its rural landscape. There seems to have been a sharp contrast between the Limagne, 'which is covered with cornfields and has no forests', where the absence of timber meant that straw had to be used to make fires and low-lying farmland was constantly threatened with flooding and a triumphant comeback by swamp, and the encircling mountains, the *saltus montenses*, the *silva*, which were the preserve of domestic huntsmen supplying aristocratic residences on the plains with game, hermits bent on escaping the world, and the sheep grazing on huge tracts of land belonging to the state, to which graziers paid pasturage taxes.

Such a contrast governed the distribution of settlements. In the *saltus* were to be found early forms of settlement pre-dating the Roman conquest, upland hamlets located by the side of ancient trackways. Their star-shaped pattern is still visible here and there on the rural landscape and differs noticeably from the regular, orthogonal network later developed in open country with centuriation. These *castella*, to borrow an expression from Sidonius Apollinaris, were quite unlike the *villae* dotted around the *ager*. The language of seventh-century writers distinguishes between the lordly residence (*domus*) standing in the middle of a big estate, flanked by farm buildings and huts where the household servants lived (each residence forming the core of a substantial concentration of settlement), and the peasant houses (*casae*) scattered among the fields and protected by hedges which also sheltered, in a number of makeshift structures, storage vessels containing reserves of provisions. Now and then a *vicus* was to be seen, a little township inhabited by farmers, of which thirteen have been identified in Lower Auvergne and about ninety in the diocese of Le Mans. These settlements, for the time being open and without defences, became the chief centres of the first country parishes from the sixth century onwards. For religious purposes at least, neighbouring *villae* were treated as their appurtenances.

These features represented a vestige of the past, rotting away like every other fruit of Roman civilization. And one of the reasons for their progressive decay was that dietary traditions were themselves undergoing slow change. In Gaul, because commercial relations were strained and self-sufficiency was essential, lard, fat and wax were replacing oil for cooking and lighting. The same changes were taking place in northern Italy under the influence of customs imported by Germanic invaders and made fashionable by the prestige of victorious warriors. In Italy the daily ration of *maestri*

Comacini, highly-skilled craftsmen, included plenty of pork, judging by regulations of the mid-seventh century, while wealthy households were becoming accustomed to eating more venison. In other words, *saltus* products from the wild were playing an increasingly important part in the human diet. But the Roman type of landscape was also deteriorating because agriculture in open country is always vulnerable. It was being threatened and destroyed piecemeal by plunderers. The decline in public order left the way clear for them, and they concentrated on places where wealth that was easy to steal had been accumulated. At the same time collective drainage authorities proved incapable of effective control of the watercourses. Imperceptibly, low-lying parts of the *ager* were being depopulated and falling into utter neglect. In the course of the seventh century countless *villae* were abandoned. Their sites have been discovered in the middle of arable districts by archaeologists, while *vici* were being drained of their substance and turning into simple *villae*. These developments are in line with the general decline in population, but it is also possible that a slow shift in settlement, a return to hill-top sites, and a revival of early forms of native habitat began in certain parts of Mediterranean Europe such as central Italy and Provence. The fall of Rome was thus made manifest in the restoration of both village types and farming practices that had formerly been features not of the *ager* but of the *saltus*, and of a culture designed not for cultivation but for the exploitation of the natural wilderness. These revived patterns of settlement were therefore very similar to those of the Germans themselves.

Landscapes of Germanic type were to be found in a pure state in regions untouched by Roman civilization, such as the Saxon homeland, or those only lightly marked by its imprint, such as England. In the northern half of Europe human occupation was thin, three times less dense, as we have seen, than was probably the case in Gaul. Climatic and soil conditions necessitated turning the ground over thoroughly prior to sowing it for cereals, either with some animal-drawn contraption, or even by hand with the aid of hoe or spade. Consequently technical difficulties and shortage of manpower caused fields to be strictly limited to soils best suited to light cultivation, to locss platcaux in Germany and alluvial riversides in England. It is likely that arable clearings were being extended in these wild regions from the seventh century. The heavy soils of the English Midlands were adapted to agriculture only slowly, perhaps by means of greater reliance on slavery and more thoroughgoing exploitation of unfree labourers in the work of the fields. In Germany, however, the rural population generally remained scattered in tiny hamlets during this period. On one site of this kind near Tübingen, in south-western Germany, archaeologists estimate that only two or three agricultural holdings providing for some twenty people at most had been laid out by the beginning of the sixth century, even though the terrain is particularly fertile and easy to till; while in the Lippe valley the settlements that have been identified rarely seem to have comprised more than three households. Archaeologists depict the arable around each of these inhabited spots as little islands no bigger than ten hectares. This pitifully small infield was taken up first of all by gardens situated in the immediate vicinity of the houses. Objects of diligent labour, and fertilized by household waste and farmyard manure, these plots constituted by far the most productive part of the cultivated area. There would also be a few fruit trees – still evidently uncommon – as provisions in the Salic Law punished fruit-stealing with heavy fines. As for the fields themselves, it appears that they were far from occupying all that remained of the clearing. The Germans did practise periodic crop-rotation for cereals, but much more irregularly than in the romanized provinces, where Tacitus had once recorded the well-known formula: *arva per annos mutant et superest ager*. They would leave fallow for several successive years parcels of land whose fertility was beginning to run low, putting their animals to graze on them and opening up new ploughlands a little farther away on ground that had recovered after resting. Thus, beyond the all-important plot devoted to gardening (that is, to tillage made permanent by manure and manual labour), extended a zone where the *rothum* (the term used in the earliest German written deeds to describe fields abandoned for the time being), lay side by side with the *nova* (land recently put back into cultivation). As soon as the seed began to sprout on these, 'signs' (*wiffa*) would be posted forbidding access and the law would punish trespassers. The cultivation area where particular patches were cropped from time to time, still carrying plenty of trees, would be marked off by hedgerows, whose legal importance is attested by all law-codes of the Germanic peoples. These enclosures were intended to protect farmland from damage by wild animals but in the main they signified possession of the soil by the hamlet's inhabitants. Across this boundary stretched a new and wider world entirely given over to collective exploitation by the village community. Herds would graze on it in spring and autumn: villagers would hunt and gather food there, and cut timber for houses, fences, tools and fires. These activities might damage the forests immediately surrounding settlements, but elsewhere large tracts of woodland survived undisturbed.

The English landscape was little different from that of contemporary Germania. In parts of the country, especially in the south-east, clearings were probably no longer so tiny; hamlets were only short distances from one another and occasionally their common arable adjoined. Continuous stretches of open field were thus laid out and around the seeded portions temporary fences would be erected and taken down again after the harvest, only to be set up once more at the first sprouting of the corn. Stipulations in King Ine's laws (from the late seventh century) disclose the existence, hard by the arable strips belonging to each family, of meadows held in common and broad expanses of woodland interspersed with islands of intermittent cultivation and great patches of grassland, or wealds, appurtenant to several villages. Tenth-century sources indicate that the whole of the uncultivated area was clearly demarcated and subdivided among the various settlements; whereas the first written documents from three centuries earlier show that peasant communities settled along the rivers had not yet shared out the territory left to the natural vegetation.

The rare signs that provide clues about human diet in this 'barbarian' part of Europe point to the use of corn virtually everywhere. In the days of King Ine subjects bound to provision the royal household are recorded as handing over loaves and beer; while archaeologists measuring the areas of byres excavated on former settlement sites along the German shoreline of the North Sea conclude that stockrearing products could have assured only half the basic requirements of the inhabitants. But it seems clear that the role of grain was more limited than in romanized countries. English peasants were also providing their kings with considerable quantities of cheese, butter, meat, fish and honey, and W. Abel has calculated, on the basis of archaeological discoveries, that the fields cultivated around the hamlets of central Germany were too small to have supplied more than a third of the calories needed by those who ploughed them. Consequently their inhabitants had to look to gardening, food-gathering, fishing, hunting and ultimately to animal husbandry for the greater part of their subsistence. Certainly the traces of the early medieval landscape that have so far been discovered suggest a system of production that was not so much agricultural as pastoral; and we know that this animal husbandry was mixed, the proportion of different kinds of animal varying with the natural capacity of the land. Oxen and cows were commonest in districts where grass predominated in the natural vegetation. On the site of one little hamlet on the North Sea coast of Germany occupied between the sixth and the tenth century, animal bones are distributed as follows: cattle 65 per cent, sheep 25 per cent, swine 10 per cent. By and large, because oak and beech forests formed the main element of the landscape almost everywhere, pig breeding was the great provider of meat products. In section two of the Salic Law sixteen articles deal with pig-stealing, setting out in detail compensation payments according to the age and sex of the animal, while English forests seem to have been studded with 'denns', or places given over to the fattening of swine.

This intimate association of agriculture with animal husbandry, this intermingling of fields with grazing-grounds and forests, is undoubtedly the feature that most clearly marked out the 'barbarian' agrarian system from the Roman one, where the *ager* was kept separate from the *saltus*. The distinction between the two systems, however, was being progressively reduced during the early Middle Ages. This was because on the one hand the Roman world as a whole was reverting to a state of barbarism, while the barbarian world on the other hand was becoming civilized. Possibly the penetration of Christianity was slowly undermining pagan taboos standing in the way of forest clearance; certainly primitive peoples were gradually becoming accustomed to eating bread and drinking wine. The study of peat-bog pollens in the heart of the German forest bears witness to the slow but steady advance of cereals at the expense of trees and brushwood in the seventh and eighth centuries, despite recurrences of plague and other diseases. Tacitus had been amazed that the Germans of his day 'demanded only cereal crops from the land' and planted no vines. Yet the vine was already an object of special protection in the penal section of the Salic Law; and whenever a great Germanic landowner in the eighth century decided to give up his estate in exchange for a life annuity in food, he would require substantial wine liveries from the beneficiaries.

It was precisely out of the fusion of these two systems of production in the West that the characteristic medieval system was eventually born. This fusion probably took place earlier and produced results more quickly in the region where the closest contact between the two cultures had been established, that is to say, in the heart of Frankish Gaul, the Paris basin. Here vast forest reserves continued to exist. The great estates whose structure is revealed in the wills of sixth- and seventh-century bishops of Le Mans were for the most part covered with woodland and waste. But those areas taken up by the natural vegetation and given over to Germanic methods of farming lay adjacent to 'plains' (*plana*), patches of ground that had been cleared long before where Roman agricultural practices had been put into operation. It so happens that the first really explicit documents to unveil the procedures adopted for exploiting the countryside, the administrative guides and manorial surveys drawn up at the behest of Carolingian monarchs at the end of the eighth century and beginning of the ninth, deal with just this zone of contact. At this pivotal point between primitive groups of peasants, a deteriorating countryside to the south, and lands relatively well favoured by climatic conditions and soil quality, these sources describe units of production controlled by agents of the king and big monasteries. These were undoubtedly the most carefully supervised and go-ahead concerns of the day. The information in these records may be relied upon if we wish to gauge farm productivity at its best.

Among these documents, those extremely rare cases which do not describe monastic property (estates where the ritualized diet of religious brethren called primarily for the production of grain and wine) reveal the considerable part played by the fruitful exploitation of the *saltus*. Chapters in the capitulary, *De Villis*, exhort stewards of royal estates to pay more attention to the care of animals and the defence of woodland against depredations by settlers, than to the cultivated fields. When surveyors visiting the royal palace at Annapes towards the end of the eighth century came to take stock of food reserves kept in its storerooms and granaries, they found relatively little grain but plenty of cheese and sides of smoked bacon. All the same, the inventory which they drew up also shows that mills and breweries (which the lord had built for his own needs but which he placed at the disposal of farmers in the neighbourhood, while deducting a fixed amount) regularly brought in substantial quantities of corn-based products to their owner. This goes to prove that even in this region, which was still a distinctly pastoral one, and even on the scale of small peasant farms, the fields were being thoroughly integrated into the system of production.

To ensure that the arable fulfilled its nutritional purpose, it was essential to keep it fertile by letting it rest every now and then, supplying it with manure and ploughing it up. The yield from cereal cultivation depended on the effectiveness of these three associated practices. But this effectiveness was itself closely related to the quality of animal husbandry. Ploughing could be more frequent and would prove more useful to the extent that draught animals were plentiful and sturdy. The bigger the herd let loose on the fallow, the more restorative was the natural fertilizer. And the amount of dung that could be spread on the fields was a function of the number of cattle and sheep kept in the byre during winter. The interdependence of pastoral and agricultural activities holds the key to the traditional system of farming in Europe.

Eighth-century documents contain hardly any information about livestock. What little they do say suggests that byres on large estates were poorly stocked. Presumably the animals reared on subordinate peasant holdings helped to revitalize the master's land: they would come to graze on his fallow and be led off to plough his fields. Nevertheless, the impression remains of a distinct shortage of livestock. An explanation for this may lie in the fact that in this backward civilization foodstuffs were hard to come by; people would look upon domestic animals as rivals competing for food, and thus fail to realize that the scarcity and feebleness of the beasts were directly responsible for deficiencies in agricultural production. Because draught animals were too few in number, the land was badly worked from the first. The calendar of labour services performed on the lord's fields is known from surveys of big Carolingian estates: in autumn the sowing of wheat, rye or spelt was anticipated by two successive ploughings, while a third ploughing preceded the spring sowing of oats. This was too little to prepare the ground properly, for the ploughing implement was rudimentary and drawn by listless oxen. Probably teams of manual labourers supplemented its action, working the land by actually digging it. Once a year dependants of Werden Abbey would break up the surface of part of the lord's field with hoes before the ploughmen passed by. The considerable importance of manual labour services among the burdens imposed on tenants of great estates may be interpreted as a remedy for the low efficiency of ploughs. But men, too, were scarce. Shortage of manpower and the fallibility of technical equipment made it impossible to restore sufficiently the soil's fertility.

This made it essential not to place excessive demands on the land, to allow it long periods of rest, and to put only a limited portion of the arable into cultivation each year. The observations of agents charged with making detailed farm inventories tell us hardly anything about systems of crop rotation. It is virtually certain that on big estates in the Paris basin during the ninth century spring corn was sown along with leguminous plants in fields that had carried winter cereals the previous year. Lands belonging to the abbey of St Amand were consequently divided into three equal parts, so that only one-third of the cultivated area was left under grass each year. A similar triennial rotation was being practised on monastic estates near Paris. Herds grazed on the fallow, between temporary fences preventing them from reaching any seeded portions, but they were probably too few in number for the soil to be properly fertilized. Spring harvests would therefore usually be far smaller than winter ones, and fields would often remain uncultivated for several years at a time. Those of the Flemish abbey of St Pierre-au-Mont-Blandin bore a crop only one year in three. Inadequate equipment and livestock compelled farmers to extend the belt of arable enormously as a result.

What evidence we have also confirms that the supply of animal manure was extremely limited. The monks of Staffelsee Abbey in Bavaria forced their tenants to spread dung regularly on the demesne fields, but in derisory quantities: each year only 0·5 per cent of the lord's land would benefit. Other surveys, when listing peasant obligations in minute detail, do not so much as refer to such a service. We can conclude that manuring had practically no part to play in the agrarian practices of those days. The small amounts of dung raked up in seriously understocked byres were in all likelihood reserved for the hungry soils of gardens and vineyards. Recourse was made to compost in certain districts, however. In the Low Countries and Westphalia archaeology has disclosed the existence of ancient terrains whose soils were completely transformed and greatly improved over the centuries, starting very early in the Middle Ages, by the deposition of turves from heathland and layers of humus brought from near-by woods. But there is nothing to indicate that such methods for regenerating the soil were widely applied elsewhere. Even in the ninth century when agricultural progress had already been under way for some time, and even in regions like the Ile de France that were arguably more highly developed than most, the yield from drudgery in the fields seems to have remained very low.

It is difficult indeed to gauge the level of these yields. One solitary document provides numerical data on this score: one, moreover, whose interpretation is an extremely delicate matter. This is the survey of the royal manor of Annapes. It contains estimates on the one hand of the amounts of grain still held in store at the time of the inquiry, that is during the winter between the autumn and spring sowings; and on the other hand of those that had just been sown. A comparison of the two sets of figures shows that, on the main farm, it had been necessary to set aside for the new sowings 54 per cent of the previous spelt harvest, 60 per cent of the wheat, 62 per cent of the barley and the whole of the rye harvest. This is another way of saying that the yields of these four cereal crops for that year had been respectively 1·8, 1·7, 1·6 and lastly 1·0 to 1 – in other words, nil. These ratios are so low that many historians have refused to accept that they could ever have corresponded to reality. But it should be remembered that the year to which these estimates apply had produced a poor harvest, worse at any rate than the preceding year's, for substantial quantities of barley and spelt remained in reserve from that particular harvest. Further, productivity was slightly higher on the subsidiary farms of the central manor, where the barley yield succeeded in reaching 2·2 to 1. But it is clear from other sources that yields of this order, between 1·6 to 1 and 2·2 to 1, were far from being exceptional in early agriculture. Such meagre returns have also been discerned in the Polish countryside as late as the fourteenth century and even from certain soils in Normandy that were not particularly infertile. Lastly, other scattered signs in written sources of the Carolingian period indicate that great contemporary landowners did not expect a higher average yield-capacity from their estates. The Lombard monastery of St Giulia of Bréscia, which consumed some 6,600 measures of grain annually, would have 9,000 sown to cover its needs, which means that the return normally available to the lord was being estimated at 1·7 to 1. On one manor of the Parisian abbey of St Germain-des-Prés, where 650 measures of corn had been sown on the lord's fields, threshing services imposed on dependent peasants were fixed in anticipation of a surplus of 400 measures. Here again the expected yield was approximately 1·6 to 1. Let us keep in view therefore a hazy but probably reliable picture of widespread cereal cultivation, extensive rather than intensive, very demanding of manpower, yet woefully inadequate to provide nourishment. Obliged to set aside for future sowings a portion of the harvest at least equal to that for food; to see their stores gnawed by rodents during the course of the year and spoilt by rot; and to suffer a reduction of even this miserable surplus whenever the autumn or spring weather had been too wet, Europeans of those times lived permanently with the spectre of starvation.

The feeble productive capacity of agricultural labour thus explains the abiding presence of famine, particularly in regions where men had adopted the custom of subsisting primarily on bread. And the halting vitality of a still very scattered population must be attributed to the exceedingly low yield ratios for cereal crops. In the most civilized part of Gaul Gregory of Tours described people who were striving to make bread out of virtually anything, 'grape pips, hazel-tree flowers and even fern roots', and whose stomachs were grossly distended because they had had to eat field grass. Graves provide the clearest proof of human biological deficiencies: the most rewarding and instructive observations have been based on the study of tenth- and eleventh-century Hungarian cemeteries,[1] and it is not unreasonable to assume that conditions of life were no better in the majority of regions farther west during the seventh and eighth centuries. The most striking of the findings is the high rate of infant mortality: though less common in graves of wealthy families, child skeletons represent about 40 per cent of the total. Out of every five deceased, one had died before the first birthday and two before the fourteenth. Among the adult population death struck especially hard at young mothers, to such an extent that the fertility rate becomes 0·22 for women dying before twenty, 1·0 for those dying between twenty and thirty, and 2·81 for those surviving until the end of the child-bearing period. We can appreciate how slow the rate of population growth was in such societies.

Nevertheless, richer graves have been located in Hungarian cemeteries, where the proportion of child skeletons is lower. No doubt there still existed in the seventh century on the most uncivilized fringes of Europe, in the far east, north and west, a few tribes of

[1] G. Acsádi, 'A középkori magyar halandóságra vonatkozó paleo-demográfiai kutatások eredménye' ('Results of early population studies on Hungarian mortality rates in the Middle Ages'), *Történeti statisztikai évkönyv*, iv (1963–4), pp. 3–34; J. Nemeskéri and A. Kralovánszky, 'Székesfehérvár becsült népessége a x.–xi. században' ('Population estimates of Székesfehérvár in the tenth and eleventh centuries'), *Székesfehérvár évszázadai*, i (1967), pp. 125–40.

hunters or fishermen unacquainted with social distinctions, but in all likelihood these were by then residual areas. Everywhere else – and therein lay the mainspring of growth – a class of lords was exploiting the peasants and forcing them by their very presence to curtail the large amount of leisure time characteristic of primitive economies, to struggle more vigorously against nature, and to produce a modest surplus for the households of their masters.

2 *Social Structure*

Neither Roman nor Germanic society was composed of equals. Both alike acknowledged the pre-eminence of a nobility, constituting the senatorial class in the Empire and comprising kinsmen and companions of war-leaders in the barbarian clans. At least in certain tribes, the lineal descendants of these overlords appear to have been endowed with legal and magical privileges by virtue of their blood. Both societies practised slavery, and perennial warfare kept up the numbers of a servile class, replenished each summer by forays into the territories of neighbouring peoples. The migrations had hardened these inequalities by ruralizing the Roman aristocracy and blending it with the barbarian nobility, as well as by extending the field of military aggression and thereby revitalizing slavery, which found renewed vigour on all frontiers where different ethnic groups were coming face to face on the turbulent confines of the Christian world. Three fundamentally distinct economic groups were thus emerging: the totally alienated slaves, the free peasants and the 'magnates' (*principes, nobiles*), masters of other people's toil and its fruits. The whole direction of the economy, production, consumption and transfer of wealth would be governed by the distribution of property and power between them.

1 SLAVES

All extant written sources reveal the presence in seventh- and eighth-century Europe of large numbers of men and women who are called in the Latin language *servi* and *ancillae*, or who are designated by the neuter noun *mancipia*, expressing more vividly their status as things rather than persons. In practice they belonged outright to a master from birth to death, and children brought into the world by a female slave would be expected to live in the same subjection as herself. They had nothing they could call their own. They were instruments, living tools whom their owner could handle as he pleased, maintain if he wished, for whom he was responsible in courts of law, whom he could punish just as he liked, whom he could sell or give away. They were valuable tools when in fit condition but seem to have commanded relatively low prices, in certain districts at any rate. At Milan in 775 a Frankish boy could be bought for twelve *solidi* (the cost of a horse was fifteen). In countries bordering on areas disturbed by warfare, it was not uncommon for ordinary peasants to own one of these drudges. The ninth-century bailiff of a manor belonging to the Flemish abbey of St Bertin, who was cultivating on his own account twenty-five hectares of arable, kept about a dozen slaves, while small farmers attached to the lordship of the Austrasian monastery of Prüm had the haymaking and reaping services for which they were liable performed by their own *mancipia*. There was no aristocratic household, lay or ecclesiastical, that did not take on domestic staff of servile status. In the *villa* bequeathed by a bishop of Le Mans to his church in 572 the staff numbered ten people: a couple with a small child, four manservants, two maidservants and a lad entrusted with the care of a herd of horses in the woods. Three centuries later, in Franconia, a small lay manor of this sort was similarly provided: one slave, his wife, children and unmarried brother, another slave with his sisters, a boy and a girl. The names borne by these folk suggest that they were descended from captives sold at least three generations earlier in the course of wars being waged by the Franks against Saxons and Slavs.

These examples show that the servile population was replenished simultaneously by natural procreation, warfare and trade. Laws also provided that a free man if hard-pressed could elect to forsake his personal status, or that as punishment for certain misdeeds he could be reduced to bondage. Christianity did not condemn slavery; it dealt it barely a glancing blow. The Church merely forbade committing baptized persons to thraldom but this ban was presumably no better respected than a great many others. At the same time Christianity did set forth manumission of slaves as an act of piety and this drew response from a number of Merovingian bishops, amongst others. The most obvious effect of the intrusion of Christianity was to bring about a recognition of family rights for the unfree. In Italy the idea gained acceptance during the seventh century that slaves could enter into legitimate marriage, as prohibition gave way to the toleration of and later to the regularization of marriages between slaves and free-born women. Mixed marriages of this kind, a sure sign of the gradual breakaway from complete segregation, like the practice of manumission, brought into being several intermediate legal categories between full liberty and its total absence. Contemporary law was concerned to fix precisely the value of individuals, in order that specific compensation payments could plainly be laid down for cases of assault. The law thus set out in minute detail the various layers of the juridical hierarchy, while an edict of the Lombard King Rothari, promulgated in 643, placed freed and semi-free persons between freeman and slave. Yet if they were no longer enmeshed so tightly in the trappings of bondage, these people remained closely dependent on lords who would claim possession of their labour and chattels. The existence within society of a substantial number of individuals subject to *servicium* (gratuitous performance of undefined labour services), whose offspring and savings would remain at the discretion of others, marks a fundamental characteristic of the economic structure of the period. This is true despite the fact that, from a long-term point of view, slow undercurrents were already preparing the way for the integration of the servile ranks with the free peasantry and tending radically to alter the economic significance of slavery.

II FREE PEASANTS

Legal provisions and the ranks they accorded to individuals kept in being a line of demarcation between servitude and freedom. What was meant by the latter was not personal independence but the fact of belonging to the 'folk' (*populus*), of being answerable to public institutions. This distinction was sharper in more backward countries, for Germanic society rested on a body of free men. The right to bear arms, to follow the war-leader on expeditions undertaken each spring, and so to share in the eventual profits of war, all constituted the basic criteria of liberty. Freedom also implied the duty of assembling at regular intervals to declare the law and to do justice. Finally, it gave men a voice in the collective exploitation of patches of wasteland and in decisions on whether or not to welcome newcomers to the community of 'neighbours' (*vicini*).

In romanized provinces peasant freedom had been eroded further and did not exclude subjection to harsh forms of economic exploitation. This subjection assumed its full force only in conjunction with landlordism. A large section of the peasantry, if not the majority, were *coloni* cultivating other people's land. Ostensibly free, they were in fact imprisoned in a whole network of services which imposed severe limitations on their independence. Their military duties had been converted into an obligation to provide for the maintenance of professional men-at-arms. The line between freedom and attenuated forms of slavery thus came to be extremely blurred and circumstances were preparing the way for its gradual disappearance. Nevertheless, the loss of liberty was not total. Notably in Gaul, free peasants in a real sense continued to exist, as inhabitants of *vici*, and as those who retained a right to use the common lands, which Burgundian documents in the tenth and eleventh centuries would still call the *terra francorum*.

The various historical sources are scarcely overflowing with information about this basic substratum of rural society. Nearly all the documents are concerned with lordship and speak of men in inverse proportion to their independence from it. Yet it was at this level that the fundamental unit of agricultural production was to be found: the team of workers linked by blood-ties and put to working the land inherited from their ancestors. The structure of peasant families is very hard to make out. The clearest indications date once more from the Carolingian period. All individuals settled on smallholdings and subject to the lord's authority are carefully enumerated in many surveys of great estates. The picture suggested by these inventories is that of a kinship group restricted to the father, mother and their children. Unmarried brothers or sisters sometimes made up part of the group but it seems unlikely that it included more distant relations, while sons usually appear to have set up a new home on taking a wife. We cannot be sure that the family structure was similar on peasant holdings not entangled in the web of lordship. We do catch glimpses of families recently incorporated into the patrimony of a monastery, which is why they are described in the surveys. We find that several couples and their offspring, or about twenty people all told, might live together on the same farm, and domestic slaves were not unknown. Yet we cannot assume the existence of large groupings with a patriarchal structure. Peasant households may have differed little as regards size from those we meet nowadays in parts of Europe where traditional country ways still survive. A capitulary of Charlemagne dating from 789, gives us an inkling of how duties were shared out among members of the family group: to the womenfolk would fall the tasks of making cloth, cutting out, sewing and washing garments, combing wool, crushing flax and shearing sheep; to the menfolk – in addition to any military and legal obligations left to them – the work of the fields, vineyards and meadows, hunting, carting, clearing new ground, hewing stone, and erecting houses and fences.

The way in which the family unit was rooted to the soil, the combination of property rights to which it devoted its energies and from which it drew its subsistence, can be discerned rather more clearly. Here again, peasant holdings can be seen only through the eyes of their owners, overlords who looked outwardly upon them as the basis of their powers of exploitation; and as a tangible, firm and far more stable basis than people, whom chance events, marriage alliances, migration and flight seem always to have kept on the move. None the less, this society was strongly attached not only to the organic bond making a single entity of the family, but also to the fixed abode where its members would huddle together round the hearth and store their stocks of food, and to the *appendicia*, the various scattered parcels in the surrounding fields providing food for the household. In England this elemental basis or major point of involvement with the soil in farming communities was called a 'hide' (*hida*), in Germania a *huba*. Bede translates 'hide' into Latin as *terra unius familiae*, the 'land of one household'. In Latin documents drawn up in the central Paris basin, the term *mansus* is used in this sense for the first time in 639–57. Little by little it spread through Burgundy, the Moselle country, Flanders and Anjou, but remained uncommon until the middle of the eighth century. This word places the accent on the *dwelling*. It denotes primarily the enclosed toft surrounded by precise boundaries marking the inviolable spot where members of the household were at home, with their animals and supplies. But, like *hida* or *huba*, the word came to designate the whole collection of properties of which this inhabited plot formed the core: all the scattered appurtenances in the belt of gardens and permanent fields, and in pasture and wasteland where they took the form of customary rights. Men even came to attribute a traditional value to the 'manse' and to employ it as a unit for defining the amount of land suitable for supporting a household. The hide or *huba* are also referred to as 'ploughlands' (*carrucatae*), meaning the arable area that a team could normally plough in the course of the year, nominally one hundred and twenty acres or 'dayworks' at the plough being spread over the three ploughing 'seasons' (*sationes*). The layout of the farm supporting the peasant household varied in accordance with the pattern of settlement. In open country, where villages were relatively compact, land belonging to the household would be widely dispersed as parcels mixed up with outlying portions of other manses, whereas in small clearings carved out of the *saltus* it would be brought together as a single unit. All the same, these household lands still owed their very existence to the tofts, whence came the labour to keep them fertile, whither all that they produced was carried off, and over which the aristocracy were making every effort to strengthen their hold, whether or not the occupants were of free status.

III LORDS

Some manses were structurally akin to those occupied by peasants but far larger and better arranged; they were inhabited mainly by slaves and livestock, and their *appendicia* were widely scattered. In regions where the use of classical Latin was being maintained, they were called *villae* and indeed were often established on the sites of former Roman ones. They belonged to war-lords, magnates and ecclesiastical foundations.

In the political system set up after the barbarian migrations, the power of command, of leading the army into battle and of seeing that justice was done among the folk belonged to the king. He owed this power to his birthright, to the blood in his veins. This dynastic tradition determined in large measure the economic position of the royal line: inheritance would favour the accumulation of wealth in the king's hands. But the rules of transmission were the same for this family as for others, and since the penetration of Germanic customs brought about a universal triumph for the principle of equal division of the patrimony among the heirs, royal estates were threatened by partition, like all lay estates, with the passing of each generation. They remained by far the most extensive, however, because a variety of prerogatives continually ran counter to the effects of partible inheritance. As a result, the royal person always found himself in the midst of an enormous 'household' (*familia*). This gathering of people bound to the sovereign by domestic ties was called the 'palace' (*palatium*) in what survived of the language derived from the late Empire, and its size far surpassed that of all other households in the realm. It joined together large numbers of young people of aristocratic origin in the kinship and comradeship of service. They would come to complete their education in the king's attendance and for periods of several years would be 'fed' (*nutriti*) in the palace. In addition, a following of 'friends' and 'comrades' (*fideles*) surrounded the sovereign, bound to him by a special sort of allegiance which conferred on them exceptional individual 'worth'. All barbarian law-codes fix their blood-price a good deal higher than that of ordinary free men. Some of these kinsmen and trusted companions would be dispatched far from the court, scattered around the countryside with the object of broadcasting royal authority. The dispersion of a section of the royal household, and the reflux that temporarily brought to it a high proportion of aristocratic youngsters, added to the interplay of matrimonial alliances weaving around the palace a tight network of kinship ties, created close bonds within the sovereign's entourage. This permanently comprised several hundred individuals, all of them nobles of the realm whom Rothari's edict calls *adelingi*. Made up from diverse elements and fused together as the descendants of chieftains of vanquished tribes intermarried with remnants of the Roman senatorial class, this nobility seems to have been a creature of kingship. We know that nobles derived their wealth from gifts dispensed by the sovereign, shares in booty which were more generous for the king's friends, powers he delegated to his 'counts' (*comites*) or ealdormen (men he would entrust with governing provinces in his name), or the high ecclesiastical offices he conferred. Part and parcel of the age, and endowed with temporal powers that everyone thought fitting for the servants of God, the Christian Church took its place among the mighty. It was deep-seated and secure. Enormous households collectively enjoying ample and steady incomes dwelt around cathedrals and in monasteries. Ecclesiastical patrimonies were benefiting from the rapid flow of pious gifts. By such means the huge landed estate of the abbey of Fontenelle in Normandy, founded in 645, was amassed inside less than three-quarters of a century. These alms came primarily from kings and nobles, but also from lesser folk as tiny parcels of land. We can see this from entries in *libri traditionum*, books in which monastic acquisitions in southern Germania were recorded and which provide the most unmistakable signs of the tenacious survival of peasant ownership in the eighth century. The

c

continuous expansion of ecclesiastical wealth was an economic factor of supreme importance and the one that written sources show up best of all.

The aristocracy exerted pressure on the entire economy chiefly by means of the power they held over land. This power was probably less absolute than it appears in the written sources (which never refer to the poor unless they are being overlorded in some way by the rich) but undeniably it was very considerable. The outlines of great estates are difficult to discern before the end of the eighth century, prior to the rebirth of writing in Carolingian times. We have to be satisfied with slight clues, scattered about some of the law-codes, the exceedingly rare wills made by bishops, and deeds preserved in the archives of certain religious houses, though these never mention the property of laymen until they begin to help themselves to the Church's wealth. The boundaries of these estates were in any case very impermanent. The laity's were continually fragmenting and recombining by accidents of charity, favours from king or Church, punishments and usurpations, marriages and partible inheritance, the rules of which varied in accordance with the customs of different peoples. The progress of civilization, the importation of the Christian Church into districts where it was unknown, and the slow expansion of production in the wildest regions, gradually making the most backward tribes capable of bearing the burden of a nobility, also played their part in constantly changing the size of aristocratic estates. If the outlines of these estates cannot be distinguished because of their instability, their internal structure remains even more elusive and we can hardly guess how magnates used to exploit their rights over land.

The existence of big estates in the seventh century is attested for all parts of Europe not sunk in total documentary obscurity: in Gaul by bequests in the wills of Merovingian bishops; in England by clauses in Ine's laws, which placed relations between lords and tenants under royal control; in Germania by laws of the Alamans and Bavarians regulating the obligations of dependent peasants; in Lombard Italy by the grading of workers on large country estates stipulated in King Rothari's edict. Latinized countries used several words to describe these great accumulations of property: *fundus*, *praedium* and, most frequently, *villa*. Such estates would sometimes cover a homogeneous area several thousand hectares in extent, like the *villa* of Tresson in Maine whose boundaries are carefully described in the will of Bishop Domnolus. Most were smaller and Latin texts use diminutives in respect of these, speaking of *locellum*, *mansionile* or *villare*. Many of them, partitioned by gifts or by divided succession, appear as fragments, 'shares' (*sortes*) or 'parts' (*partes*), while still others comprised multifarious parcels scattered around various localities or dispersed along pioneering margins of settlement. All would be cultivated only partially. Variations in their compactness were due to their own individual histories. In Gaul, for example, the large compact estates held by kings and old aristocratic families often seem to have been successors of the *latifundia* of ancient Rome. Sometimes their extent simply arose from the lie of the natural landscape. In the territory of present-day Belgium the most spacious *villae* were laid out in districts with favourable soils, largely cleared during the Roman period; whereas manorial units on the less fertile sands, constricted by difficulties of development and low densities of human occupation, covered very much smaller areas.

These huge concentrations of land were initially subject to direct exploitation. The farming of estates was based on the employment of a body of slaves assisted periodically by reinforcements of auxiliary manpower when need arose, like the labourers at work in the fields of an Auvergne nobleman at harvest time depicted in a passage from Gregory of Tours. We know of no substantial farm that does not produce evidence of domestics of servile status, and in several instances the only workers on record are slaves maintained in the master's household. Already, however, we come across a phenomenon that was to become increasingly common in the most advanced regions, that is, *villae* where the land was not entirely worked by household servants but was partly subdivided into holdings, or subsidiary farms granted to peasant families. Hard by the *villa* of Tresson, which was inhabited only by slaves, lay another manor likewise furnished with a gang of slaves but counting amongst its farming personnel ten peasants called *coloni*. The term comes from the language of Roman lordship and indicates men who were not masters of the land they cultivated but who, in a legal sense, nevertheless preserved their freedom. Use of the word *colonica* in contemporary documents to describe holdings incorporated in a *villa* expresses the direct link between this mode of exploitation and the colonate of the late Empire. Yet these 'manses', as they were beginning to be called in the Paris region in the seventh century, were not inhabited solely by free men. Some were occupied by slaves who are styled *servi massarii* in Rothari's edict, meaning 'set up on a self-contained farm'. As early as 581 we find among the bequests of a bishop of Le Mans a *colonica*, the holding of a *colonus*, being granted 'with two slaves, Waldard and his wife, and their children who dwell there'. Both the appearance and proliferation of peasant tenements in the seventh century were the result of a far-reaching innovation, a new method of utilizing dependent labour. In this period great landowners seem to have been discovering that it was profitable to marry off some of their slaves, settle them on a manse, and make them responsible for cultivating its appurtenant lands and feeding their own families. The process would relieve the master by reducing costs of staff maintenance, generate enthusiasm for work on the part of the servile task-force, increase its productivity and ensure its replacement, since these slave couples would be entrusted with seeing to their children's upbringing themselves until they became of working age. By degrees this last advantage probably turned out to be the most important. Slaves became increasingly rare on the majority of western European markets all through Merovingian and Carolingian times. Possibly this decrease stemmed from a growing strictness in religious morality in relation to the enslavement of Christians; more certainly it was the outcome of an expansion of trade with the southern and eastern Mediterranean. Most of the slaves procured through war could be sold outside Latin Christendom and their market price was rising, with the result that landowners had an interest in having them brought up locally. The best way to manage this was to leave the matter in the hands of the parents, so as to obtain slaves from domestic procreation and let them live in their own homes. At the centre of many *villae*, therefore, the staff of servants was dwindling at the same time as the amount of land subject to direct exploitation was declining and the number of tenants increasing. Among these, former slaves were becoming more usual. A slow transformation can now be discerned in the status of slaves, gradually bringing their circumstances closer to those of free tenants. This is one of the great landmarks in labour history and was undoubtedly a decisive factor in economic development. It caused a new type of estate structure to spread from the end of the sixth century based on the juxtaposition of a demesne and tenements, and on the participation of the latter in the exploitation of the former.

We are poorly informed about the duties of dependent cultivators to their landlords. The practice of recording these obligations in writing had fallen into desuetude, except perhaps in regions where the elements of ancient farming had deteriorated least, that is to say in central Italy. There, a few manuscript fragments have been preserved in which tenurial responsibilities are recorded. In the most romanized provinces it is also possible that the use of contracts had survived, whereby land was granted for an agreed period in return for renders in kind only. Tenants in Auvergne as late as the ninth century, many of whom were still slaves, had to carry to the *villa* little more than fixed proportions of their harvest: they were virtually free from labour services. Farther north, on the other hand, it looks as if the grant of a holding obliged the free peasant not only to hand over grain, livestock or wine, but also to commit his energies and draught animals to the service of the manor with certain specified tasks: repairing manorial buildings, constructing enclosures, carting crops, carrying messages and sometimes putting a portion of the lord's fields into cultivation. Chapter 67 of Ine's laws deals with the case of a peasant who has been granted a 'yard of land' to plough: he does not lose his liberty but has to supply rent in kind and a contribution in labour fixed in amount by agreement with the landlord; if he has received a house and the first year's seed from him, he cannot quit the land without leaving behind the harvest. The law of the Bavarians, which was committed to writing in 744–8, lays down the duties of a Church *colonus* as follows:

There is the *agrarium* [ground-rent] assessed by the bailiff, who should take care that the *colonus* gives according to what he has. He shall give three measures of corn out of every thirty and pay for grazing rights in accordance with the custom of the country. He is to plough, sow, fence, reap, cart and get in the crop on *andecingae* [predetermined portions of the lord's land] of the proper size. . . . He is to enclose, mow, toss and carry [the hay] on one *arpentum* of [the lord's] meadow. As regards the spring grains he must set aside up to two measures of seed, sow, reap and take in the crop. . . . Let them hand over every second bale of flax, every tenth pot of honey, four chickens and twenty eggs. They shall provide post-horses or else themselves go wherever they shall be directed. They shall perform carrying services with their wagons within a radius of fifty leagues, but they shall not be compelled to go farther. For repairing the lord's houses, hayloft, granary and hedge, reasonable tasks have been assigned to them . . .[1]

[1] 'Lex Baiwariorum' in *Monumenta Germaniae Historica*, section I, *Leges Nationum Germanicarum*, vol. v, part 2 (Hanover 1926), pp. 286–9.

Besides a levy of about one-tenth of what was produced on their own farms, the lord could force his free tenants to provide regular and substantial support for the labourers on the estate. The contribution he might expect from the slaves he had settled on tenements was heavier still and less clearly defined. Let us now turn to the law of the Alamans drawn up in 717–19, the text of which, moreover, is closely related to that of the law of the Bavarians:

> Slaves of the Church shall render their tribute in accordance with the law: fifteen measures of barley-beer, a pig worth one *tremissis*, two measures of bread [it should be noticed that these liveries, whether of beer or bread, concern cereals that had already been prepared for consumption in the slave's dwelling], five chickens and twenty eggs. Female slaves shall carry out their prescribed tasks conscientiously. Male slaves shall perform half the ploughing service on their own account, half on the demesne and, if enough [time] is available, they are to do as slaves on ecclesiastical estates: three days on their own account, three days on the demesne.[1]

For half their time, as can be seen, slave tenants remained bound to the service of the magnates.

These magnates owned an enormous share of the food-producing area. Most slaves belonged to them, while numerous free peasants held from them the tofts they inhabited, fields they cultivated and common rights in woodland and waste. This enabled the aristocracy to squeeze a good deal of their personal strength from this undernourished population and to draw off for their own use the meagre surpluses from small peasant farms. By means of their rights over land, kings, noblemen, cathedral clergy and monks accumulated in their barns, cellars and storerooms a considerable proportion of what this wild, unprofitable countryside and destitute peasantry produced. But in addition the aristocracy had at their disposal authority that gave special backing to their economic power and extended it far beyond the bounds of their own landed estates. By rights, this authority belonged entirely to the king. He owed it to his military functions and to the magical powers passed on to him by his ancestors; even so he would regard it as a private possession, as one element of his patrimony, and would therefore treat it as he thought fit. As war-leader he took the lion's share of the loot

amassed on pillaging expeditions. As guardian of law and order he

[1] 'Leges Alamannorum' in *Monumenta Germaniae Historica*, section I, *Leges Nationum Germanicarum*, vol. v, part 1 (Hanover 1888), pp. 82–3.

was the fount of justice. Slaves were punished by their own masters, but free men who had broken the public peace by committing some kind of heinous crime had to make good the harm they had thereby caused the sovereign. They had to purchase his clemency, to pay for it with one of those fines for which tariffs were meticulously laid down in barbarian law-codes and, if the offence were exceptionally serious, to place all their possessions and even their lives in the king's mercy. The entire area of the realm was the king's personal property; that is to say all territory that belonged to no one else was his and anyone farming unclaimed land would in theory owe him something. A few remnants of the Roman Empire's fiscal system still survived and were taken over by barbarian overlords, in particular a group of taxes levied on commercial traffic, the tolls collected at town gates and along rivers. At the principal court assemblies aristocrats would certainly not show their faces without bringing gifts. The masses on the other hand were expected to provide for the maintenance of the king and his whole following as the royal household travelled around. For this purpose Anglo-Saxon free men, the *ceorlas*, were combined in groups of villages to supply what was called the *feorm*, sufficient to feed the sovereign and his escort for twenty-four hours. In addition, what Latin documents in certain regions call the *bannum* (French *ban*), the duty of maintaining law and order, the right to command and punish, was the source of considerable transfers of wealth and legalized fresh inroads into the peasants' resources. And because kingship was prodigal by its very nature; because the monarch relinquished a large part of his prerogative to those who served him, whether out of love or fear; and because, in a country subdivided into small districts by so many natural obstacles and by the extreme dispersion of its inhabitants, the ruler was generally absent and in no position to make use of his powers himself, local overlords, owners of big *villae*, whose grain-stores were full amid the general scarcity, usually exercised power most effectively from day to day, assisted by squads of armed retainers. These were the men who profited from power. The long-term tendency during this obscure period seems to have been a progressive strengthening of the aristocracy, through the slow maturing of what would constitute the main framework of the medieval economy – lordship.

The magnates' hold over the population presumably increased first of all in the most developed regions. From the seventh and eighth centuries onwards, peasant independence comes to look like a residual element, a survival from the social structure on which the political institutions of classical antiquity had formerly rested and whose strength was still preserved among the most backward of the barbarian tribes. But everywhere it was now under threat from progress.

In primitive Germania the free man had been first and foremost a fighting man, called up in the summer months for military undertakings pursued over short distances. Mounted essentially for pil-

lage, these expeditions ranked among the enterprises on which the group's livelihood would normally depend. Like food-gathering or hunting, they provided complementary foodstuffs. The inconveniences of this seasonal mobilization were minimal in a community of graziers and itinerant farmers, in which the part played by strictly agricultural tasks was limited. They became more serious when permanent fields took on greater importance, and, with tribes entering a wider political setting, the scope for warfare expanded. At the same time military techniques improved and the conduct of war needed less rudimentary equipment to be effective. From then on, warfare became a crushing burden, whose incidence most peasants could bear only with difficulty at a time of year when fields demanded close attention. In order to survive peasants had to give up the essential mark of freedom, the military role. Like rural labourers in the Roman state beforehand, they were defenceless, *inermes*. They became what the language of Carolingian documents calls the 'poor' (*pauperes*). It was still considered that they ought to co-operate in military activity, but their contribution assumed the degrading form of a 'service' (*obsequium*). They had to supply provisions for the troops. For the dependent *coloni* of the monastery of St Germain-des-Prés the *hostilicium*, or former duty to fight, was no longer distinguished from the dues and labour services imposed on each manse by the beginning of the ninth century. Such a development found its sharpest expression in a narrowing of the gap that separated free peasants from unfree ones, and in the institution of levies on the crops and labour power of small farmers who had not yet been incorporated in a manor. These demands would be heavier than usual wherever the big local landlord was entrusted with the supervision of the service.

Bowed down not only by nature's hostility but also by obligations of this kind, many of the 'poor' of those days would seek out the patronage of some powerful figure who could protect or feed them. The texts of Merovingian formularies are very illuminating here:

> As it is well known to all that I have not the means to feed and clothe myself, I have begged your pity, and your will has granted it to me, to allow me to be delivered into and consigned to your protection. This I have done under the following conditions: you are to help and sustain me, in respect of both food and raiment, according as I shall be able to serve you and be worthy of you. As long as I live, I shall owe you service and obedience compatible with liberty, and for the rest of my days I shall not have the right to withdraw from your power or protection . . .[1]

This is how a new dependant, along with his family and all that he had been able to accumulate in land, would be incorporated in a great estate. Sometimes it was piety, a desire to ensure for themselves the blessings and safeguards of the world to come that would persuade humble folk to give up their independence like this and enter into the *familia* or patronage of a religious house. More often it was plain destitution, the wish to evade the burden of the state, to refuse the demands of its tax-gatherers, or to resist pressure from local potentates who in seventh-century Gaul were transforming so many *vici* inhabited by free men into *villae* of dependent tenants.

At the same time kings, willy-nilly, were giving away their powers of exploitation to the magnates, and all the more freely as the territory subject to their authority grew in size. The Church was persuading them to relinquish such powers to herself as a guarantee of the benevolence of Heaven; the lay nobility were able to demand more and more generosity in return for political co-operation. By the seventh century, Anglo-Saxon kings were consigning to bishops and abbots the *feorm*, the right to hospitality and construction services due from *ceorlas* over a whole range of territory. Somewhat later similar concessions to secular lords occur in the written record, though it is certain that these favours were granted earlier and were even more extensive than those to ecclesiastics. In this way royal rights were attached to private domains and dues whose collection they sanctioned were mingled with charges demanded from manorial tenants. Inside manorial custom, confusion quickly arose between burdens of public origin and payments constituting ground-rent. In England labour services were rapidly substituted

[1] 'Formulae Turonenses,' §43 in *Monumenta Germaniae Historica, Legum*, section V, *Formulae Merovingici et Karolini Aevi*, vol. i, part 1 (Hanover 1886), p. 158 (dating from the second quarter of the eighth century).

for provenders of victuals gathered together for the *feorm*. All was subsumed in the notion of *servicium* or *obsequium*. Imperceptibly, this process was reducing the rural population to a state of bondage. A nexus of economic subjection plain and simple gradually embraced the whole of Europe, submitting all the 'humble' to the 'great', all the 'poor' to the 'powerful'. This machinery for exploitation thenceforth controlled everything. Kings, when conscious of their mission, strove to check the abuses, but in vain. Inexorably it channelled towards the households of their lords the surplus product of workers in the fields.

The distribution of power over land and people posed a problem of liaison between the dwelling places of the aristocracy and the numerous clearings where peasants were struggling to extract from the land the means to survive and to meet their lords' requirements. This problem was all the more acute where the population was low and thinly spread and where the resources of the aristocracy, whether of monarchs, churches or great families, were dispersed over a vast area. Faithful to Roman tradition, kings in Italy, presumably like most Lombard nobles, continued to reside in towns. Bishops had established themselves in 'cities' (*civitates*), with the majority of monasteries close by. The chief palaces of Merovingian kings were also urban residences, though they would spend long periods on their country estates, such as Compiègne or Crécy-en-Ponthieu. On the other hand, Frankish rulers ceased to frequent *civitates* in the course of the eighth century, while mere villages served as stopping-places along routes used by Anglo-Saxon kings. Undoubtedly, recurrent changes of abode were a means by which rulers and magnates would take advantage of the various components of their resources. Further, it was essential for them to put in an appearance here and there, if only to prevent their authority from becoming too remote and therefore non-existent. At every major centre on an estate, ample stocks of provisions would await the lord and his train to pass by. Let us not imagine, however, that they were always on the move. Certain lords were liable to stay put, including some of the wealthiest and all heads of monastic communities. The rest would settle down for a while in the best prepared of their houses, and visit their subsidiary manors every now and then. Consequently the aristocracy's economic power and the scattered nature of their landed possessions suggested methods of indirect management. Responsible individuals had to be placed in charge of each head manor, entrusted with keeping it in working order between the sojourns of the lord, supervising the farming, exercising authority over servants, tenants and dependants, collecting dues and eventually dispatching surplus produce to wherever the owners had taken up residence. The structure of wealth and authority thus called into being the intermediate economic powers wielded by so many poorly supervised managers, like the stewards (*villici*) to whom the body of instructions in the capitulary, *De Villis*, is addressed. Between workers and lords came men who were often slaves, yet who would do their utmost to derive maximum personal profit from their jobs. In this way the great estate was breeding its full share of parasites.

The economic position of the aristocracy was the source of another form of loss, for it necessitated constant transfers of wealth. This explains the enormous weight of messenger- and carrying-services imposed on dependent peasants. A large part of the labour supply might be sent away along tracks and waterways on errands of communication and conveyance, which reduced further the forces available for working the land in a world that was already underpopulated and badly equipped for production. It was the desire to cut down such wastage that prompted people to trade as much as possible, to sell in one place in order to purchase somewhere else, and so to avail of money. Recourse to the monetary medium was considered quite normal by administrators of the day. The Benedictine rule, for instance, assumed the use of cash, instituting a special office in monasteries, that of the cellarer who was in charge of the money and who threw open the domestic economy to the external world. *De Villis* recommends stewards to sell some of the produce from royal manors. At the beginning of the eighth century, abbeys in the Po valley, which were exploiting olive-groves in the lakelands and salines in the Comácchio lagoons, also had warehouses where manorial surpluses were sold to river-traders at Pavia, along the Ticino and towards its confluence with the Po. And so it was that because agricultural production was under the control of the aristocracy, and because, within the framework of the great estate and through the agency of dues exacted from dependent cultivators, consumers were often far removed from producers, the fruits of peasant toil inevitably entered the world of commerce.

3 *Mental Attitudes*

In order to define accurately the real function of commerce in the economy of those times and to discern the profound repercussions of the transfer of wealth, we still have to investigate mental attitudes. These were as decisive as the factors of production, or the realities of power at various levels in society. Two major behavioural characteristics should be mentioned. First, this uncivilized world was wholly imbued with the habit of pillaging and with the need for offering. To despoil and to proffer were two complementary actions governing in very large measure the exchange of goods. An intensive circulation of gifts and return gifts, of ceremonial and hallowed offerings, permeated the entire social structure. These offerings partly destroyed the products of labour, yet they ensured a certain distribution of wealth and they procured above all a boon for men and women that to them seemed priceless: the goodwill of the dark forces governing the universe. Secondly, Europe in the seventh and eighth centuries was bewitched by memories of an ancient civilization whose material forms had not been completely obliterated and whose remains she would endeavour to re-use as best she could.

I TAKING, GIVING AND CONSECRATING

The culture born of the great folk migrations was a culture of war and aggression; the status of freedom was first of all defined as fitness to participate in military expeditions, and the principal earthly mission of kingship was to lead the army, in other words, the whole folk massed together for the attack. Between warlike activity – all that we call 'politics' – and pillaging, there was no line of demarcation. P. Grierson has drawn attention to stipulations in the laws of Ine, king of Wessex, which call for the following distinctions to be made between aggressors: if there are less than seven, they are simply thieves; if they are more numerous, they constitute a band of brigands; but if there are over thirty-five, they may fairly be taken for an army.[1] Foreigners were indeed objects of prey. Beyond the natural frontiers marked out by marshland, forest and wilderness, any territory they occupied was regarded as a hunting preserve. Every year, the young men would set out in a body to roam round it, with their chieftains as guides. They would try to despoil the enemy, to lay their hands on everything they could carry off from his lands: ornaments, weapons, cattle and if possible men, women and children. The captives' tribe could retrieve them for a ransom; otherwise they would remain the property of their abductors. In this way war was the source of slavery. At any rate it represented a regular form of economic activity of prime importance, as much for the profits it secured as for the losses with which it threatened rural communities. This explains the presence of weapons in peasant graves, the prestige of the warrior and his absolute social superiority.

Natural hostility between ethnic groups was not unleashed by raids alone. It was also the origin of regular and peaceable transfers of wealth. Annual tribute was nothing more than the collection of booty made orderly and normal, for the benefit of any tribe that was sufficiently menacing for its neighbours to sense an interest in buying peace. For long this was the policy of Byzantium: to buy peace in her outlying provinces by offering sumptuous gifts to barbarian kings. By this method, certain peoples drew rents from their military strength. These rents were basically similar to dues that lords of big *villae* were imposing on neighbouring farmers, forced by their very weakness to come under the lords' protection. The greater the military superiority, the higher stood the rent. Thus, the Frankish folk were receiving twelve thousand gold *solidi* as tribute from the Lombard folk in the late sixth century. Commenting on the Hungarians in the ninth century, one Arab writer, Ibn Rustah, could say: 'They lord it over all the Slavs who are their neighbours and impose a heavy tribute on them; the Slavs

[1] P. Grierson, 'Commerce in the Dark Ages: a critique of the evidence', *Transactions of the Royal Historical Society*, 5th series, ix (1959), pp. 123–40.

are at their mercy like prisoners.'[1] Lastly, whenever peace was made between tribes of equal strength, it would be prudent to preserve it carefully with return gifts, the essential tokens of its permanence. What was 'peace' for the author of *Beowulf* but the prospect of exchanging gifts between peoples! The risky policy of alternating raids was being replaced by a regular round of mutual offerings.

In the collective psychology of those times giving was the necessary counterpart of taking. At the end of a successful campaign no war-leader would keep the loot for himself. He would share it out, and not only among his comrades in arms. It was his duty to offer up part of it to the invisible powers. This is how many English churches, for example, acquired their share of the treasures that Charlemagne and the Frankish army brought back from their campaign against the Avars. This sharing and consecration were the very condition of the power wielded over his companions by an overlord and delegated to him by the gods. They were also the condition of a purification, a periodic rejuvenation of the social group. Men whose existence was still precarious were anxious to proffer and to sacrifice, partly for protection against aggressors, partly for useful and productive purposes. To their way of thinking, their survival would depend alike on these two actions. For in all societies many of the needs governing economic life are by nature immaterial. They proceed from a respect for certain rites, which entail not only profitable consumption but also the apparently senseless destruction of the wealth acquired. Because many economic historians have misunderstood the significance of these attitudes, it is important to place heavy stress on them here by referring to one of the great masters of ethnology, Marcel Mauss:

> In economies . . . that have preceded our own, we can never postulate (so to speak) simple exchanges of goods, wealth and products through the medium of a market operating between individuals. In the first place, it is not a question of individuals, but of groups of people who had mutual obligations towards one another, made exchanges and entered into contracts. . . . Furthermore, what they exchanged were not just material goods and riches, movables and immovables, things useful economically. They were primarily courtesies, feasts, ritual acts, military services, womenfolk, children, dances, festivities and fairs where the market was but one feature. . . . Finally, these favours and return favours were endorsed by the giving of presents in a more or less voluntary

[1] Ibn Rustah, *Les atours précieux*, trans. G. Wiet (Cairo 1955), p. 160.

fashion, although basically they were strictly obligatory, under pain of private or open warfare.

As a result, a considerable proportion of what was produced was drawn into the heavy traffic in necessary generosity. Many of the payments and offerings that peasants would have no option but to deliver to their lords' homes were for long referred to in contemporary parlance as 'presents' (*eulogiae*). They were apparently regarded as such by all concerned. The same holds true of blood-price payments, whereby peace would be secured between the victim's family and that of the assailant after a murder; of grants of land on precarial tenure by which churches, often against their will, would endow neighbouring magnates with benefices; and of the vast transfer of wealth occasioned by every marriage. When Chilperic, king of the Franks, handed over his daughter, the bride-to-be of the king of the Goths, to the latter's ambassador in 584, Queen Fredegund gave 'an immense quantity of gold, silver and clothing', while Frankish noblemen offered gold and silver, horses and finery.[1] Magnates of the realm would have to come to court with their arms full. Their periodic gifts did not simply constitute a public manifestation of their friendship and submission, a peace-token similar to those maintaining security between peoples: when offered to the sovereign, universally regarded as the natural mediator between the entire folk and the powers above, they guaranteed prosperity for all and promised fertile soils, abundant harvests and an end to plagues.

All these offerings had to be matched by open-handedness on the part of those who received them. No rich man could close his doors to petitioners, send away hungry folk seeking alms at his grain-store, or turn down wretched men offering him their services in return for food, clothing and protection. Of all the goods that possession of land and authority over the lowly channelled in the direction of lordly residences, a substantial part would be redistributed like this among the same people who had brought them. It was through seigneurial munificence that early medieval Europe achieved some degree of social justice and reduced total destitution to mere poverty. And monks were not alone in organizing a 'gate' service, whose role was to normalize this redistribution among the poor. As for kings, their prestige was a reflection of their liberality;

[1] Gregory of Tours, *Histoire des Francs*, book VI, §45, ed. R. Latouche, vol. ii (Paris 1965), p. 69.

they would plunder with seemingly insatiable greed only to give more generously. Not only would they bring up all their friends' children in their households, not only would they share out all the proceeds of pillage and tribute among their comrades in arms; they would also arrange between themselves and magnates coming to their courts on the occasion of great assemblies a sort of gift-competition, the prize going to the provider of the most splendid presents. Every gathering around a ruler appears as the high point of a regular system of free exchange, permeating the whole social fabric and making kingship the real regulator of the economy in general.

But kings were the principal accumulators, too, for they needed a reserve to dip into. For ever being whittled away by gifts and replenished with presents and stolen goods, the ruler's treasure-house was the seat of his power. He needed to amass the most delectable treasures hidden within the earth: silver, and above all gold and precious stones. Kings had to live surrounded by marvels, which were the tangible expression of their glory. Treasure could not simply consist of a heap of priceless materials. Rather it had to be put on show on grand ceremonial occasions. Folk-leaders had to arrange their treasure about their persons, like a halo of splendour. As he showed Gregory of Tours the medallions he had been given by the Emperor Tiberius II, and a large, plate-gold dish decorated with precious stones, King Chilperic said: 'I have made this to highlight the brilliance of the Frankish nation; if God should grant me life, I shall make still more of them.' The whole folk would thus derive glory from the riches piling up around their king. It was important for these riches to be handsome, since treasure was for adornment. As a matter of course, therefore, royal treasure-houses had workshops as outbuildings, in which the best craftsmen were brought together. They were employed in transforming the multifarious objects arriving as gifts into a coherent collection. Such men were primarily goldsmiths, like St Eligius who served King Dagobert I. They would add the infinite and unrecognized value of their labour to the intrinsic value of the objects themselves. Courts like those of Paris and Soissons in the days of the early Merovingians, Toledo in the seventh century, or Pavia during the reign of the Lombard King Liutprand were focal points of the finest craft techniques. They were centres of artistic creativity whose brilliance was as radiant as the prince was powerful. Open to all, their products were scattered abroad through the ruler's generosity, the fount of his prestige. What Westerners might see of the glory of contemporary Byzantium would largely depend on the wonderful quality of articles made in imperial workshops, which the *Basileus* would dole out among barbarian overlords so that they could measure the full extent of his superiority. But rulers in the West would give generously, too, and of their finest possessions; items which in their value and formal perfection stood in harsh contrast to the destitution of the half-starved peasants whose exploitation was the principal source of their wealth.

We should not suppose, however, that the good things of life were reserved only for kings and magnates. The humblest workers in this poverty-stricken world would indulge in merrymaking, the object of which was now and then to rekindle a sense of brotherhood and to command the goodwill of the invisible powers through communal, short-lived and joyful destruction of wealth in the midst of a universe of privation. Such were *potationes*, ritual drinking bouts of alcoholic beverages, aiming at one and the same time to half-open the gates of the unknowable and to reinforce group cohesion for mutual protection.

Nor were the lowly without ornaments. Pathetic replicas of those adorning the remains of kings are to be found in the poorest graves. In seventh-century Germania goldsmiths and itinerant metal-founders were producing, for a rustic clientele, fibulas and belt-buckles in impressed bronze, whose decoration popularized the artistic themes of royal and aristocratic treasure-houses.

The lowly too, as much as the exalted, were subject to superstitious fears and anxieties. The need to conciliate the invisible powers gave rise to a series of prohibitions on the one hand, and demands for consecration and sacrifice on the other, whose influence on economic change it would be perilous to disregard. Worship of trees and forests had erected powerful taboos, holding back the activities of settlers and hindering food-production on margins of clearings, and Christianity was an unconscionable time in rooting them out. An entire section of canonical decrees by the council of Leptines, held in Frankish Gaul in 743, urged people to combat idolatry, and even in the eleventh century Bishop Burchard of Worms was to condemn its tenacious survivals. Religious attitudes would themselves prescribe gifts, which were all the more precious and necessary for being offered up to implacable forces whose bounds were known to no man.

Pious gifts represented a crucial loss at the expense of production and consumption since, unlike gifts enjoyed by lords and kings, they were not compensated for by any redistribution of visible advantages. These were real sacrifices of livestock, horses and even human beings, which we know from recent excavations were still being practised on the confines of the Christian world in the tenth century. In pagan rites a great many of these offerings would go to the dead, whom we therefore have to regard as an important category of consumers in an economic system that broadened out into the supernatural. Apart from food supplies, the dead man would be permitted to take with him into the grave all his personal belongings: pieces of jewellery, weapons, and tools. The homes of those left behind would be deprived of all these possessions at one blow. Presents from next-of-kin would be added to this luggage for the journey. The wealth of archaeological finds, though fortuitous and applicable to a tiny proportion of burials, proves how serious these inroads into the resources of the living might have been over the generations. To be sure, these expropriations involved mainly luxury items, the personal treasures that every human being, no matter how poor, would keep about him. But they also drew upon tools, especially metal ones, with which contemporary society seems to have been so badly provided. These indeed were assets so tempting that certain individuals were prepared to brave the terrifying vengeance of departed souls to steal them, as the harshness of penalties against despoiling tombs goes to show. But grave-robbers were never common, and the majority of the goods offered to the dead were not put back into circulation. No form of investment could have been more unproductive than this, yet it was the only one to be widely practised by this infinitely penurious society.

The progress of conversion to Christianity put an end to the custom of burying artifacts with the dead. This was perhaps the way in which it contributed most directly to economic development. But it was a very gradual process. Carolingian capitularies carried on the struggle against offerings to the dead, yet prohibitions laid down in general assemblies of the Empire did not prevent Charlemagne from being lowered into the tomb bedecked with magnificent jewellery. And heathen practices were being replaced by others just as demanding. Now it was the Church that claimed the 'dead man's share', given him by his heirs for his future life. Treasure-hoarding, centred until recently in burial-grounds, was simply transferred to Christian sanctuaries where consecrated valuables were deposited. Men great and small would bequeath their treasures so that these might eventually adorn the service of God. Thus Charlemagne shared out his jewellery among the Empire's metropolitan churches. Round altars and saints' relics, precious possessions began to accumulate, of which the finest items were to come from royal treasuries. These offerings became steadily more bountiful. Barring accidents, they would not be squandered. Taboos protected them from pillage, and an echo has been preserved of the holy terror that seized Christendom when Vikings, still heathen, violated these proscriptions by taking gold and silver from monastic sacristies. The taboos were so powerful that many of these offerings remain to this day precisely where they were originally deposited. All that survives of contemporary jewellery, apart from that found in graves, comes to us in this way. Even so, precious metals bequeathed by the dead were not buried in the earth, as in former times, and thereby withdrawn from use by the living. The future would consider it in keeping with God's glory to avail of these treasures for other purposes, and reserves of gold and silver would be drawn upon to rebuild churches or to assist the poor. The conversion of Europe to Christianity did not suppress treasure-hoarding for funerary purposes, but it did radically alter its character. From being final and therefore sterile, it became temporary and potentially fruitful. In the course of these dark centuries, savings in metal accumulated which were to foster the rebirth of a money economy after the year 1000.

The Church received much more besides. Ancient beliefs were engulfed in Christian practice, making sacrifice of earthly goods the surest means of acquiring Divine favours and atoning for sin. God's pardon could be purchased with offerings just as the king's peace could be bought for a fine. To offer the Lord the first crop, every tenth sheaf after reaping, was likewise a propitiatory gift. None the less, these consecrated goods were not destroyed, and again this change was far-reaching. They were handed over to men entrusted with a special office – prayer. Thus, the penetration of Christianity led to the establishment within the community of a large group of specialists, who took part neither in working the land nor in warlike pillaging expeditions and who formed one of the most important sectors of the economic system. They produced nothing. They lived off subventions on the toil of others. In exchange for these payments, they would offer prayers and other sacred gestures for the well-being of the community. Not the whole Church was in an economic position of this nature: the lower clergy in the countryside would farm holdings themselves and were barely distinguishable from peasants. But even the humblest of priests were *rentiers* with respect to at least part of their incomes. As for monks, and clerks associated with bishops in serving cathedrals, they occupied a truly seigneurial position as idle consumers. The universal practice of giving, of making ritual sacrifices to Divine authority, went on adding to their landed estates. We have already recognized in the flow of gifts of land to the Church one of the broadest and most regular economic currents of this period.

How false it is therefore to regard this economy as a closed one! Undeniably, there prevailed in all households, whether those of kings, monks or the poorest peasants, a desire to provide for themselves and to obtain from their own lands the bulk of what they needed for consumption. This leaning towards self-sufficiency, the wish to live independently and to ask for as little as possible from the outside world, would for instance make monasteries in districts where viticulture was unrewarding acquire vine-growing outliers, sometimes situated far away but enjoying a more favourable climate. Society as a whole was shot through with an infinitely varied network for circulating the wealth and services occasioned by what I have called 'necessary generosity' (*les générosités nécessaires*): gifts of dependants to their protectors, of kinfolk to brides, of friends to party-givers, of magnates to kings, of kings to aristocrats, of all the rich to all the poor, and lastly of all mankind to the dead and to God. True, we are here dealing with exchanges, and there were plenty of them. But it is not a question of *trade*.

Let us consider by way of an example the traffic in lead during the ninth century across Gaul, where since none was produced it was imported from the British Isles. For covering the roof of a side-chapel in his abbey at Seligenstadt, Einhard had to pay a large sum of money to buy enough. But Lupus, abbot of Ferrières near Orléans, wrote to the king of Mercia asking him to have a quantity of lead sent over and promising him prayers in exchange. Through Charlemagne's generosity Pope Hadrian acquired a thousand pounds of it, which court officials transported all the way to Rome with their luggage in one-hundred-pound loads. There was not a merchant in sight on this occasion, nor was any payment made. Yet this rare commodity was in circulation over great distances, like the spices that Roman friends used to send St Boniface in return for reciprocal generosity. Because they have uncovered few traces of real trade, many economic historians have attributed to Dark Age Europe a turning inwards that did not take place; or they have wrongly regarded as commercial, exchanges that were nothing of the kind. In actual fact the expansion of trade in medieval Europe, the course of which we shall endeavour to follow in this book, was only the very gradual and always incomplete dovetailing of an economy of pillage, gift and largess into a framework of monetary circulation. And that framework was already in existence; it was the legacy of Rome.

II FASCINATION WITH CLASSICAL MODELS

Another basic psychological characteristic of this period was that all barbarians aspired to live in Roman style. Rome had passed on to them imperious tastes: bread, wine, oil, marble and gold. Amid the ruins of her civilization, sumptuous dwellings, towns, highways, merchants and money still survived. Victorious overlords had set themselves up in cities; they had occupied palaces; they had become familiar with baths, amphitheatres and the forum. The part of their wealth that most excited their pride bore the superficial gloss of what had once been Roman. In this way town vitality was sustained, more pronounced at Verona, Pavia, Piacenza, Lucca or Toledo, but reaching as far as the ruins of Cologne or the 'chesters' of England. It is true that urban activity in a strictly economic sense had experienced a considerable setback. Cities had taken on a country aspect. Vineyards were planted and flocks put out to graze among the remains of ancient monuments. Shops were deserted. To find commodities of distant provenance was becoming more and more a matter of chance. But they certainly did not disappear altogether. In any case, the town remained the centre of public life because it would contain the palace of the ruler or his representative, the bishop's residence, the *xenodochia* where travellers could put up for the night. Around all towns in Gaul, a ring of monastic foundations had been established a short distance from the fortified nucleus since the sixth century: St Vincent and St Germain-des-Prés at Paris, St Médard at Soissons, St Radegund at Poitiers, St Remigius at Reims. Eight monasteries and hospices could be counted outside the fortifications of Le Mans in the seventh century. Retinues of political leaders and household staffs of churches would thus bring together on the town site a large group of permanent residents whose standard of living was relatively high. Their very presence would give rise to regular importation of food-supplies and sustain the activity of specialized craftsmen. For the successors of Roman city-dwellers intended to follow the lifestyle of their predecessors. They strove to keep in being as best they could the material culture that had been left behind. They were particularly keen on building. At the end of the sixth century the poet, Fortunatus, praised Duke Leunebold ('this man of "barbarian" origins') for having built a church, 'and having accomplished what no "Roman" had ventured to undertake'.

Equal concern not to allow a tradition of comfort and stupendous lavishness to fade away was displayed in the countryside, in *villae* still inhabited by the most well-to-do and least unmannerly landowners. About 585 the same Fortunatus depicted as follows the residence near Coblenz where Bishop Nicetius of Trier, a native of Aquitaine, loved to stay:

> An enclosure flanked by thirty towers encircles the mountain; a building rises up on a spot covered until recently with forest; the wall spreads its wings and drops down to the valley floor; it rejoins the Moselle whose waters close in the estate on that side. On the summit of the high rock a magnificent palace is built, like a second mountain perched on top of the first. Its walls encompass an immense area and the house alone constitutes a veritable fortress. Marble columns hold up the imposing structure; from the top you can see boats gliding by on the surface of the river in summertime; it has three storeys and when you reach the top, the edifice seems to overshadow the fields lying at its feet. The tower commanding the sloping approachway contains a chapel dedicated to the saints, as well as weapons for the warriors' use. There, an engine of war still stands whose missiles speed away, dealing out death as they go before vanishing out of sight. Water is channelled off along ducts following the contours of the mountain; the mill which it turns grinds corn for feeding the inhabitants of the district. On these slopes, formerly sterile, Nicetius has planted juicy vines, and green vine-shoots clothe the high rock that used to bear nothing but scrub. Orchards with fruit-trees growing here and there fill the air with the perfume of their flowers.

We must make allowance for rhetorical grandiloquence in this description, but it does provide a striking picture. On the one hand, it shows the close interweaving of religious, military and rustic elements in the aristocratic way of life; on the other, the implanting in the forests of Germania, on the initiative of an élite imbued with ancient traditions, of a colonial type of economy represented by the stone building, vineyard and mill. Among those who were diffusing Roman models bishops played a considerable part, as did monks. In Gaul alone more than two hundred monasteries were founded on the sites of former Roman *villae* during the seventh century, and their buildings might cover an area twenty or thirty times greater than that of classical Lutetia (Paris). The construction of these vast buildings involved the transportation and working of an enormous mass of materials. Some would come from far afield, like the marbles from Pyrenean quarries used for decorating monastic churches in the Paris region.

To transplant Roman styles of living into the wild north in this way did not simply entail a revival of vestiges of former colonization and a transformation of the landscape by acclimatizing viticulture. It would still be necessary to maintain links with sources of supply for exotic commodities, such as oil, papyrus or spices. Now these links were being threatened by the steady decline of the communications system built up by Rome. Although the events he is recalling relate to as late as 991, evidence left behind by Richer, a monk of St Remigius at Reims who set out on a journey to Chartres, draws attention to the profound delapidation that had finally overtaken the road system: 'Caught up with my two companions in a maze of woodland by-ways, we were exposed to all kinds of misfortune. Misled by a fork in the road, we covered six leagues more than was necessary.' Six miles from Meaux the pack-horse died, and the narrative continues:

> I left the servant there with our luggage, after telling him what to say to any passers-by and . . . I reached Meaux. Daylight would barely permit me to see the bridge across which I was proceeding and, when I examined it more closely, I saw that I had met up with further calamities. . . . When he had looked in every direction for a boat without finding one, my companion came back to the dangerous bridge-crossing and prevailed upon Heaven that the horses might cross over in safety. Where there were gaps, sometimes he would place his shield beneath their feet, sometimes bring together planks that had come apart; now bending down, now standing upright; now moving forward, now retracing his steps, he crossed the bridge successfully with the horses, and I followed on.

Overland transport by cart did not come to an end, however. According to a record drawn up at St Denis before 732, this method was still considered normal. It relates to a royal decision granting tax exemption on merchandise to a religious household:

> We have accorded him this favour: that his agents who are trading, or travelling for some other necessary purpose, shall not pay toll or any taxes whatsoever at our *fiscus* on a certain number of carts each year when on their way to Marseilles or other ports in our kingdom to buy what is needed for lighting [i.e. oil]. Accordingly . . . you shall neither claim nor exact any toll on so many carts of this bishop at Marseilles, Toulon, Fos, Arles, Avignon, Valence, Vienne, Lyons, Chalon and other towns or districts, wherever they are demanded in our realm, whether it be a matter of carriage by boat or by cart, on highways or at bridging-points; whether on account of the dust that is raised, the safety guaranteed or the fodder consumed.[1]

But in the first instance this document mentions boats and the route along which it pinpoints the stages was one for coastal and river shipping. Waterways were becoming the main lines of communication, favouring settlements close by rivers compared with others. It should also be remarked that this *formula* contains clear allusions to the making of purchases and passing of toll stations by *mercatores* or traders.

Traffic in long-distance commodities, then, was not stimulated solely by exchanges of gifts. Specialists in trade were undoubtedly stepping in as well. Sometimes, as the text we have just read suggests, it was a case of servants dispatched by a lord to handle business abroad in his name, but probably also of merchants pure and simple. It is hard to discern whether *negociatores* appearing in the documents were independent individuals or household servants of a master. It is likely that, from the late Empire, magnates had been accustomed to engage commercial agents, who would be better informed of trading practices. These professionals would take advantage of their temporary attachment to the household of a powerful lord: thanks to him they could benefit from safe-conducts and privileges facilitating their own business transactions. There is no doubt as to the existence of dealers who were independent, at least in part, and who made a living from their function as middlemen. Rome had left behind in her cities the remnants of colonies of Oriental traders, the *Syri*, who are frequently mentioned in sixth-century Gallic sources and from whom Jewish merchants were later to take up the challenge. Jews figured among those whom Dagobert called 'his merchants'. They commanded intellectual

[1] A. Uddholm (ed.), *Marculfi Formularum Libri Duo* (Uppsala 1962), pp. 332, 334.

equipment well suited to commercial undertakings and enjoyed the close ties maintained between the many small communities of Jews scattered all over the former Empire as a result of the Diaspora. Their position as outsiders in relation to the mass of the population and to Christianity too, tended to cast them in the specialist economic role of traders. Indeed, communities for whom commerce was still a fringe activity, tangential to a gift economy and consequently suspect (as it was in the eyes of the Christian Church), would gladly leave its practice to foreigners. Yet there were certainly some Christians among professional traders. These native merchants were commoner in regions where the imprint of Rome had left more trace. From the time when Italy emerges from the profound obscurity in which she was submerged by a succession of disasters during the whole of the seventh century, we see Lombard kings taking a keen interest in them. The laws of Liutprand in 720 made special provision for free men to absent themselves from home because of commercial interests, or to practise skilled handicrafts. Aistulf in 750, allocating the services due to him among members of the folk, distinguished *possessores*, those whose wealth lay in land, from *negociatores*, a class so large and diversified that the law subdivided its members into three groups, depending on their means. The richest traders were expected to serve in the army on horseback with full military equipment. What marked them out from the wealthiest landowners was leave to acquit themselves of their obligations by bringing money to the royal treasury, for the greater part of their wealth was in cash.

For all the tribes occupying western Europe silver and especially gold were given the highest material value. Yet precious metals assumed a monetary guise only marginally and usually briefly. Considered in bulk, they served to create a halo of magnificence around the gods, and the persons of kings, overlords and the rich, as well as of the dead. Plunder, tribute and gifts normally circulated only in the shape of trinkets. Then the craftsmen enjoying the highest prestige were commissioned to work them into forms fit to reflect the glory of their owners.

But everywhere, even in the most uncivilized countries, coins were in circulation. To appreciate precisely what role they played in contemporary societies is a difficult task, perhaps the most difficult of those facing the economic historian. In the first place, the sources here are peculiarly deceptive: the only evidence that can justify firm conclusions is provided by the coins themselves. Many have been recovered but always as a by-product of archaeological discovery, in graves and above all in hoards. The reasons for concealment are always unknown but the coins were probably hidden as often as not in the hope of protecting reserves of power from some temporary danger. All numismatic documents stem from a sequence of fortuitous accidents, which places considerable limitations on their value as evidence. In the second place, a serious effort is called for in order to shake off habits of thought imposed by the modern world, where all economic change is regulated in terms of monetary values.

If money was omnipresent in the seventh and eighth centuries, it was far from being minted everywhere. East of the Rhine there was no mint before the tenth century. In England the earliest may have been in operation at the beginning of the seventh century, but for a long time their activity remained very limited: the Sutton Hoo treasure, which archaeologists believe to have been buried either *c.* 625 or *c.* 655, contains no more than thirty-seven coins, all of them Frankish. Mintage made sudden progress after 660, but stayed strictly confined to the south-east of the island until the ninth century. There are no grounds for assuming any kind of economic change in this part of England round *c.* 660, so we should bear in mind that it is rash to associate too closely the opening of a mint with a process of growth. It is probably better to regard the introduction of minting in 'barbarian' countries as simply an aspect of borrowing from a superior and fascinating culture: coins must have had the status of other vestiges of Roman civilization. The manufacture of coins, like making bread, drinking wine, taking baths or being converted to Christianity, did not necessarily represent an economic step forward: it could be a sign of a 'renaissance', or of cultural absorption.

Coins were struck in all regions remaining faithful to ancient traditions in the early seventh century. But in each case we must ask ourselves about the use being made of them and about their real significance. Let us take the case of seventh-century Gaul. In the south and as far northwards as the Seine, currency was used for making monetary calculations and prices were expressed in terms of a number of coins. This means that people had confidence in their weight and degree of fineness; in men's minds they were coming to be recognized as measurements, symbols of worth, units of valuation. Yet the further we probe into the barbarian world north of the Seine, the more this function of money seems to diminish. Here, apparently, coins were weighed and assayed, and were therefore presumably regarded as uncertain and varied. This was partly because the currency supply was irregular, mints distant and their issues inconsistent in quality. But above all it was because local tribes were not used to accepting coins at the face value attributed to them. For these people, coins were bits of metal that it was wise to sample one by one.

Though ubiquitous, coins were everywhere scarce, as is proved by written documents which frequently show very rich men incapable of raising the cash they needed. This was the case with one magnate from Neustria who, in default of joining up with the royal army, was sentenced at the end of the seventh century to the crushing fine of six hundred *solidi* by which military defection was punished. He had to turn to the abbot of St Denis and to pledge a large estate in the Beauvaisis in exchange for the requisite number of gold coins. He died without having been able to free himself from his debt and his son had to give a recognizance to the monastery of full ownership of the pledge. In deeds recording sales, prices are expressed in monetary values; but at all levels in society the purchaser is seen, as often as not, making payment by giving objects in his possession that were coveted by the seller. 'The price is fixed at fifty-three *librae* in gold, silver and horses': this *formula*, coming from north-eastern Gaul and dating from 739, is most revealing. It is even more amazing to see an Italian landowner selling a plot worth one *solidus* in 760 and accepting a side of bacon as one half of the price and six *modii* of millet as the other; or again a moneyer at Lucca, a man who could procure cash more readily than most, giving a horse as equivalent to thirteen of the twenty-eight *solidi* he owed. More characteristic of the limited part played by money in the development of exchange is the absence, in the most advanced societies of those times, of small change suitable for minor transactions. The ancient world had struck small currency in bronze. This no longer appears in Italy or Gaul after the sixth century: from then on only gold and silver coins were in circulation. These had very high values as legal tender. In exchange for a single silver *denarius*, the Frankfurt capitulary of 794 enjoins the king's subjects to part with one dozen wheaten two-pound loaves, fifteen rye-bread loaves, or a score of barley-corn loaves. How then did people pay for one loaf, a man's daily ration? Of what possible use in everyday life were gold coins, worth at least four times as much as Charlemagne's silver *denarius*, and yet the only ones to be minted in Gaul between the mid-sixth and mid-seventh centuries? Historians have been reluctant to admit to the non-existence of small change and have wondered whether the dearth of evidence has not deceived them. Its absence from hoards, they say, proves nothing; it was not worth sufficient to hide away. This argument is weak. Down to the sixth century hoards do contain bronze coins as well. Some historians have put forward the hypothesis that former Roman coins continued in use. Now it has been shown that contemporary coins would have quickly worn out whenever they remained in circulation, to the point of disappearing in less than a century. Thus we have to take our stand by the evidence: the coins used in this period were very heavy. Ethnologists tell us that primitive societies can manage perfectly well without small change, without for that reason being unacquainted with petty exchanges, or even with genuine commercial ones. As we have just seen, seventh-century Europe practised barter on a large scale. A multiplicity of offerings of different kinds between rich and poor households took place, making purchase an exceptional or at any rate intermittent operation. Coins with low values were not indispensable to this still open economy. The basic reason for their disappearance is that rulers were uninterested in minting them, since they would add nothing to their prestige: they preserved only the magisterial elements of the Roman system. It was gold currency that they struck because their immediate concern was to imitate the Emperor.

In the period with which we are dealing, monetary phenomena seem thus to relate less to economic history than to the history of culture and of political structures. It is primarily in terms of cultural and political evolution that we have to try to explain the gradual spread of the monetary medium and of fluctuations affecting the circulation of coins. To issue coins was properly a matter of state. Such an act required a minimum of political organization, without which the regular manufacture of identical objects like coins, under guarantee from a recognized authority, was not possible. Above all, the concept of sovereignty needed to reach maturity, the idea that the prince was the upholder of order, in control of weights and measures, and responsible for placing the requisite standards for regulating transactions at people's disposal. Like justice, coinage was an institution of public order, emanating from the personage who, by his eminent magistrature, was commissioned to maintain in harmonious and beneficial partnership the visible world and God's designs. This supreme mission of peace and stability was the Emperor's. For long the Emperor alone was judged capable of carrying it out. Consequently, very early on in the Middle Ages Europe used exclusively coins bearing a likeness of Caesar on one of their faces. The gradual withdrawal of these coins and the appearance of others issued in the names of 'barbarian' kings were thus bound up with the general process of acculturation, which integrated barbarism imperceptibly into the political framework inherited from Rome.

The latest Byzantine gold coins to have been found in the West north of the Alps come from hoards buried in Frisia between 625 and 635. Imperial mints continued to issue gold coins, *solidi* and *trientes* (the *triens* was one-third of a *solidus*). In Italy, which remained under Byzantine political tutelage for longer, these mints kept up their activities in the Emperor's name: at Ravenna until the city was taken by the Lombards in 751; at Rome until papal authority was decisively substituted for that of Byzantium *c.* 770; at Syracuse until the Arab conquest in the middle of the ninth century. In the barbarian kingdoms rulers had gained possession of mints, but for a long time they did not dare to take over mintage entirely. They allowed coins with the Emperor's head to go on circulating. To have the audacity to substitute their own for his, they needed to be persuaded to carry on not as representatives of imperial power but as governors actually responsible for public order. First to take the plunge were the Frankish kings *c.* 540. The Lombards soon followed them. In Spain the initiative was seized by King Leovigild (568–86) during a general effort to reorganize the state, renew acquaintance with the legal tradition and restore Roman symbols of sovereignty – proof once more that the resumption of coinage denoted primarily the rebirth of a sense of majesty. In the same way, the first issues of gold coins in Kent at the beginning of the seventh century signified an advance of political institutions which found expression in the laws of Æthelbert. What is also striking about the decisions of barbarian kings is the respect they showed for the ancient tradition of coinage, a fidelity that was evidently most marked in Lombardy, where memories of Rome were more persistent than anywhere else. In imitation of Byzantium, King Rothari restored the colleges of moneyers, whose members, sworn in as hereditary holders of their offices, came to dominate the economy of Lombard towns until the twelfth century. He stressed the monopoly of issuing coins as a fundamental attribute of sovereignty; he reserved to the monarch all gold panned in rivers by gold-washers, and he inflicted the Byzantine penalty of the loss of a hand on anyone attempting to counterfeit gold coins. Mintage was centred in Pavia, Milan, Lucca and Treviso, and the moneyer's name did not appear on the coins, the better to impress the mint's public character.

The role played by royal coinage seems to have been threefold. First, it was an affirmation of the monarch's prestige. Second, it was a symbol of order, of the stable and as it were Divine values that had to preside over all transactions, even those innumerable ones without any recourse to coins. Third, the main function of money in those days was probably to concentrate such exchanges as were taking place around the king's person. Coins were beautiful objects, made from precious metals, like the jewellery manufactured by gold- and silversmiths attached to the royal treasure-house (and who were often responsible for mintage as well). Did they not serve primarily to convey favours emanating from the palace; and subsequently to deliver to the king sums levied by his agents on convoys of merchandise along highways and rivers, the proceeds of tribute exacted from subject peoples, the income from fines imposed in public courts? Do not the majority of references to monetary values occur in the stipulations of barbarian law-codes fixing tariffs of cash fines? Of the many ways of transferring wealth, there were some where it was impossible to avoid using money: those relating to levies in any shape or form. There was no room for barter here. The Neustrian nobleman condemned to hand over 600 *solidi* to the royal treasury was forced to pay up in cash, notwithstanding all difficulties. Through his generosity the king would dole out to members of his entourage pieces of gold stamped with the insignia of his personal power; they would come back to him through the agency of taxation. In this way a localized and almost entirely closed circuit was made to operate, of which the nerve centre was formed by the palace. Such seems to have been the fundamental role of this heavy currency, whose inconvenience at the level of strictly commercial exchanges is so striking to the economist. Let us not forget that money belonged to Caesar and had to be rendered unto him. But if coin was the medium for taxation, it was equally one of its instruments. The ruler quite legitimately took a share of any precious metal conveyed to mints for manufacture into coins. And whenever kings happened to relinquish these profits to those on whom they conferred the right to strike coins, the new custodians of mintage would in turn be motivated to maximize the circulation of money.

Because money was primarily a political institution, the state's vicissitudes were reflected in its history. The case of Frankish Gaul is instructive here. In contrast to Italy, power was less concentrated and Roman models more shadowy; coin manufacture was accordingly scattered amongst a whole battery of mints. Their geographical distribution indicates the direction of the main routeways to the Mediterranean: those along which tolls were collected and necessarily handed over in cash, and those used by merchants since money naturally served for commercial purposes as well. The mint at Marseilles was for long the most active. It underwent considerable development *c.* 600, reaching its peak in the middle of the seventh century, when the Lombard invasion of an Italy ruined by Justinian's wars had diverted the principal channels for importing oriental goods towards the Rhône valley. In northern Gaul coins were first struck *c.* 650, once again along the busiest routes, at Huy and Maastricht on the Meuse, and at Quentovic where traffic for the British Isles was concentrated. What is especially significant is the steady spread of mints. In eighth-century Burgundy, the main ones were in former Roman towns along the road from the Saône towards Neustria, first at Chalon, then at Sens, Autun, Auxerre and Mâcon. Nine others have also been identified. There were more than a thousand of them in the whole of Gaul. Many were set up in tiny settlements, so small that 20 per cent of those in the west have not been located. Dispersion is much more marked in the north, where real commercial activities were apparently less intense. Thus, the minting of coins was not a response to users' needs but a reflection of the decay of royal authority. Gradually stifled by the furtherance of aristocratic power, Frankish kingship was unable to preserve its monopoly. Along with other favours, kings had granted the right of striking coins to churches. Moneyers – who were becoming increasingly common and of whom over fifteen hundred are known, some of them itinerant – had been allowed ever-greater independence. They demonstrated it by substituting their own names for that of the king on the coins. The first moneyer's name appears in 585, while the royal name disappears from gold coins at the beginning of the eighth century. This process is certainly related to a decline of regal authority, resulting in irregular mintage and a deterioration of the coins, whose weight decreased little by little and whose degree of fineness was altered.

It is tempting to connect these developments, which followed on from political disaster, with the most important monetary phenomenon of the age: the gradual but total victory won by silver over gold coins. Just when the enhancement of royal prestige in the Lombard state was causing the minting of gold coins to increase and that of silver ones to be abandoned, mints in Gaul, whose public character had been almost entirely lost, can be seen issuing the *denarius*, a silver coin, at Clermont, Lyons and Orléans *c.* 650. Its weight varying from 1·13 to 1·28 grams, was clearly greater than that of the *triens*, which weighed scarcely one gram. It remained stable until the end of the eighth century. Gold coins gradually disappeared: they ceased to be struck at Marseilles *c.* 680 and are no longer found in Frisian hoards concealed after the last third of the seventh century. In three decades a new monetary system was established. It drew forth an immediate response from the other side of the English Channel: when mintage was resumed in south-eastern England *c.* 660, the mints issued those silver coins which numismatists call 'sceattas'. They were disseminated far and wide: some were discovered in a hoard buried in 737 at Cimiez near Nice. This silver system triumphed completely. By the close of the eighth century the minting of gold was no more than a relic. The Carolingian conquest had driven it first from the Lombard kingdom, then from Rome in Pope Hadrian's time. It had been pushed back to outlying parts of the West where Byzantium still maintained a presence.

I shall not dwell on the long-drawn-out controversy conducted by historians about this change. Let us simply bear in mind that Western Europe has no sources of gold. How much was likely to be gleaned by gold-washers in the fast-flowing streams of the Lombard kingdom? The West had either to live off her own reserves, which were running low, or to obtain supplies abroad. Contributions from the outside world ceased at precisely the same time as the minting of gold coins was slowing down, but this was for political rather than commercial reasons. Byzantium had been the chief gold supplier during the sixth century and remained so at the beginning of the seventh. And gold had reached the West not through trading activities (merchants were strictly forbidden to send coins out of the Empire) but as presents offered to barbarian princes, wages paid to mercenaries and tribute that pride made her disguise as free gifts – the exarch of Ravenna was having three hundred pounds of gold transported to the Lombard kings each year in the late sixth century.

As the Eastern Empire retreated into political isolation, however, these liveries gradually became less bountiful. Soon they ceased altogether. There remained the accumulated stock, which was considerable, for gold pervades the writings of Merovingian times, and the Frankish and Saxon goldsmiths' craft was possibly never more active than during the second half of the seventh century, when the *denarius* was making rapid strides. Gold was thus tending to become immobilized in the treasure-hoards of rulers, churches, and in those consecrated to the dead. Silver, on the other hand, was a local product. Tacitus had been amazed to see Germans preferring it to gold. To the Gallic moneyers of private lords who, unlike kings, were unconcerned about majesty, silver seemed a handy raw material. Those who were making use of money for long-distance trade showed greater interest in the *denarius* as, with a slow tilting of the balance, direct relations with the Byzantine world declined and exchanges with the tribes of Germania and the North Sea area intensified. Trade with the Moslem world, where the currency was the silver *dirham*, was also expanding. There is every reason too for supposing that the silver coin, of slight value, was regarded as a more practical device in a society growing accustomed to relying on money for an increasing variety of transactions.

The abandonment of gold currency might therefore be the sign not of economic contraction but, on the contrary, of a gradual expansion of commercial exchanges. This is consistent with the fact that the new currency appears to have had only a marginal effect on the workings of the economy, primarily because money, of whatever kind, remained extremely scarce. When Alcuin wanted to please his English friends by offering them rare commodities, he sent them spices, oil and coined silver. In England, where King Offa was minting solely at Canterbury, the use of silver coins did not become common until the tenth century. The same was true in Germania. The *denarius* was evidently not small change designed for everyday dealing. Its adoption is mainly indicative of shift in the underlying significance attached to money. As fascination with the Byzantine world faded, its prestige value diminished and it became a practical tool.

Such was the role of money at the onset of the changes that

carried forward the development of the European economy from the seventh century. It was a legacy inherited from the much more advanced economies of the ancient Mediterranean. This legacy had for long been neglected by a West that had become uncouth and rustic. Currency had accordingly lost one of its principal functions: coins were no longer considered as reserves of wealth. It was in the form of jewellery that precious metal was being accumulated. There remained a second function, a symbolic one, as a measure of value, but the growing scarcity of commercial exchanges had severely limited its importance. The end of this gradual decline restricting the role of money can be placed within the seventh century. From then on it seems that the evolutionary process was put into reverse. As soon as the political structures of any tribal group became sufficiently mature for mintage to become regular, the latter tended naturally to be stimulated by the combined effects of two factors: first, the advantages that using money would offer anyone wishing to exchange goods; second, the desire on the part of those in authority to derive greater profits from mintage. Only with the growth of institutions under state control did the habit of paying cash gradually take root as medieval civilization advanced. From this point of view, the rise of Carolingian power marks a decisive phase in the economic history of Europe. During and after the eighth century, and step by step from the romanized parts of the West, the *denarius* was accepted as the most convenient means of effecting the transfer of assets, whether it were a question of a gift, the payment of a due or tax, or a sale. Its use became increasingly common, slowly at first, then more rapidly as silver immobilized in hoards was steadily released. Here was a change of great moment. Throughout this book, it will be essential to register its progress, and its effects on the growth of the Western economy.

The directions taken initially by this growth were to a large extent determined by a number of disparities, to which this brief introduction has drawn attention in turn. First was the uneven development of different parts of the European landmass. The folk migrations and slow diffusion of residual forms of Roman culture, including the spread of Christianity and familiarization with the use of money, were encouraging the north and distant east which had not yet emerged from prehistory, to join together in a single unit with the ports of the western Mediterranean. Here, near amphitheatres still frequented, Greek or Hebrew could be heard spoken and cargoes of dates and papyrus were being unloaded in the middle of the eighth century. Between Rome and England, between Narbonne, Verdun and the perimeter of the Slav world, the layers of a gradual acculturation were built up on a common basis of peasant toil, while the flow of commercial traffic was developing in a southerly direction. This traffic and even the process of acculturation were advanced by the increasing stratification of wealth and social status. To the rich minority who commanded the labour of hundreds of farmers and herdsmen, and who could wring the whole meagre surplus from hundreds of peasant holdings, the fascinating models of the Roman way of life were not inaccessible. Meanwhile, on the plane of mental attitudes, tensions were being generated between the idea of the state, which was coloured by memories of the Empire, and the notion of lordship, whose roots went down to survivals of tribalism and the *latifundia*; between the ideal of peace, as the image of Divine justice, and the ingrained habits of warlike aggression. All these overlapping contradictions made the pattern of development extremely complicated.

In any attempt to outline this pattern, the demographic impulse has to be placed in its centre. To be sure, it is practically impossible to measure its strength, not only because all basis for quantitative estimation is lacking before the Carolingian surveys, but also because absolute uncertainty reigns with respect to the composition of the family. True, we have remarked how limited was the capacity for population renewal, held back as it was by the feebleness of productive techniques and the active survival of domestic slavery. This capacity was not however at zero. The study of tenth-century Hungarian cemeteries lends credibility to the hypothesis of a natural rate of increase of approximately 4 per cent, which would have succeeded in doubling the number of human beings within eight generations, or hardly more than two centuries. The voids created by the disasters of the sixth century invited reconquest. Abandoned lands were available: indeed their attractions had been responsible for the initial migrations, particularly the slow infiltration of Slav tribes towards the West. Early in the seventh century the Obodrites entered eastern Holstein to found their little circular settlements on the edges of lakes and rivers. Slav colonization in Thuringia and on wooded hillsides flanking Bavarian territory on the north-east began at the same time. But in every direction the same appeal was stimulating the vital push forward after the plagues. Just when owners of slaves were starting to establish them in what they hoped would be fecund settlements, a movement of expansion was set in train which did not stop short at repopulating deserted tracts. In Gaul seventh-century place-names indicate that new settlements were appearing here and there on the margins of former clearings. This evidence, together with what we can infer from the plateaux of Picardy where special soil conditions greatly reduced the obstacles posed by the forest cover, suggests that we cannot dismiss the idea of a far-reaching and creative opening up of new lands. More than half the inhabited places in the region bear names that date from this period, implying that the decisive phase of rural settlement here should be located in the seventh and first half of the eighth century. This instance may be untypical, but it is certainly not unique. The initial impetus behind all future progress in the West, carrying forward the rise in agrarian production and stimulating technological innovations, was to all appearances released well before the increase in documentary material casts a glimmer of light over economic history. The England of Domesday Book was indeed 'an old country'. This was true even two and a half centuries earlier. And older still was the Ile de France of the Carolingian 'polyptyques'.

In this pattern of development it is equally necessary to find a place for political factors, whose intervention caused the movement of growth to divide into two broad phases. Behind the first, which continued until after the year 1000, the most obvious driving forces were the military ones of aggression and conquest. They maintained the vitality of important economic institutions, such as slavery and periodic quests for booty. This phase of growth was in its early stages primarily that of a war economy. Nevertheless, conquerors soon aspired to reconstitute a state, modelled on Rome, within which peace might be established. One after another they attempted 'renaissances', like that which the Carolingians temporarily succeeded in kindling. Little by little a new order was founded during the course of the tenth century, durable because better adapted than the Roman one to the deep-seated realities of a civilization that had become completely rural. Thereafter, Western Christendom was spared from invasion, as the menacing turbulence slowly ebbed away towards its frontiers and subsequently beyond them. Then, inside the framework of what is customarily called 'feudalism', a second phase of growth began to materialize, sustained within an economy of relative peace by agricultural expansion.

Part Two
Profits of War

(NINTH TO THE MIDDLE OF THE ELEVENTH CENTURY)

Among the contrasts still distinguishing regions impregnated with Latin culture from those where barbarian elements predominated in the eighth century, one of the sharpest was in attitudes to war. The Germanic invasions had made reverence for the warrior's virtues penetrate the aristocratic mentality even in the most romanized districts. But long after the peasants of Aquitaine, Auvergne or Provence had been disarmed, those of Thuringia or Northumbria continued to regard the seasonal pillaging expedition as a normal means of obtaining supplies. In these areas especially the first fruits of economic growth were employed to supplement the incomes of war-leaders; and made possible the formation of an aristocracy of select warriors in places where this did not yet exist. The warriors in turn used these extra resources to improve their military equipment. In the most barbarous communities of the West weaponry seems to have been the earliest and most profitable of productive investments. It was certainly with an eye to greater effectiveness in battle that technical innovations in iron-working, horse-breeding and ship-building were first promoted, innovations that later on were to serve to increase the peaceable production of wealth. Well before the seventh century, in a world where farmers were tackling the land with pitifully inadequate wooden tools, ironsmiths in Germania were fashioning by means of a series of semi-magical operations those masterpieces of skill – the long, shining swords of which Cassiodorus used to boast and which had once borne down on Roman legions. A sacred art, metal-working was first and foremost a military one. The advances it made in the service of warriors went on out-stripping its application to peaceful works. But they did prepare the way for them, and that is why the aggressive tendencies harboured by the primitive societies of barbarian Europe can be counted among the most powerful expansive forces at the outset of medieval Europe's economic growth.

They had one other effect, no less direct. Equipped with better weapons, mounted on better horses and sailing better ships, warrior bands between the eighth and eleventh centuries launched out on the conquest of areas whose relative prosperity aroused their greed. Initially these ventures were destructive and many did not pass beyond that stage; they resulted in the ravaging, pillaging and  impoverishment of any districts that were attacked. Spoils brought back by the aggressors to their native lands served for little else than the unproductive adornment of gods, overlords and the dead. But some conquerors carried their actions further, and their expeditions ended by creating conditions favourable to the growth of productive forces. They built up states. Their military enterprises brought about the destruction of tribal structures and the strengthening of the aristocracy's economic position as the victors stepped in and perfected the system of seigneurial exploitation. The establishment of internal peace promoted capital accumulation, the formation of contacts between different regions led to the opening up of vast areas of exchange. Thus war hastened the march of progress. Two principal stages in this slow process stand out, corresponding to the two most important political and military adventures of the period: the Carolingian and the Viking.

4 *The Carolingian Stage*

In Austrasia, the most uncivilized region in the Frankish kingdom, an aggressive force gradually crystallized during the first third of the eighth century round a great family, that of Charlemagne's forebears, and the men who had been attached to it by bonds of vassalic loyalty. It sallied forth successfully against other aristocratic clans, then against other ethnic groups. The bands thus formed extended their depredations in a circle, on all sides: into the depths of Germania in response to hostile incursions; on punitive expeditions even farther afield, heading for Neustria, Burgundy and the most romanized parts of southern Gaul; then towards Lombard Italy. The example of Aquitaine shows that these attacks, over the course of many decades, initially entailed devastation and decay. But out of these ruins was eventually built up the new Empire, an immense state which was kept firmly under control for half a century. From the historian's point of view, one of the chief consequences of this political reconstruction was the restoration of writing in administration. Conscious of being heir to the Caesars, Charlemagne wished to renew acquaintance with Roman tradition in this respect also. He gave instructions for his own decisions to be written down, and for careful surveys to be made of his estates and those of the churches for which he felt himself responsible. These orders were carried into effect very imperfectly and only in the old Frankish homeland between the Loire and the Rhine, in Bavaria and in Lombardy. But at least some records have come down to us and this sudden, short-lived renaissance of documentary evidence from the period around 800, together with the quite new desire for quantitative precision to which it bears witness, rescue some of the broad features of economic life from the impenetrable darkness. This is the chief interest of the Carolingian stage – the relative clarity of the picture it provides.

I POPULATION TENDENCIES

In the pattern of growth described above, a central place was assigned to demographic change. This was mainly a matter of guesswork; but now, for the ninth century and for some parts of Carolingian Europe, the changes can be discerned more clearly. When inquiries were made in order to construct what is called a 'polyptyque', a detailed inventory of a large landed estate, the people settled on tenements were counted, sometimes with immense care. Indeed, they were worth much more than the bare earth, constituting as they did the estate's prime resource. Of course, surveys of this type never provide anything but a partial view of rural settlement. They do not concern villages but manors, whose shape frequently did not coincide with that of the actual farmland. Slaves employed on the demesne and fed in the master's house were not included in them on principle: they were regarded as movable goods. Peasants who had entered a great landowner's clientele without being granted a holding, and whose dues were therefore purely personal ones, were counted, but only as individuals, and the document says nothing of their families. By way of compensation, for the tenants, free or not, the whole family group usually appears in the survey, in the context of the manse, the basis of seigneurial exactions. In this case, the particulars are invaluable. They verify the hypothesis that a population rise is likely to have followed the restoration of political security, the retreat of the plague and changes in the nature of slavery.

The first impression conveyed by these documents is one of very dense settlement. The most famous of the polyptyques, which Abbot Irminon commissioned for the estates of St Germain-des-Prés in 806–29, enables us to calculate without too wide a margin of error the density of inhabitants per square kilometre for a number of villages in the Paris region. It reaches twenty-six at Palaiseau and thirty-five at Verrières, the same figures as those for rural population density in Poland and Hungary on the eve of World War II. The lands of the abbey of St Bertin, on the borders of Artois and Flanders appear to have been more closely settled. According to the data of this polyptyque (844–8), the density stood at between twelve and twenty-one adults, that is to say, from twenty-five to forty inhabitants per square kilometre. Here densities are far higher than the astonishingly low ones suggested for the beginning of the seventh century by the investigations of archaeologists. Even if they are valid only for patches of settlement, small islands of tillage where people were crowded together, separated by vast empty spaces, and if on that account the average density of a region was much lower, it still seems that in Gaul, as in Germania, the population had increased between the age of Gregory of Tours and that of Charlemagne. This is our first hypothesis

It is confirmed by other signs. The ninth-century surveys were all written in the context of great estates, or more exactly of the farming units occupied by the households of dependent peasants, the manses. Irminon's polyptyque, like the others, shows that these units, each representing in theory the 'land of one household, no longer coincided with teams of workers united by ties of kinship. The system lived on because manorial officials were anxious to preserve the basis for apportioning dues and services. But, in two or three generations, demographic change had caused it to break down. Some of these manses were settled by several couples and apparently overpopulated. If forty-three manses at Palaiseau were occupied by a single household, eight were held by two households and four by three of them. Thus 39 per cent of the recorded population were concentrated on only 20 per cent of the tenurial units. On the whole of this manor, the survey shows that there were 193 family groups to 114 manses. The names borne by tenants further suggest that overpopulated manses were often occupied by a family man and his sons-in-law, or by several married brothers. The evidence indicates that pressure was being exerted internally by population growth on the ancient component parts of the manorial economy. But this pressure also seems to have been contained: a section of the population could not find anywhere to expand freely and so was condemned to overcrowding.

Overcrowding was apparently caused by the nature of the households. If some holdings in the same village or on the same manor were overpopulated, others were underpopulated. Hence the unequal fertility of couples and the rigidity of inheritance rules prevented an even redistribution of the working population on the available farmland. The proportion of bachelors is striking: they formed close on 30 per cent of the tenant population in the *villa* of Verrières near Paris, more than 16 per cent at Palaiseau. More striking still, and posing more serious problems, is the proportion of men in relation to women. The sex ratio sometimes appears to have been abnormally high: 1·30 at Palaiseau and 1·52 at Verrières. Presumably the dangers of childbirth increased the death toll among women, but not sufficiently to account for such an imbalance. We can explain this only by a hypothesis of massive immigration by men, who were summoned to fill up gaps in the work force due to the barrenness of some marriages. Traces of high mobility among the rural population frequently come to the surface. On manors described in the polyptyque of St Remigius of Reims, *forenses, forestici* and *foranei* are mentioned, outsiders who made up at least 16 per cent of the recorded population in each manorial complex. Was this situation peculiar to more open and secure ecclesiastical estates? Were not lay lords better armed, on the other hand, to ensure effective protection? Whatever the explanation, the phenomenon seems to have been widespread.

This mobility occurred from one clearing or cluster of settlements to another. To all appearances men were under no compulsion to conquer the wasteland. Except in Germania and perhaps in forested areas of Champagne, references to assarting in districts illuminated by Carolingian sources are rare. Chapter thirty-six of the capitulary, *De Villis*, contains this advice to stewards of royal estates: 'If there are patches for clearing, let them be cleared, but let not fields gain ground at the expense of the woods.' This sets distinct limits on the amount of assarting thought desirable, which was restricted to the routine organization of periodic crop rotation in the heart of the ancient farmland. This injunction finds an echo in chapter sixty-seven: 'If there are not enough tenants for the unoccupied manses, or room for recently acquired slaves, let them ask our advice.' Such counsel shows once more that rural workers were migrating from one manor to another and not to places where land was being cleared. If there was any agrarian expansion, it appears to have been confined to more methodical and intensive farming of the cultivated area. This intensification of tillage, made imperative by demographic pressure unaccompanied by any improvement of techniques, can perhaps explain the low yield-levels suggested by the data in Carolingian documents. It was at this point that the second and more decisive obstacle was placed. Whenever possible, boys from families that were too big would take over vacant holdings on their native manor, or on some other manor; otherwise, they would stay on their father's farm, so overburdening it that it would become too small to feed its occupants. Empty tracts were close at hand, but rare indeed were men who would embark upon pioneering ventures. The reasons for this are not clear. The most compelling can probably be sought in technical inadequacies making it impossible to tackle virgin ground. Signs of overpopulation can be explained in this way; also the existence, constantly denounced by the capitularies, of a floating and dangerous population of beggars and petty thieves. The disquieting presence of this social flotsam and jetsam, half-famished and rootless individuals whom the moralizing legislation of Carolingian rulers strove in vain to rehabilitate, is one of the clearest indications of the imbalance between the system of production, whose rigidity was upheld by the absence of technical innovations, and the naturally expansive tendencies of the population. But in the middle of cultivated areas, the unequal distribution of farming units, that is of the means of subsistence, among heads of household, bred instability and malnutrition in a section of the manorial population. By restricting births, voluntarily or otherwise, and by making temporary or permanent emigration necessary, this instability curbed the natural tendencies to expand.

Statistical information provided by the polyptyques sheds some light on the rate of this potential growth. The most carefully executed surveys distinguish adults from others in each household. We can be virtually certain that unrecorded children were not of full age, but youngsters who had not yet come out from their legal minority. Where those who were had stayed on in the paternal home, the surveyors follow their names with a reference to their personal status. A comparison of the number of adults and minors in the tenant population of a manor enables us to size up, albeit in a rough-and-ready fashion, the prospects of replacing one generation. Many of these households turn out to be without any children, either because they were young couples, or ageing ones whose offspring had found room elsewhere. Into this category come thirty of the ninety-eight married heads of household in the *villa* of Villeneuve-Saint-Georges near Paris, described in the polyptyque of St Germain-des-Prés. The net effect of so high a proportion, along with that of bachelors, is that in the total tenant population of this manor, the number of youngsters to have survived the heavy death toll of infancy is exactly the same as that of adults.

They were somewhat more numerous at Palaiseau and Verrières, averaging 2·4 and 2·7 per household. If all the data of Irminon's polyptyque are combined the result is an average of slightly under two. There was no growth, therefore; only stagnation, which by and large was the outcome of overpopulation and consequent undernourishment.

The light suddenly thrown upon the rural scene by the first Carolingian documents reveals in the heart of the Frankish kingdom a peasant population that was not making progress but passing through a crisis. Expansion was apparently brought to a halt at the very beginning of the ninth century, after an early rise that had upset the balance between population and farming units, and had increased the number of mouths to such a point that the arable area, incapable of being extended for technical reasons, was unable to provide them with enough food. Each agrarian unit was being subjected to unquestionable but wholly contained demographic pressure. This state of affairs seems to have been a passing phase. The probability is that internal tension, gradually building up over subsequent decades, became powerful enough to release the pressure a little and perhaps to bring about an initial improvement in techniques of production. The polyptyque of St Remigius of Reims, dating from 881, records an average of 2·7 children per married couple. At one village in the Ardennes, described in the survey of the possessions of Prüm Abbey in 892–3, people were exerting much greater pressure on the land than in the earliest polyptyques at the beginning of the century. Here, 116 dependent families were occupying thirty-four manses. To all appearances they were managing to subsist on this basis, which suggests that the agrarian system had become more productive. In the same locality these families were farming an additional eleven manses, said to have been 'unoccupied' (*absi*), which look like privileged holdings burdened only with cash payments, and there is no reason to doubt that these were farms that had recently been laid out after ground had been cleared. A count of the number of unfree inhabitants mentioned in Burgundian documents of the ninth and early tenth centuries produces a ratio of 384 children to 304 adults, that is to say, conditions allowing the population to increase by one-eighth with each generation. In northern Gaul, focal point of the relative order achieved by the Carolingian conquest, the first half of the ninth century seems therefore to have been a critical moment in demographic history between two upsurges of growth. The first had ceased in default of any technical improvements, after filling up the voids created by early medieval depopulation. But inside the lock formed jointly by seigneurial restrictions and unchanging techniques, it seems that the spring was then set, in at least some settled areas, for a future expansion of population. On this occasion it was released by technological advance. Just when raiding parties of Norsemen were gathering strength, this second phase of expansion had already apparently got under way.

II THE GREAT ESTATES

The Carolingian records reveal clearly the nature of the great landed estates. Starting with the most explicit of these documents which tell us only about the largest accumulations of property, those of the king and above all the Church, and making particular use of Irminon's polyptyque, medieval historians have long since built up a standard picture of what were undoubtedly the most powerful economic institutions of the age. The main features of this picture were present in outline from the seventh century. I shall dwell only on those which appear in more detail, or are quite new, in the ninth-century sources. The 'classic manorial system' (*régime domanial classique*) is presented to us in the context of *villae* described one after the other by the surveyors. These were great concentrations of land, several hundred and occasionally several thousand hectares in extent. The names they bear are generally those of present-day villages and it is sometimes possible to demonstrate that the area of the manor actually coincided with that of the village. Even so, the land would be divided up into several farms: one very large and managed directly by the lord himself; the others variable in number, far smaller in size and granted out to peasant households.

The manorial demesne is referred to as the lord's manse (*mansus indominicatus*), arranged around an enclosed, built-up area called the 'court' (*curtis*). This is how the one on the manor of Annapes is described:

> . . . a royal palace built of excellent stonework, with three large rooms and an upper storey [*solariis*] all the way round the building comprising eleven small rooms [the arrangement of a big country residence had not changed since Roman times]; down below, a storeroom and two porticoes [*porticus*]. Inside the court are seventeen other buildings made of wood, with as many rooms, and other outbuildings in good condition:

a stable, kitchen, bakehouse, two barns and three sheds. The court is provided with a strong palisade and a stone gateway with an upper chamber [*desuper solarium*]. There is a little court, this also enclosed by a well-kept hedge planted with trees of different kinds.[1]

In addition there would be one or more mills and a chapel which had become, or was in process of becoming, the parish church. To this centre would be attached long ploughing strips or 'furlongs' (Latin *culturae*, French *coûtures*), the best meadowland, always some vineyards wherever their cultivation proved feasible, and finally the greater part of the untilled wilderness. At Somain, an outlier of Annapes, the area dependent on the lord's home-farm covered 250 hectares in fields, 44 in meadow and 785 in woodland and waste. The portion assigned to the various peasant farms, whose tofts (manses) we can visualize lying huddled together somewhere near the lord's residence, was usually smaller. On manors in the Boulonnais described in the polyptyque of the abbey of St Bertin, it was equivalent to two-thirds, or even two-fifths of the manorial demesne. It might happen that this land, almost all fields, was shared out among the tenants in uniform parcels of about a dozen or fifteen hectares. But this was not normally the case. Most of the time, striking inequalities are revealed, some of them due originally to the legal status of the holdings. Some, indeed, are called 'free' (*ingenuiles*) in certain surveys and stand out as better equipped than others, which are called 'servile' (*serviles*). But the disparities between one manor and another are generally much more profound. At four places in the Paris region described in the polyptyque of St Germain-des-Prés, the average arable area attached to each manse comes to 4·8, 6·1, 8·0 and 9·6 hectares respectively: within a few kilometres, then, it could vary to the point of doubling. Furthermore, the survey reveals enormous differences on each of these manors between adjacent farms of the same status. Hence we can see one particular servile manse with forty-five times more land than another. Such unevenness betrays the effects of the prolonged mobility of landed property in the hands of the peasantry. The interplay of inheritance divisions, purchases and exchanges had brought about the enrichment of some, the impoverishment of others. This same mobility had destroyed the coincidence between the status of the manse and that of the husbandman who farmed it. Free manses might be held by slaves; servile ones by *coloni*, that is

[1] *Monumenta Germaniae Historica*, *Legum*, section II, *Capitularia Regum Francorum*, vol. i, part 1 (Hanover 1883), p. 254.

workers deemed free. And while certain manses were occupied by a single household two or three and sometimes four households were settled on many others. Notwithstanding all this disorder, a more or less chaotic reflection of the antiquity of each great estate's organization, the lord did nothing to remedy it. He merely imposed equal burdens on all tenements in the same legal category, whatever their size and the number of labourers farming them (in other words, their productive capacity). Such indifference contrasts oddly with the sense of numerical precision displayed by many surveyors, who were at pains to measure areas and enumerate the occupants of tenements. There is nothing to suggest that a survey was intended to distribute peasant obligations more fairly. But to ignore economic realities was dangerous. It was one of the weaknesses of these major units of production. What hope was there that tenants of tiny or overpopulated manses could discharge their duties as readily as others? Was it not inevitable that they should try to shirk them? Constantly disrupted by changes that the lord was powerless to obstruct, the basis of the whole manorial system – the division of the work load – seems to have been invariably in a state of serious imbalance.

From dependent manses the lord expected a rent, dues brought to him in his residence on the appointed day. These periodic liveries of a few eggs and chickens, a sheep or a pig, occasionally a few coins, represented the ground-rent for the toft. They paid for the customary rights by which tenants put their animals out to graze and gathered wood from the uncultivated part of the demesne. Others were burdens of public origin, equivalent to requisitions formerly made in aid of the royal army, whose collection had been consigned by the ruler to the manorial lord. These levies on small-scale animal husbandry in the home, or on the minimal profits of casual trading activities, did not overburden the peasant's farm and what they brought in to the lord's dwelling was of little value. The lord, as depicted in the polyptyques, was a *rentier* only in a minor way. He was primarily a farmer. Basically, he demanded from the tenants a contribution in labour power for the needs of his land. The fundamental economic role of the small satellite farm was to co-operate in working the big one.

Because of technical shortcomings, the home-farm required workers in enormous numbers. Some were entirely at the lord's beck and call. A gang of male and female slaves was maintained in the 'court' of every manor. Carolingian surveys have little to say about these household slaves. The surveyors do mention the occasional 'women's workroom, where there are twenty-four women', where they had found 'five pieces of serge, with four bandages of the same, and five pieces of linen cloth'; but while they took care to count mares, oxen and sheep, they paid no attention to the total strength of the permanent staff of servants. A few casual references bear witness to their presence. The bishop of Toledo reproached Alcuin for keeping more than twenty thousand unfree workers in the service of the four abbeys of Ferrières, St Martin of Tours, St Lupus of Troyes and St Josse. We know that on the sixty manors owned by the monastery of St Giulia of Bréscia in the early tenth century, where 800 families were settled on holdings, 741 slaves were toiling away on the demesne lands to which they were attached. In another connection, there are hints of unfree servants in the homes of ordinary peasant tenants: a peasant couple were given to Amiens Cathedral in 850 'with their children and slaves'. And how could single men farming the biggest manses in the *villae* of St Germain-des-Prés cultivate their lands without calling upon the services of household dependants? We can hardly suppose that residences of lords were relatively less well provided for than those of their tenants. Inside the 'court', wooden huts flanking the lord's dwelling would shelter large numbers of full-time workers. On one Bavarian manor given in alms by the Emperor Louis the Pious, twenty-two of them dealt with eighty hectares of arable. Lords liked to feel that close at hand were human beings whose persons belonged to themselves alone and who were ever ready to carry out their orders. As far as we can see, domestic slavery still remained very common in the ninth century throughout the countryside described by the polyptyques, playing a leading role in the exploitation of farms large and small. This role, however, was plainly diminishing. The ninth-century system was only a substitute for one based on slavery, which an already long-standing combination of circumstances had condemned. The same reasons as before were encouraging masters to settle the unfree on holdings. As demand for cereals and wine rose, slavery proved increasingly ill-suited to the manpower requirements of a large farm. Tasks in fields and vineyards were unequally spread over the course of the year. Off-seasons alternated with others when the calendar required a superabundant labour force for ploughing or harvesting. It would have been ruinous for the farmer to maintain year in and year out all the personnel necessary for peak periods of activity; he would therefore retain permanently a mere skeleton staff. But the need to supplement it from time to time was more imperative than before.

Reinforcements would sometimes come from wage-earners. It was easy to take on hirelings from among tenants who had little land, or from bands of itinerants always present on the confines of the manor. These piece-workers were fed, but might also receive money. Sixty *denarii*, for instance, were set aside in the annual budget of the abbey of Corbie for the temporary employment of extra gardeners. But the main contribution of manpower came from the tenements, which provided it in many different ways. As a rule, tenants of servile manses would owe a higher proportion of their time. Holding less land, but detained for longer periods in the lord's service, they would have been unable to spare as much time for cultivating their own plots as tenants of free manses. More directly engaged in domestic service, the household's womenfolk had to work in the 'court' workshops or manufacture pieces of cloth in their own homes. The men were compelled to attend at the lordship's headquarters three mornings a week and carry out orders. The nature of their obligations ensured that servile workers were fed partly at the lord's expense – another reason for granting them smaller holdings. In any case, their services were in general manual ones and undefined in character. Larger and better provided with ploughing equipment and draught animals, so-called free manses were usually burdened with more precisely defined works. Their holders would have to fence in the manor's fields, meadows and 'court' over a particular stretch; fully cultivate some specified portion of the demesne ploughlands for the lord's benefit; drive their teams on the lord's land for a given number of days at appointed seasons; accompany carts over a precise distance, and carry messages. Here the imposition on the household's productive forces was lighter, yet its value was greater from the lord's point of view because the requisitions (*corrogata*, meaning 'demands' in the strict sense of the word) placed at his disposal not only men and women, but also draught beasts and the least ineffectual implements.

When the combined labour services of all the holdings are added together, surprising figures result. The eight hundred tenant families of the monastery of St Giulia at Bréscia were liable to perform about sixty thousand dayworks at the beginning of the tenth century. Everything leads to the conclusion that the great estates were not making full use of the labour forces they were able to command: a reserve was formed on which to draw according to need, which would vary from season to season and from year to year. It should not be forgotten, however, that the land was most unyielding and a devourer of manpower. Even in Picardy (anything but a backward region) many fields were still being turned over with the hoe. The manorial system had been built upon the basis of extensive agriculture; it did nothing to improve productivity. On the contrary, it made enormous demands on the strength of an undernourished peasantry, badly equipped and too unevenly distributed over the food-producing area. The lords' capacity for unrestricted requisition of free manpower made great property owners indifferent to technical improvements. Therein lay the system's gravest defect, giving rise to a suspicion that the great estates arrested to an appreciable extent tendencies towards growth.

Even in the country between the Loire and the Rhine, the chosen land of the great polyptyques, the 'classic' manorial system never looked so neat and straightforward as in the brief outline we have just sketched. Primarily this was because every manor was a living organism. Partible inheritance (when the lord was a layman), gifts, purchases, forfeitures – all these pressures from concurrent forces would keep on altering its boundaries and internal structure: whenever the area of the demesne was increased; whenever dependent tenements and the labour force they provided were detached from the big farm; conversely, whenever new, duty-bound peasants whose labour was superfluous were added to the manor, these changes were constantly upsetting the balance between land and work. They introduced into the manorial system difficulties that would mar its operation and necessitate endless adjustments. According to prescriptions in the capitulary, *De Villis*, it was the stewards' task to carry out transfers of manpower and duties if they could manage it. In reality, the picture normally presented by the surveys is one of ungovernable chaos, but at least it brings out four features clearly enough.

First, the system we have described seems to have spread further in the ninth century. It infiltrated less advanced parts of Latin Christendom in particular. Great estates arose in Flemish territory at this time and were gradually put into working order. The manorial system then spread into Germania, which was steadily colonized by the Frankish aristocracy and great ecclesiastical foundations. In England blocks of landed property similarly assembled had been forming since the seventh century, in the cradle of that agrarian prosperity which was to tempt first Vikings, then Normans. Thus unfolded that long-term evolution which, on the one hand, changed imperceptibly the position of slavery in the workings of the economy by increasing the number of tenements for slaves, and, on the other hand, continued to tighten the upper aristocracy's hold over those peasants who were still independent.

Secondly, great estates were far from extending over the whole Western countryside. They happen to be all that the sources disclose for us, or nearly so. Almost total darkness prevails beyond their boundaries, yet the presence of smaller estates can still be detected. Among the written documents concerning Picardy, which bring into focus only what was owned by great religious establishments, one deed in three reveals the existence of medium-sized properties. This suggests that they were in a majority in this area. Peasant farms without an overlord also appear in the sources. Carolingian capitularies allocating military obligations among the holders of one, two or three manses point to the tenacious survival of small free proprietors. We might guess as much from tiny gifts in alms received by religious institutions. The polyptyques themselves describe modest family possessions that had just been incorporated in an ecclesiastical estate, but which had been independent until recently and certainly did not constitute exceptions. And at monasteries like St Gall in the ninth century or Cluny in the tenth, we can see the full extent of large numbers of allods in their well-preserved archives. These were properties that were entirely free from seigneurial control. Their size corresponded to the needs and manpower resources of a peasant household; they had been slowly pieced together through their owners' patient thrift. Here was an important sector of the rural economy that continued to operate in the background; it was in the hands of a middling aristocracy and the peasantry; it did not come within the ambit of the 'classic' manorial system, or only indirectly.

Thirdly, the features of the manorial system become seriously distorted as soon as we leave Neustria, Austrasia or Burgundy. Profound regional differences come to the surface. In Germanic districts the structure of the great estates appears to have been much looser. Some tenements, inhabited almost exclusively by slaves, were alone in their proximity to the 'court'; the rest were scattered about at a distance, sometimes so far away that peasants occupying them could scarcely have brought anything to the lord but rents. They did not actively assist in farming the demesne. In Lombardy large gangs of household slaves were maintained at manorial headquarters, supported by the unlimited services of a few peasants, also of unfree status, settled on near-by holdings. But most of the tenants were free men who possessed allods elsewhere. Some owed labour services, though light ones; the majority were ordinary share-croppers (*métayers*) handing over a well-defined portion of their harvest to the lord. A similar separation between the demesne, its exploitation resting almost entirely with unfree servants, and the tenements, providing only rents or a few occasional services, can be found in Flanders and in western, central and southern Gaul. We may well wonder whether the system portrayed most clearly in Irminon's polyptyque was not in fact a rare phenomenon.

Fourthly, already antiquated when surveyors visited the possessions of St Germain-des-Prés in the early ninth century, the manorial system underwent during the course of the century developments that distinctly altered the way it worked. These changes can be discerned only with difficulty. The polyptyques were intended to ascertain the current state of affairs on an estate and stabilize its structure. The description they give is therefore static. In order to detect long-term tendencies inside the manorial system we have either to interpret the corrections made to survey-texts during the decades *after* they were drawn up, or to compare surveys of successive dates (though these commonly relate to different manors, which considerably reduces their value for comparative purposes). Some of these tendencies do allow us a fleeting glance. The most obvious is the gradual disappearance of all distinction between free and servile manses. Population changes, mixed marriages, inheritances and property transactions had long since destroyed the coincidence between a peasant's status and that of his land. Free men would have to do service like slaves if their manses were not free. They would be more harshly exploited than their neighbours of servile origins who were in possession of a free tenement. Custom found it hard to accept these discrepancies; they were therefore simplified. Little by little, identical burdens were imposed on every homestead, but this standardization took place in line with a general increase in peasant obligations. This can be detected especially in Germanic countries and can be explained in part by the development of the agrarian economy, by a slow conversion of the system of production to the more demanding cultivation of cereal crops, and by the improvement of peasant equipment. Unfree holdings in Germania might be subjected by degrees to compulsory ploughing services in the ninth century, but at least their holders now had the use of a team of draught animals. Even so, free peasants in particular suffered as the gap separating them from slaves narrowed imperceptibly. This was one further step along the road leading from slavery to serfdom, as the dependent population became fused into a single, homogeneous mass of exploited labourers.

If this tendency is most evident in the barbarian part of Europe, another stands out more clearly in the most advanced areas, those where Roman survivals still lingered in the south. It is connected with the ever deeper involvement in dues assessed on manses of cash, the use of which had been revived by the restoration of the machinery of central government. For example, on one Burgundian manor surveyed in 937, each holding was expected to supply about sixty coins annually in several instalments. Some of these money payments are described as being equivalent to former liveries of livestock or woodwork; another eventually replaced a labour service: 'He does two fortnights' work; otherwise he redeems them with eleven *denarii* in mid-March.' Conversions of this type point to the flexibility of the monetary medium and its gradual penetration of the peasant's mode of existence. Lords and workers were coming to an understanding for the wider use of *denarii*. It is hardly surprising that commutation was most usual in northern Italy, where the rural economy was stimulated early on by the circulation of coins. By the end of the tenth century, tenants of the cathedral chapter of Lucca were almost entirely exempt from labour services and payments in kind; instead they were meeting most of their obligations by handing over money. Arrangements of this kind had the effect of further separating the big farm from the smaller ones surrounding it. What the tenant was paying for, with the proceeds earned by selling his labour or the surplus from his domestic output, was the right to dispose freely of his energies and devote them to his own land in order to increase its yield. With the cash in hand, the lord would aim to replace workers liable to compulsory labour services by wage-earners, whose voluntary and paid work seemed more productive. In short, this great innovation has to be viewed in terms of mental attitudes: as people became accustomed to using money less exceptionally, they discovered that labour was a value in itself, capable of being measured and exchanged. This revelation struck at the root of relations between lord and tenants on the manor. The cash nexus entered the heart of the farming system and since all this was bound up with a new awareness of *prices*, the elasticity introduced into the workings of the manorial economy led quite naturally to a rise in productivity.

Diverse in structure, adaptable, yet less widespread than has sometimes been thought, the great estates were nevertheless the centrepieces of the whole economy of the period, because of the function they fulfilled and the influence they exerted upon the surrounding countryside. Their role was to sustain a chain of large aristocratic households. As units of production they were therefore in the service of a consumer economy. When lords were engaged in exploiting their resources more rigorously their first care was to determine in advance, with maximum accuracy, what the requirements of their households would be. This is what a few skilful monastic administrators had striven after in the ninth century, notably Abbot Adalard of Corbie who in 822 turned his attention to defining meticulously the quality and quantity of the commodities demanded by the various departments of the domestic economy. Wherever economic planning existed, it was seen in the context of needs to be satisfied. What was expected of manorial production was that it should be equal to foreseeable demand, and lords were satisfied if their farm managers could provide them on the spot with all they actually required. The correspondence of Einhard, Charlemagne's friend, with the stewards of his various estates illustrates this attitude well. It was not a question of maximizing output from the land, but rather of maintaining it at such a level that it could respond to any request at a moment's notice.

Two consequences ensued. First, in order for there to be sufficient at all times, manorial production had to operate at a high rate because capricious weather conditions made possible enormous differences between one harvest and another. Normally there was more than enough. This explains, for example, why the surveyors inspecting granaries at the royal manor of Annapes found more seed from the preceding year than from the current one, despite losses incurred through vermin. Because the size of the harvest was extremely variable, at a time when needs were inelastic, the economy of the great estates was wasteful with respect to both land and manpower. Apart from technical shortcomings, irregularities in output made the support structure of large seigneurial farms an excessive burden on the productive area and on the peasantry. Thus the upkeep of just one of the sixty monks in the abbey of St Bertin depended on the provision of about thirty subordinate households.

Since the manorial system's productivity was pathetically low, the foundations of the economic and social structure underpinning the aristocracy were extraordinarily massive. This prompted magnates to defend jealously their rights over land, even more over men and women, and strive to extend them still further.

Secondly, because consumption dictated manorial production, the real motive force for growth has to be sought in the increasing needs of the upper ranks of the aristocracy, who tended irresistibly to use their power over land and people for bigger spending. The gradual consolidation of a social élite, at least in certain parts of Carolingian Europe, already appears as one of the most powerful stimulants of development. Every magnate wished to have as large a following (*mesnie*) as possible, since his prestige was measured by the number of people in his entourage; he aimed to treat these habitual guests better than other overlords, because generosity and lavish hospitality were the outward show of his strength. These desires urged lords to squeeze more out of their land, though apparently less by striving to increase yields from their fields and vineyards than by endeavouring to acquire new ones. Concern for ostentation bred rapacity and aggressiveness well before it led to improved methods of exploiting landed resources. Lords scarcely dreamt of such means of enlarging their incomes until other opportunities for enriching themselves disappeared – in other words, when the chances of readily laying their hands on other people's property had diminished. The reconstruction of the state and consolidation of public order in the ninth century may therefore have stimulated growth by deflecting seigneurial greed towards the quest for higher manorial profits.

As the manorial system spread further and further, it generated its own momentum. Not without reason, the decrees issued by Carolingian rulers called owners of great estates the 'powerful' (*potentes*) and made every effort to wrest the 'poor' (*pauperes*) from their grasp. In the clearing where his property lay, the lord, and in his name his bailiff, could in practice act unchecked. Peace and justice depended on them. They alone could offer to provide for itinerant families or younger sons of village peasants, by endowing them with newly created small-holdings on the perimeter of the demesne – *hospitia* or *accolae*, as Latin documents call these marginal plots of land. The manor's grain-store, still full when others were empty, was the hope of starvelings thronging its doors and promising anything in exchange for corn. Compilers of polyptyques did not describe this seigneurial power, which sprang from the remoteness of public authorities and the affluence of magnates in a human environment assailed by a thousand dangers, for it was not included in the legitimate rules for making customary payments. Their power was none the less considerable; indeed, it was through its agency that manorial boundaries were extended in all directions. It subjected small, still independent farmers to the authority of the big landowner. Because of the sheer size of his landed possessions, the lord dictated the whole round of agrarian practices, fixing times for reaping and grape-picking while controlling the labour market through his enormous need for auxiliary manpower. He dispensed help; he lent seed and flour. In return he would expect services. One is struck by the extent of the complex network of 'commendations' (*commendationes*) that eventually attached the majority of autonomous peasants in the neighbourhood to a *villa*. These dependants (*protégés*) were counted in certain polyptyques because they paid an annual due called *capitagium*; there were twenty of them on the manor of Gagny, belonging to St Germain-des-Prés, as against sixty-eight customary tenants. Their personal submission looks like a first step towards stricter dependence, which was leading to the integration of their land with the lord's and bringing the status of their descendants close to that of *servi casati* slave tenants. The most important gains made by the great estates took place at the expense, not of neighbouring estates, but of the still independent peasantry.

Some peasant resistance was encountered within the nascent village community. Associations of 'neighbours' were gathering strength around the parish church and the collective possession of customary rights. It is even possible (for the class struggle may now have assumed this basic pattern) that peasants had been forming special associations to protect them from oppression by the rich. A capitulary promulgated by the king of the West Franks in 864 denounced *villani* (villagers) who were organizing themselves in *conjurationes*, groups bound by oaths of mutual aid, to oppose those who had despoiled them. Were such sworn associations entirely ineffectual? It may be doubted when we see how powerless were lords to come to terms with recalcitrant tenants even inside the manorial framework. A protracted lawsuit was necessary to enable monastic lords in Aquitaine to compel the dependants of one of their *villae* to discharge certain obligations in 883: these had been written down in an earlier polyptyque but in face of the peasants' passive resistance they had fallen into disuse. In the end the quarrel had to be brought before the royal court. At other times the ruler's judgement came to the assistance of workers who were jibbing at new seigneurial demands. The continual and muted struggle between peasant forces and landlords was not so unequal as it might appear, and its results were varied. Small independent farms were absorbed in huge numbers by the extension of seigneurial authority, but in the very heart of the manor inertia, deception, considerations bought from the bailiff, the threat of absconding into the wilds where pursuit was impossible – there to join up with the bands of outlaws that Frankish capitularies strove vainly to disperse – all constituted effective weapons against any pressures from the economic system. No great landowner had the means, nor perhaps even the intention, to ban the sale or exchange of land, which was leading to a gradual fragmentation of the basis of peasant burdens:

> . . . in certain places, tenants of royal and ecclesiastical manors sell their inheritances, that is, the manses they hold, not only to their peers but also to chapter clerks or village priests and other men. They retain only their homes and thereby manors (*villae*) are destroyed, for dues can no longer be levied and it is no longer possible even to know which lands are dependent on each manse.[1]

Charles the Bald's edict of 864 deprecating this phenomenon attempted to take remedial measures which we can be sure were quite fruitless. Because it lacked strength, the shell of the great estates crumbled away, undermined by the resistance, conscious or otherwise, of those 'poor', 'humble' and 'weak' men who toiled in the fields. They, notwithstanding their deprivation and the moving epithets the language of our sources applies to them, were none the less forerunners of economic growth. Every polyptyque describes a partially decomposed organism, whose disintegration it was trying unsuccessfully to slow down. By its propensity for wastefulness, its unlimited demands, the excessive dues keeping its subordinate masses in a state of chronic malnutrition, the manorial system could countervail the efforts of the peasantry. Yet its links were weak; it could not contain the sudden rise in population apparent during the second half of the ninth century. Changes began to occur. Lords in pursuit of higher profits built machines

[1] *Monumenta Germaniae Historica, Legum*, section II, *Capitularia Regum Francorum*, vol. ii, part 2 (Hanover 1897), p. 323.

for grinding corn, so releasing part of the rural labour force for other duties; they gradually came round to prefer cash payments to labour services; by enlarging the sector of self-supporting farmers, they encouraged them no longer to cultivate solely to subsist but also to sell; they endowed their slaves with holdings, thus whetting appetites for work in a substantial section of the populace; they were aware of the value of generosity and willy-nilly distributed their surplus harvest among those who were famished. Despite themselves, the great estates were nurturing progress in the rural economy.

In the long run the manorial system played an important part in speeding up the development of exchange and monetary circulation in the countryside. This happened because money was slowly filtering into the system of payments, and because the need for small farmers to hand over commodities to their lords was forcing them regularly to frequent those little weekly markets that had been spreading far and wide in villages of the Empire during the ninth century. As soon as the habit of using silver coins was adopted as the most convenient vehicle for transferring wealth, the extremely scattered nature of the great estates prompted their administrators to dispose of surplus produce from each *villa* and send the cash-product of these sales to their master's residence.

> We wish [says the capitulary, *De Villis*] that every year during Lent, on Palm Sunday, stewards shall see to it that the money arising from our sales is brought in according to our instructions, so that we might know the sum total of our profits for that year.[1]

The most profitable royal manors were located on the main trading routes, which their presence was helping to bring back to life. All along the Meuse exchanges based on the use of money were providing regular connections between the waterway and the great estates that flanked it. The monks did not consume one-seventh of the fifteen thousand measures of wine produced on the lands of St Germain-des-Prés; the rest went by boat along the rivers to be sold in countries to the north and west. The role of commercialization was not always 'marginal' and this traffic was collectively generating an ever greater volume of cash transactions. The abbot of St Riquier was able to amass some seventy thousand silver coins annually in the early ninth century, equal in value to one hundred

[1] *Monumenta Germaniae Historica, Legum*, section II, *Capitularia Regum Francorum*, vol. i, part 1 (Hanover 1883), p. 85.

and fifty horses. Part of these he would use for buying commercial goods. The economic concentration represented by the great estate made a powerful contribution towards associating the work of the land and its fruits with trading activities.

III TRADE

These activities occupy a large place in the sources of Carolingian economic history. This was one of the effects of the restoration of the monarchy. It would be incumbent upon the ruler (whose ambition was to revive the Empire, and who, anointed by bishops, was becoming more fully aware of being God's instrument) to act as guarantor of order and justice, and keep special watch over this unfamiliar sector of the economy. Morally suspect because it brought into play the profit motive condemned by the Christian ethic, trade called for strict control. Consequently, the king was in duty bound to pay particular attention to it. He supervised and legislated, and writings emanating from the palace bear numerous traces of his preoccupations. This in itself might lead the historian into error, by making him attribute a disproportionate role to trade.

The new-found state was concerned in the first instance to keep the peace wherever commercial transactions occurred, and thus fix precisely the times and places for merchants to meet. If references to country markets increase in areas under Carolingian control during the ninth century, is this simply a sign that the commercial exchange of goods by peasant producers was growing? Was it not also partly the outcome of a consolidation of royal authority over living institutions, and the ruler's generosity in granting to churches the proceeds from tolls on trade? One fact is certain: Pepin's instruction to the bishops in 744 to ensure that a market was held regularly in each diocese meant that markets were not yet to be found everywhere. A century later they had become common in the old Frankish lands, too common even, with the result that a restoration of order was called for lest royal control should lapse. The edict of 864 bade counts draw up lists of markets in their administrative districts, distinguishing those that had already been active in Charlemagne's day from those that had been established in the time of Louis the Pious, and later under Charles the Bald. Any that seemed to them unnecessary were to be suppressed.

The attention paid to coinage was even more scrupulous. Indeed, the Divine order whose guardian the ruler wished himself to be would demand regular activity: 'It is needful,' proclaims the *Admonitio Generalis* of 789, referring to the Book of Proverbs, 'that weights and measures should be identical and fair throughout the realm.' Carolingian monetary reform resembles an act of political morality. Taking regal power back into their own hands, the new leaders of the Frankish people intended to reserve the monopoly of mintage for themselves. Their subjects were compelled to melt down foreign coins, which explains the absence from hoards concealed in the Carolingian Empire of those Arab *dirhams* that abound on the more barbaric fringes of Europe. Its rulers prescribed a uniform type of coin. Directly after his coronation in 755, Pepin the Short decided that twenty-two *solidi* should be struck from every pound of silver; one of these would be set aside as wages for the moneyers who, with the restoration of royal authority, again became paid assistants. Their names soon disappeared from the coins, which were indeed the king's own. Mint workers were combined in the Lombardo-Byzantine fashion into colleges, over which counts were expected to keep a watchful eye. Later, Louis the Pious was to adopt the imperial sanction of the loss of a hand for false moneyers and to punish with exile and confiscation anyone striking coins outside state workshops. Mintage had well and truly recovered its uniformity, so that in a hoard buried at Wiesbaden before 794 the five thousand *denarii*, issued by various mints, are all of the same weight. In 806 Charlemagne even attempted to centralize mintage completely: 'Let there be no minting in any place other than our palace.' The measure was unenforceable in such a vast state. Because coins remained an exceptional phenomenon and because it was necessary to strike them as required whenever a money payment could not be avoided, it was essential for mints to be established within reach of all those localities where currency was in regular use, especially near seats of justice, where money still served primarily for payment of fines. Thus irresistibly mintage spread. An edict of Charles the Bald in 864 tried, for the last time, to arrest the process by concentrating mints in the royal palace and nine public buildings. It failed but, at all events, order had been re-established by his predecessors for at least a century.

Even after the imperial coronation, Charlemagne did not go back to a gold currency. The gold *solidi* commissioned by his son, Louis the Pious, in imitation not of Byzantine coins but of those of the ancient Caesars, represented a short-lived affirmation of the *renovatio imperii*, the cultural renaissance. Possibly the easier circulation of silver in comparison with gold had made the white metal flow into northern Gaul in the late eighth century. Nevertheless, loyalty to silver for coinage was apparently dictated mainly by essentially political considerations: the king had to place himself in the tradition of Pepin, restorer of Frankish power, and especially to avoid giving offence to Byzantium, rather keeping a respectful distance from her. The Frankish kings intended at least to make a strong and stable currency of the *denarius*. They raised the weight of the Merovingian coin, first up to 1·30 grams, then to 1·70 and even up to 2·03 grams in the time of Charles the Bald. In northern Italy they substituted it for the gold *triens* after their conquest of the Lombard kingdom. They fixed the ratio between silver and gold, and between the *denarius* and the *solidus*, in accordance with the market price of precious metals then obtaining in north-western Gaul, and so instituted a monetary system based on a *libra* of twenty *solidi*, each worth twelve *denarii*. In the ninth century this was adopted by Anglo-Saxon rulers.

The rebirth of the state had fostered the development of monetary circulation. Increasingly employed for the exchange of goods silver *denarii* possessed an economic value more and more clearly recognized by their users. In his attempt at reorganization, however, Charlemagne soon discovered that control of their value was slipping from royal hands, and that the weight of coins could not be altered without causing fluctuations in prices and the use of money. Further attempts were made at readjustment. At Frankfurt in 794 he fixed commodity prices in terms of the new system. After 803 glosses were inserted in the Salic Law in order to overhaul the tariff of fines. Between 794 and 804 he took measures against those who were refusing to handle the new coins. But resistance was strong and apparently common to all sections of society: he had to threaten free men with a fifteen *solidi* fine, slaves with corporal punishment, and proceedings against bishops and counts who were not showing themselves sufficiently vigilant. The opposition proves that the use of money was already widespread in certain parts of the Empire by the end of the eighth century. Yet the king was strong enough to overcome his opponents, and if the Frankish monetary system took root all over Europe, this was (a political factor once more) because it was controlled by the decisions of the ruler whose military conquests had made him the most powerful in the West.

It also lay within the ruler's responsibility to keep a close watch on long-distance trade, the special activity of those whom the sources call *mercatores* or *negociatores*. In countries through which they passed merchants travelling over great distances were by that very fact foreigners, inadequately protected by local custom and all the more insecure in that the precious wares they were known to be carrying might well excite covetousness. They therefore needed special protection, suspect as they must have been in a world where the boundaries between peaceful exchange and plundering were ill-defined. How could people distinguish between pillagers and these unknown traders, who likewise moved about in a band and often spoke another tongue? Alfred the Great's laws, for instance, show them in company with a body of servants who were probably armed. Such men could sow seeds of discord; their passage through a locality might provoke brawls and riots. In cases of murder, who would assume judicial responsibility for their actions on the victims' behalf? Who could be sure that the goods on offer had not been stolen? For such reasons it was important for commercial dealings to be controlled by public authority, to take place openly and under strict supervision. Accordingly Carolingian legislation banned all trafficking at night-time, apart from the sale of provisions and fodder to travellers; the count or bishop was to be present whenever the exchange concerned items evoking the liveliest suspicions – slaves, horses, objects of gold and silver. It was essential that the king should guarantee the status of merchants dealing in foreign trade and that certain times and places should be set aside for their activities.

We gain some insight into the status of merchants in a decree by the Emperor Louis the Pious dating from 828. Merchants were described as the ruler's 'vassals' (*fideles*) and this personal tie placed them within the special peace extended to royal dependants. Because they belonged to the prince's household, they were exempt from tolls levied on goods traffic, except at Alpine crossings and in those wide-open gateways to the northern seas, Quentovic and Duurstede. They had their own means of transport but when their travels were ended, in mid-March, they came to the palace to make customary payments to the treasury. They then had to distinguish fairly what was their own private business from what they had handled on the ruler's behalf. These seasonal yet regular activities made these men beyond all question professionals. Presumably they were enlisted as subordinates of the royal household, whereby they obtained fiscal benefits and added security, but they retained a substantial share of the initiative, which was capable of being enlarged. Of these and others not attached to the royal palace but to abbeys or aristocratic households, or even operating free-lance, how many were free men, Frankish or Lombard, and how many were Christians? All that can be said is that eighth- and ninth-century sources, when referring to *negociatores*, frequently allude to two ethnic groups whose colonies were dispersed along the main routeways and reached far beyond the frontiers of the Empire: Jews and (in the North Sea area) 'Frisians'.

All these suppliers of items of long-distance trade met at specially organized sites, where they displayed their wares and exchanged them among themselves. Documents refer to these places by the Latin word *portus*, equivalent to the word *wik* in Germanic speech and the word *burh* used in King Alfred's England. They were spaces enclosed by stockades to protect stores from raids by thieves. Expert witnesses subject to royal control were on hand as guarantors of the validity of contracts. By the time of Louis the Pious we may assume the presence of a representative of the ruler. He was responsible for passing judgement on merchants and for collecting the tribute-money that constituted the price of royal protection. Before the ninth century, *portus* had appeared in the north of the Frankish kingdom in districts that were still without active towns: Dinant, Huy, Valenciennes, Quentovic and Duurstede. After this, more frequent references in the same area show *portus* established near the sites of Roman towns, such as Rouen, Amiens, Tournai and Verdun. We do not meet any farther south, where their functions were probably fulfilled by existing *civitates*. Fairs served as other meeting points. Some of these were integrated into the regular cycle of weekly markets: on a known date during the year one of these gatherings would attract more people. But in that case the nature of the occasion changed completely: legally, because the ruler's protection would be extended to all who wished to come, even from far afield; economically, because its aim would be to arrange regular contacts on the appointed day between productive areas separated by enormous distances and for that reason normally isolated from one another. The fair held near the Parisian abbey of St Denis took place in October, after the grape harvest. It was probably a wine fair. In 775 a second fair was added in February, likewise placed at a strategic point in the agricultural calendar. They were evidently no longer mere outlets for produce from the surrounding countryside. Deeds granting tax exemption mention that boats laden with honey were finding their way there and that monks from Corbie would turn up to buy cloth for their cowls. We come across Englishmen from the beginning of the eighth century; Frisians and *negociatores de Langobardia* after 750. At the other end of the Empire, a fair was held at Piacenza. Early on, this lasted for just one day in the year; but in 872 three new gatherings, each of eight days' duration, were initiated; then, in 890, a fifth fair of eighteen days. This is how the expansion of trade was making a real impact. As for the geographical distribution of fairs and *portus*, there were two areas, to the north-west and south-east of the Carolingian Empire, where long-distance traffic seems to have been heaviest.

These two areas, which were to remain the magnetic poles of medieval *grand commerce*, were situated at meeting points of the sea and the main arteries of the European river system. By way of the Po, leading to Byzantine-dominated waters, the first gave access to more prosperous economies, sources of high-quality luxury goods, exquisite fabrics and costly spices. The second looked out via the Seine, Meuse, Rhine and North Sea on less civilized lands, continually disrupted by tribal warfare but, for this reason, valuable markets for slaves.

The consequences of a terrible war, then migration by the Lombard folk, had left northern Italy crippled throughout the seventh century. All trace of maritime activity at Genoa disappears in 642, whereupon the barbarians' sway was consolidated. For a short while the Rhône valley became the principal route to the Orient. This was when the Frankish king, Dagobert (629–39), granted privileges in the ports of Provence to monasteries in northern Gaul. The house of St Denis received an annual sum of one hundred gold *solidi*, levied on the toll at Fos near Marseilles, for purchasing oil and other provisions; and tax exemptions were granted in the ports of Marseilles and Fos for buying papyrus and spices, privileges that were renewed up to 716. But by then they were out of date. The route that had been established along the Rhône, Saône and Meuse heading for Maastricht, along which active Jewish communities from the Midi towns were settled at intervals, was beginning to be affected by Moslem raiding parties. The route did not go out of use but thereafter ran through Catalonia to Moslem Spain. Hither merchants from Verdun took companies of slaves, and no doubt magnificent swords from Austrasia, carefully concealed since their exportation was strictly forbidden. Meanwhile, Lombardy had once more become the gateway to Byzantium. The foundation of the monastery of Novalesa in 726, at the foot of the busiest pass across the western Alps throughout the medieval period, marked the first stage in a reorganization of Alpine crossings. King Liutprand came to an agreement with merchants from Comácchio, by which their boats were to travel up the River Po laden with salt, oil and pepper. Round the Adriatic lagoons, still under Byzantine control, were slowly gathering forces from which Venetian vitality was soon to come surging forth. By the end of the eighth century, Pavia was the place in Western Europe where the most beautiful objects were to be found. Notker of St Gall, writing *c.* 880, tells us that court magnates of Charlemagne's time used to obtain there silken fabrics from Byzantium. This surely was still valid for the late ninth century, pointing to the lagoon sailors as the chief intermediaries between the treasures of the Orient and Carolingian courts. It was these long-distance exchange operations centred on Lombardy that gradually brought the Rhineland route back to life, supplanting Maastricht by Duurstede, and ultimately stimulating 'Frisian' trade.

The early conquests of the Austrasians had subjugated Frisia, which missionaries were laboriously to bring within the Christian fold. Commercial adventurers from this region were visiting England by the end of the seventh century. Bede mentions one Frisian trader who was buying prisoners of war in London, and the London Frisian colony was already important in Alcuin's time. On the Rhine Frisian boats were carrying wine, grain, pottery, salt extracted from Lüneburg, and slaves. They were settled in special quarters at Cologne, Duisburg, Xanten, Worms and above all at Mainz. They could be seen at the fairs of St Denis. In the ninth century it was in the company of Frisian merchants that St Anskar reached Birka in Sweden. This network of boat traffic became more active at the close of the eighth century. Centres for the collection of tolls are referred to in the *diploma* of exemption granted by Charlemagne to the abbey of St Germain-des-Prés in 779 – Rouen, Amiens, Maastricht, Quentovic and Duurstede. They mark the boundary of the area inside which the new *portus* and silver currency developed. The two principal intersections were Duurstede, whose coins radiated in all directions in Charlemagne's reign, and

Quentovic (mentioned for the first time in 668 by Bede). This was where Anglo-Saxon monks about to make an assault on Germanic paganism, and pilgrims for Rome disembarked; through it passed cargoes of wine, slaves, and those pieces of cloth whose quality was regulated in an agreement of 796 between Charlemagne and King Offa of Mercia.

We may add to this the traffic that developed along the Elbe and Danube, though it was less distinct from pillage than trade elsewhere. This traffic took the form of contacts with Slav tribes, whereby traders could get supplies of slaves (whom a capitulary of 805 attempted to channel towards a chain of frontier markets) and gives a clear impression of sustained growth, causing genuinely commercial activities to spread at the expense of a gift economy. Growth was promoted essentially by political reconstruction; that is to say, by internal peace, by the reorganization of the monetary system, above all by the consolidation of an aristocracy who until early in the ninth century divided among themselves the abundant spoils of incessant and victorious wars. How exactly are we to measure this growth? Is it inflated by the written sources, which (as I have suggested) tend to distort true perspective by assigning too much importance to mints and merchants? Let us tread warily, guarding against the excessive attention that historical writing, in the wake of Henri Pirenne, has paid to monetary and commercial aspects of the economy of this period. Was it the first wave of real growth, or a mere surface ripple? Three observations spring to mind.

First, it is on the perimeter of the Carolingian Empire that signs of increasing trade are particularly plentiful. Yet this was still due to the structure of the state, bounded as it was by frontiers. Following the example of Byzantium, the state set up fixed stations where duty was charged to merchants. As there were few towns in the north and east, only this desire to regulate and control can account for the appearance in the documents of new urban settlements. Is this to say that the interior of continental Europe had not been penetrated by the revival of communications? We have already explained why foreign coins hardly ever turn up in hoards and, if traces of urban expansion cannot be detected, this is because many towns already existed there, big enough to encompass further activity. In ninth-century Burgundy annual fairs were held in the region's five *civitates*, in the chief towns of the county and in the vicinity of the principal abbeys. The absence, then, of *portus* and of foreign coins by no means implies commercial sluggishness. Nothing entitles us to regard the apparent awakening as exclusively peripheral in character. We must not be deceived by the fortuitousness of documentary evidence.

Secondly, this revival seems to have been a partial one as regards the items of long-distance trade. These were essentially high-quality luxury goods. In the last analysis, trade was simply a substitute for pillage. It supplied what war could supply only uncertainly and irregularly. Like war it brought into the homes of overlords, via professional merchants who were usually their household servants, things to be worn, to amuse, to embellish and to be given away as presents. Ermoldus Nigellus expresses this outlook most succinctly in the poem in praise of the Rhine that he composed in the mid-ninth century: 'It is advantageous to sell wine to Frisians and other seafaring nations and to import superior products. This is how our people can clothe themselves with finery, for our merchants and those from foreign parts carry attractive wares for them.' No doubt we should except salt, a product of prime necessity, loads of which probably constituted the principal item of long-distance trade, in weight if not in value. The list of charges at the Raffelstetten toll station on the Danube shows that nearly all traffic between Bavaria and Slav countries was based on this commodity, and we may guess that the production and carriage of salt destined for Lombardy lay at the source of early capital accumulation in Venice and Comácchio. Wine sold at the St Denis fairs was also transported in great quantities. It came in jars made in the vicinity of Cologne, examples of which have been revealed in enormous numbers by excavations at London, Canterbury, Winchester and in farthermost Scandinavia. Like honey and slaves, wine made noble junketings even more resplendent and impressive. As for fabrics, the rough products woven on servile manses or in manorial workshops by the tenants' wives and daughters were deemed unworthy of the self-esteem of their lords. They demanded more finely-textured materials, dyed in brilliant colours, with which to clothe themselves or to flatter their friends. The purchase of these materials probably comprised the greater part of their outlay. According to the rule followed in Benedictine monasteries, the community's needs were classified under two headings: one was the *victus* or food supply, care of which devolved upon the cellarer, the official in charge of farm management; the other was the *vestitus*, or provision of vestments, purchases for which the chamberlain was responsible as receiver and keeper of cash revenues. This division implies that cloth was normally supplied by merchants and paid for in *denarii*. The 'cloaks of Frisia' were in no sense articles of mass production but robes of splendour: Charlemagne made presents of them to Caliph Harun ar-Rashid, and Louis the Pious to the Pope. The business deals that traders under royal protection were reporting back to the palace belonged to the realms of excess, luxury and rarity. For the most part, they were conducted on a small scale and for the sole benefit of an élitist minority in a still rustic society.

Thirdly, let us consider the repercussions of these activities on contemporary towns. Can the *portus* on the banks of the Meuse, Rhine or Scheldt, still operating on a seasonal basis, be regarded as genuine towns? What was Duurstede? Archaeological investigation has revealed it as a narrow street, one kilometre in length: a road lined with warehouses wherein a few traders, for whom a parish church had been erected, lived as permanent residents. Similar was the *pagus mercatorum* growing outside the walls of Regensburg between the Danube and the abbey of St Emmeram in the ninth century, like other merchant quarters along the Rhine nestling against the walls of the Roman towns of Mainz, Cologne or Worms. They were simply outgrowths, little different from the clusters of specialized workshops huddled at the gates of big monasteries and answering the needs of the lord's household; or the 'streets' (*vici*) in which metalworkers, weavers, tailors, skinners, men-at-arms and domestic helpers of a large country estate were allocated places close by the abbey of St Riquier in the second half of the ninth century. The real towns of this period remained first and foremost centres of political and military activity, based on a few stone buildings, and focal points of religious life. The great building projects undertaken by bishops at Orléans, Reims, Lyons and Le Mans shortly after the year 800 possibly made a more direct impact on the economy's vitality than did passing merchant caravans. In Germania the towns that were coming to life during this period sprang from fortified royal palaces flanked by an episcopal seat and a few monasteries. Commercial expansion was ushered into an environment still that of a peasant society dominated by war-leaders and priests. Trade was not influential enough to reshape it except locally.

Our conclusion must be, therefore, that these developments amounted to a mere surface ripple. Yet limited though it may have been, it somehow linked up with that other, fundamental exchange sector which the increasing use of money was activating in the context of villages, great estates and agrarian production. Unfortunately the circumstances of this interaction are completely shrouded in obscurity. We know that such end-products as salt and wine were flowing directly along the arteries of overseas trade. We can guess, too, from capitularies dealing with the regulation of bread prices or (like the edict of 864) with the purchase of wine by the *sextarius* (a few litres), that produce from the land was being sold retail everywhere, in towns and at major river crossings. The function of the retail trade was to feed a small population of specialized servants, detached by their crafts from the soil, and those whom Carolingian law and order enabled to move about in greater numbers along trackways and rivers.

The political reconstruction engineered by the Carolingians imprinted another decisive characteristic on the economy of the West. Rulers were anointed. Their principal calling was to lead God's people to salvation, and their spiritual office could not be separated from their temporal acts. Under the influence of the churchmen in their entourage, and especially the monks who came into prominence in the time of Louis the Pious, they were careful not to allow economic activities to disturb the order willed by God. Referring always to scriptural precepts, they wished more especially to purify commercial practices, the handling of money, and all transactions wherein the spirit of charity was endangered. Whenever disasters or Divine wrath brought confusion to the natural order, it would be incumbent upon the king to act. In years when poor harvests and famine drew their attention to the unsettled condition of commercial life, they would enact decrees or restrictions and spell out the distinction between what was pure and impure, lawful and unlawful.

> All those who acquire corn at harvest time or wine after the vintage, not from necessity but with cupidity as the ulterior motive – for example, by buying one *modium* for two *denarii* and holding on to it until it can be sold for four or six *denarii*, or even more – are making what we call an improper gain. If, on the other hand, they purchase it out of necessity in order to keep it for themselves or distribute it to other people, we call that *negocium*.[1]

[1] *Monumenta Germaniae Historica, Legum*, section II, *Capitularia Regum Francorum*, vol. i, part 1 (Hanover 1883), p. 132.

This definition of trade, taken from a capitulary of 806, not only throws light on the substantial price variations of victuals between harvesting seasons and summer dearth, caused by deficiencies in production, but also pinpoints the needs that would justify recourse to buying and selling. These were to supply one's own household and procure goods to give away to others. The morality underlying Carolingian decrees was derived partly from biblical teaching, partly from traditional ideas about self-sufficiency and necessary generosity. It tolerated commerce only when its purpose was to make good occasional shortages in domestic output. Morally, trade was an exceptional, almost unwarranted activity, and those who indulged in it should not as a rule be allowed to make a higher profit than a fair return on the trouble they had taken. Commissioned by God to extirpate evil on earth, it therefore rested with the king to condemn those 'who by diverse schemes fraudulently conspire to amass goods of all kinds with the intention of making a profit', or 'who covet the possessions of others and do not give them away to other people when they have obtained them'. According to the order that the ruler was expected to uphold, the only legitimate forms of wealth were those which came from forebears through inheritance or which were due to the generosity of an overlord. Riches were a gift, not the outcome of some kind of speculation, and the word 'benefice' (*beneficium*) in contemporary usage denotes quite simply an act of beneficence.

But the capitulary just cited, promulgated at a time when foodstuffs were in short supply, also shows that profit-making based on the use of money had penetrated the substructure of the economy down to the level of the production and consumption of the most basic goods. Taking advantage of the needs of others, men were winning money at the expense 'of those who sell wine and grain before the harvest and who thereby become poor'.[1] Commerce was a reality, and no doubt rare indeed were traders who confined themselves to a role as benevolent intermediaries. In order to prevent merchants from committing too great a wrong, it was necessary at least to try to contain their activities within certain limits: by making them observe the sabbath, by suppressing Sunday markets save those recognized by ancient custom (809), and by fixing a just price for commodities (794).

Two features of the exchange economy where the danger of

[1] *Monumenta Germaniae Historica, Legum*, section II, *Capitularia Regum Francorum*, vol. i, part 1 (Hanover 1883), p. 152 (dating from 809).

sinning was most acute, the slave trade and money-lending, attracted still more attention from Frankish kings. It seemed reprehensible that Christians should be reduced to slavery, and downright scandalous that the lure of profit could cause baptized men and women to be enslaved by infidels. During the eighth century, the slave trade had increased considerably in volume along a route leading from the borderlands with the East, through the Frankish kingdom by way of Verdun, the Saône and Rhône valleys, to the cities of Moslem Spain. Most of the slaves passing that way were Germanic or Slav heathens, yet they were seen by prominent churchmen, fired with the missionary spirit, as souls to be won. Furthermore, Christians were often rounded up on the way and added to the slave caravans. From 743, rulers issued prohibitions forbidding the sale of slaves to non-Christian buyers, who were debarred from crossing the frontiers. These injunctions had little effect and had to be promulgated over and over again. In the ninth century Bishop Agobard of Lyons, in his treatise against the Jews, besought the faithful in Christ 'not to sell Christian slaves to Jews and not to let them be sold in Spain'.

As for usury, it was normal practice in a primitive rural society, short of monetary reserves yet permeated by complex exchange networks, for every man, no matter what his economic status, might from time to time find himself forced to borrow in order to discharge his obligations. The Christian ethic bound people to assist freely their fellow men. Based on a passage in Exodus, the capitulary of 806 proclaims that 'lending consists in providing something; lending is right when only what has been provided is claimed back'. It defines usury as 'claiming back more than has been given; for instance, if you have given ten *solidi* and claim back more, or if you have given a *modium* of wheat and then demand one more in return'. Usury was condemned, but presumably just as ineffectually as was the export of baptized slaves. Even so, the principle had been clearly enunciated, with the support of venerable texts whose memory was not lost. This moral philosophy prevented the peasantry of medieval Europe from ever being as helplessly in debt as peasants of the ancient world had been, or as those unfortunates in Moslem countries continued to be. One of the most lasting achievements of Carolingian policies was the institution of an ethical code bearing upon this slowly evolving but still peripheral sector of the economic system.

Morality impinged on economic development in yet another

way, for at this juncture Carolingian kingship became peace-loving. Aggressive wars launched against outlying tribes had lost some of their edge in the early ninth century when Louis the Pious became Emperor, because conquest had been pushed so far that plundering expeditions were no longer very lucrative. Forays to the north and east encountered a world that was too wild and impoverished to offer much scope for stealing. In the south they came up against resistance that was difficult to overcome. These material circumstances gave rise to an ideology of peace inside the narrow circle of Church intellectuals surrounding the Emperor. The expansion of the kingdom had ended by uniting almost the whole of Latin Christendom under a single authority and giving 'actuality' to the City of God. Was not the ruler's first preoccupation thenceforth to preserve peace among the people? Following the example of the *Basileus*, the Emperor had no longer to concern himself with leading the attack but with defending the flock of baptized Christians against pagan incursions. These considerations, broadcast by ecclesiastical propaganda, strengthened those natural tendencies which, by a dramatic reversal of fortune, were now keeping on the defensive the Frankish war-parties that had so long been victorious. For a century aggressiveness had enabled the aristocracy of Gaul and Germania to adorn themselves with a modicum of luxury and to arouse the initiative of their household merchants, while hardly drawing at all upon their enormous landed resources. That this aggressiveness began to subside was an economic factor of paramount importance. By reducing the value of spoils brought back to court by the armies in late summer, it gradually exhausted the main source of royal munificence, striking at the sole means whereby the king might keep the aristocracy in check. Thus the political structure built up through conquest started to disintegrate. Thereafter economic development was to take place in an entirely new setting. And Latin Christendom, forced back on the defensive yet made marginally richer by the hesitant growth we have been investigating, was now to be a prey to aggressors in her turn.

If we take advantage of the relative clarity diffused by ninth-century written sources, we may hazard the following conclusions: first, by leading their comrades and vassals on annual pillaging expeditions, Charles Martel, Pepin and Charlemagne had amassed wealth from all quarters. They had also given away a good deal of it. This necessary generosity through distributions of movable goods had added appreciably to the resources the aristocracy were able to dedicate to self-indulgence. Such an increment in spending-power, in a culture growing accustomed to the use of money, had the effect of stimulating the development of real trade in expensive items.

Secondly, immersed in this affluence, magnates made little personal effort to exploit their landed wealth. This task was handed over to farm managers, that is to say, more often than not, to routine practices. When surveys lay bare their structure after the year 800, the great estates look like fossilized organisms whose unwieldiness tended to stand in the way of demographic expansion.

Thirdly, in the course of the ninth century, two developments forced these organisms to become less rigid and to adapt themselves. These were the gradual influence of monetary circulation and the sudden end to wars of conquest. To preserve their way of life, the diminishing returns from booty and tribute led magnates to stir up enthusiasm on the part of their farm managers: manors had to be made to yield more. A slow change therefore came about. Mounting pressure from the authority wielded by the 'powerful' over the 'poor' prepared the way for the peasantry as a whole to sink into a condition modelled on a new version of slavery. At the same time an improvement in technical equipment was taking place and this may have triggered off the resumption of population growth to which polyptyques of the late ninth century bear witness.

5 *The Final Assault*

It is not without misgivings that we venture to make room in a history of the economic development of the medieval West for the last waves of invasion to which Latin Christendom was subjected. Extending from the end of Charlemagne's reign until the new dawn after the millennium, these raids were long regarded by historians as a watershed. Some, like Henri Pirenne, saw in Carolingian times the final phase in the gradual decay of the system bequeathed by the ancient world. Others placed the real onset of growth in Charlemagne's day and age. Such views are understandable, for a great void is encountered in the documentary record. After the light thrown on economic affairs by writings from the Carolingian cultural renaissance, the chasm of the Dark Ages yawns wide open; for over a century, historical knowledge is deprived of most of its sources. Careful examination of the rare surviving evidence nevertheless bids us revise this judgement. For by and large, continuity was not broken, and in certain sectors the hesitant advances of the Carolingians were even encouraged. This leads us to take in at a single glance the period from the early decades of the ninth century until the middle, if not the last quarter, of the eleventh.

I THE ATTACKS

Let us first briefly pinpoint the incursions that befell the Christian West. The earliest came from Scandinavia. Prolonging an expansion that probably had its origins in the late seventh century, Norwegians came into contact in Charlemagne's time with the area of civilization whose history can be written. Annals place the date of their first appearance off the coasts of England in 786–96, Ireland in 795 and Gaul in 799. Simultaneously the Danes embarked upon sea-borne ventures now made easier by the absorption of Frisian sailors into the Frankish kingdom. Initially they launched lightning pillaging raids, but after 834 their expeditions were on a larger scale. Raiding parties set up permanent bases at the mouths of rivers, along which they sailed farther and farther upstream, attacking London (sacked in 841), Nantes, Rouen, Paris and Toulouse. Between 856 and 862 Gaul was under very heavy pressure. After 878 more than half of Anglo-Saxon England was held by Vikings.

From ports in North Africa and particularly in Moslem Spain, corsairs harassed Christian ships in the Mediterranean. They raided coastal districts as well: evidence for attacks on Italy comes as early as 806. The slow strangulation of shipping made piracy less rewarding and bands of robbers installed themselves on the mainland, holding to ransom passers-by over mountain roads. They appeared in southern Italy between 824 and 829. At the end of the ninth century, permanent robber camps were established to the north of Campánia ('the Saracens went on the rampage from the Tyrrhenian to the Adriatic and the Po, returning time and again to the Sabine Mountains and the River Liri beyond, where they had their ships and whence they carried everything back to their homelands'). Brigands based at Fraxinetum in the Massif des Maures in Provence controlled the Alpine passes for several decades.

Finally, Hungarian horsemen ventured westwards from the plains of Pannonia. The records allude to thirty-three raids between 899 and 955. These took them as far as Bremen in 915, Mende and Otranto in 924, Orléans in 937; and almost every year the countryside of Lombardy and Bavaria suffered springtime attacks. While Saracens followed trackways and Vikings the river-courses, Magyars were making use of Roman roads, carrying off their loot by the wagon-load.

In order to explain the vigorous, simultaneous and far-reaching nature of these attacks, we have first of all to bear in mind that Latin Christendom was a tempting prey. Pirates from the Moslem world, a more advanced economic region, were seeking prisoners to sell at slave markets, especially in Spain. If they turned out to be persons of rank, they would try to extort a ransom. Saracen pillaging was a kind of renewed slave-trading, stimulated, just like that long practised in Slav countries by *negociatores* from the Frankish kingdom, by extensive outlets in the Islamic Mediterranean. And slaves too comprised a high proportion of the booty seized by Hungarians and Scandinavians. These raiders from the more barbaric parts of Europe were also looking for the jewellery and precious metals hoarded in abundance in Christian sanctuaries. By amassing her treasures for the glory of God or of princes, the West had transformed herself into an enchanting Eldorado in their eyes. The incursions of the ninth and tenth centuries were deeds of men who came for the most part from native aristocracies. They set out primarily in pursuit of glory but also, as the runic epitaphs of Scandinavian warriors clearly demonstrate, in search of riches to enhance their own standing when they returned. Viking leaders, especially after the mid-ninth century, were searching beyond the seas as well for places of permanent settlement for themselves and their comrades in arms. Most of the invaders in fact were motivated by the same ambitions as the conquering war-bands that had sprung from the Frankish nobility during the seventh and eighth centuries: they were seeking adventures by which to earn their reputation, treasure from which to replenish their hospitality, slaves with whom to furnish their homes, and lands upon which to quarter their weapons.

Such ventures may have been successful at this moment in European history because of certain modifications in the conditions of life in the raiders' native lands. It may be that slow climatic changes quickened the westward drive of the peoples of the steppe and favoured a population rise in Scandinavia. But even if the theory of population expansion holds good for Norway during the seventh century, it does not seem applicable to Denmark, homeland of the most ferocious aggressors. The formation of bands of adventurers may also have been encouraged among northern peoples by the development of political institutions, by the transition from tribe to monarchic state. Be that as it may, the main cause of the last invasions Europe was to experience lay in her military inferiority. The Frankish army had shown itself to be a highly effective offensive weapon against tribes who fought on foot as the Franks did, who were equipped with rudimentary arms and were easily forced back on the defensive. It was invincible on familiar terrain. But it was cumbersome, slow to mobilize, and incapable of coping with unforeseen attacks by stealth, except perhaps on the military marches that Charlemagne had set up in Germania. Its new adversaries were fighters to a man. They had at their disposal instruments that made them difficult to catch – the Hungarians' horses and the Vikings' ships, which the initial rise of Scandinavian culture had turned into marvellous weapons. The first plunderers appeared on the horizon along a maritime front unprepared for war. They met with no resistance. They brought back news of this to their homelands and came again in even greater numbers. These sea-borne forays sowed disarray and terror. They hastened the disintegration of the state, with the result that Magyar raiders found the defences already abandoned. Hence the Frankish aristocracy, who for generations had relied on warfare as the principal source of their ostentation, now had to hand over their treasures to freebooters. The history of military technology explains this sudden reversal.

II THEIR EFFECTS

Written sources may overstate the seriousness of all this. They come from churchmen, quick to bemoan the misfortune of the times and give play to every apparent manifestation of Divine wrath. Moreover, they bore the brunt of the devastation, since they were sitting on the most tempting treasures which they were ill-equipped to defend. Their testimony must be put in proper perspective. The trials of Picardy, situated in one of the most exposed areas, are referred to in only two of the fifty-five extant charters and *diplomae* for the period 835–935, when the Scandinavian danger was at its height. Yet it cannot be denied that the shock was severe, as the lasting memory in the collective consciousness goes to show. How can we measure its impact on the economic structure of the West?

The freebooters had evidently taken everything they could carry: men and women, precious objects, gold, silver, wine, anything circulating visibly in the shape of gifts or trade. Later on the Danes organized a more rational exploitation of the hidden wealth of Latin Christendom. They forced the population to pay them tribute money, as they had in Frisia by 819. These ransom payments were at first local and private; afterwards leaders of Scandinavian warbands dealt with the public authorities. Beginning in 845 and continuing until 926 the kingdom of West Frankia was subject to payments in *denarii* to buy peace from the Northmen: in 861 Charles the Bald had five thousand *librae* delivered to the Somme Northmen and six thousand to those of the Seine. A military tax was imposed on part of England in 865 and became a regular tribute: in 991 its successor 'danegeld' amounted to £10,000. Eventually Vikings replaced the native aristocracy in certain areas (as early as 841 at the mouths of the Scheldt), appropriating in their stead the surplus product of peasant labour. They founded states around the two towns of Rouen and York, where they concentrated surpluses derived from their exploitation of the rural population. A large part of such little jewellery and precious metal as had been accumulated by the impoverished, rustic civilization of Carolingian Europe and Anglo-Saxon England thus passed into the victors' hands. Many a district saw its monks take flight. Carrying with them their relics and what they could salvage of their treasure, they stole away to secluded spots well inland on the Continent, making for regions far enough from the front line to look safe. For nearly a century the monastery of Novalesa, at the foot of an Alpine crossing controlled by Saracens, remained deserted. Raids and migration seriously depopulated coastal districts of the Tyrrhenian Sea. In Frisia all trading activity subsided during the 860s.

Yet it would be wrong to see the Scandinavian, Saracen and Hungarian raids as agents of unlimited destruction. Many towns were sacked, but few were as totally devastated by the attacks as Fréjus, Toulon, Nice or Antibes on the Provençal coast (and even they were repopulated in the late tenth century). Though very close to the North Sea, Saint-Omer repelled every assault. Fortified in 883, the *burgus* formed at Arras outside the abbey gate of St Vaast withstood the attack of 891 and was never abandoned by its inhabitants. Coins were still being struck at Quentovic in 980. The towns therefore survived for the most part, even the most exposed. But they did change in appearance. While the Carolingians were keeping the peace, town walls had served as quarries for constructing new cathedral buildings, large enough to push economic activity towards the outer edges of these pre-urban nuclei. From the middle of the ninth century fortifications began to be erected around Gallic towns or the monasteries in their *suburbia*, which mostly held out against the attacks. Their defensive role became the mainstay of urban vitality. It encouraged refugees and their wealth to pour into the towns. This concentration helped to accumulate resources for future growth. Thus, not only was there no general break in urban activity but the towns were in some sense stimulated by the dangers besetting the surrounding territory.

Isolated monasteries and the countryside were most exposed to devastation by robber bands. Many manors and villages lost a proportion of their workers, carried off by slave-traders. But the rural economy was too primitive to suffer serious loss from these visitations and the farming equipment too simple to be put out of action completely. In most regions it is doubtful whether these incursions by pagans caused much more material damage than was committed annually by continuing rivalries among Christian magnates. The populace would flee before the invaders with their livestock; they usually returned after the alert to labour on land that had been in no way harmed. It would not have cost them much to rebuild their huts and many peasants presumably settled down again very quickly within the customary framework of lordship. The institution of lordship itself may have experienced some disruption. We can discern from written sources indications originating between the Loire and the North Sea that country-folk tried to defend themselves against their assailants. Armed groups were raised which also harassed the local aristocracy. These risings, quickly suppressed, failed to loosen the grip of seigneurial authority, but the attacks and terror they inspired frequently brought about substantial peasant migrations, depriving great estates of the manpower indispensable to their exploitation. In the capitulary he issued in 864, Charles the Bald tried to mitigate the losses incurred by his magnates, by making peasants living in areas subject to emergency warnings attend at their customary places of work at least at sowing and harvest times. Such a decree, of uncertain application, was by implication recording a fact of great significance: that the farmworkers were indeed being uprooted from their manors. As they fled from Vikings, Saracens or Hungarians, many slaves and dependants took the opportunity to break the bonds tying them to their lords. They settled elsewhere in the service of new lords, ones who treated them as free men and exploited them less harshly. For in order to repopulate their estates with workers, big landowners were probably forced to make the system of rents and services more flexible. It may well be, therefore, that the shock of the invasions caused tenurial burdens to be modified. As soon as detailed documents reappear at the end of the eleventh century, we can see that conditions of tenure were far less arduous than at the time of the earliest Carolingian polyptyques. In that part of

England subject to Danish authority sokemen were to all appearances survivors of a middling class of peasants whom the Scandinavian conquest had prized from the grasp of the Anglo-Saxon aristocracy. Accordingly, a considerable relaxation of the excessive rigidity of large country estates is a reasonable hypothesis. This, by easing the burden on workers in the fields, spurred them on in their daily task and promoted land clearance and population growth. By the turn of the ninth century, traces have been uncovered in the countryside flanking the River Meuse of forest colonization which led to the creation of new holdings and manors. Compulsory labour services had already been replaced by money rents and country churches were evidently being extended during the ninth and tenth centuries. All these signs bear witness to a *détente* that allowed the pressure of energy long contained by customary constraints to be released for development. The last invasions seem to have been responsible for a sudden shock that was ultimately beneficial to the economy. It gave scope to expansive tendencies which numerous restrictions still held in check in the rural world of Charlemagne's day.

The most violent agitation occurred on the surface of economic realities represented by transferable wealth, and in the main by precious metals. Through show-case windows in Scandinavian museums today, we can gaze enthralled at a tiny part of the gold and silver brought back from their expeditions by the Vikings. The plundering of monastic treasure-houses, then the imposition of danegeld, liquidated a considerable portion of the reserves hoarded in the churches and palaces of Latin Christendom. From an inventory drawn up after a visitation by Northmen, we know that three-quarters or even seven-eighths of the pieces of jewellery comprising the treasure of the monastery of St Bavon at Ghent had disappeared. But the likelihood is that they were not all taken by freebooters to adorn their persons or graves at home. The invaders were not the only ones to indulge in pilfering: natives too took advantage of the disorders to carry off whatever they could steal. Further, Vikings gradually adopted the habit of staying for a time on the sites of their raids. Some of them settled permanently. In such cases they shared with their companions part of the proceeds of their depredations. This was exchanged for other possessions, particularly for the great swords forged by the Franks and, above all, for lands. Many may well have set out with the intention of finding an estate for themselves. To their way of thinking, rural lordship was the supreme prize, to win which they would part cheerfully with the precious metals they had seized. As a result, Frankish and Saxon countries also benefited from the increase in liquidity that stimulated the circulation of silver, enlarged the number of coins and by degrees made economic institutions work more smoothly. Around the spoils amassed by the Vikings developed a whole complex of exchanges, redistributions, acts of generosity and real commercial transactions. Permanent camps set up by the conquerors in England and north-western Gaul were open to visitors from the neighbourhood, who came to do business. In 873 Northmen based on the Loire obtained royal permission to found a market on the island where they had settled. Slaves formed the main item of this traffic. Prisoners were set free in exchange for ransoms. Many were redeemed by monastic establishments, drawing still further upon their reserves. Others were sold to the highest bidder and trafficking in human livestock, which Carolingian law and order had banished to the Slav or Moslem frontiers with Christendom, started growing again. The slave trade would still be practised in Normandy during the last third of the eleventh century. Hence, from centres near the English Channel and the North Sea, trade gradually became more widespread, penetrating deeply into the rural world. Proof of this is supplied by the evolution of the monetary system. Whereas the early Carolingians had striven to raise the weight of the silver *denarius*, Charles the Bald in 864 gave orders for lighter coins to be struck. He probably intended to increase the number of coins in circulation and by reducing their value to adapt them to the commercial practices of people further down the social scale. Thus began in France that slow process which, by devaluing coins in terms of their content in precious metal, more rapidly popularized their use.

Far from marking a break by wrecking the initial development represented by the foundation of *portus* during the Carolingian phase of reconstruction, Scandinavian pillaging established continuity between this and the well-documented expansion after *c.* 1075. During this period the shock administered by the invaders was cracking the shell enclosing the rural economy of the West; hitherto unconnected networks of boat traffic were being linked up from the Atlantic all the way to the Slav plains; the area of Europe was being extended by the Carolingian conquests and missionary expeditions; and the incorporation of Hungary into Christendom was being anticipated by the opening of the Danube route to

Byzantium. Accordingly the turmoil of the invasions reinforced climatic changes and released dynamic forces that were given full rein as soon as the raids stopped.

Their cessation seems to have coincided with social changes among the aggressors, whose success gradually made such expeditions less necessary or less profitable. From the middle third of the tenth century, Magyars began to give up the nomadic way of life and to cultivate the Danubian plain. The influx of African slaves to the Moslem world may have lessened interest in slave-trading in the Tyrrhenian Sea. But of course the invasions also ceased because the West had at last succeeded in overcoming her military inferiority by constructing a network of effective strongholds and adopting some of the techniques of her assailants. The castle, the armoured knight and familiarization with naval warfare had released Christian Europe from danger. In the mid-tenth century warriors from Germany, supported by Saxon forts, put a stop to the Hungarian raids. Saracen lairs by the Liri and at Fraxinetum were reduced in 916 and 972 respectively, and Barbary Coast pirates no longer had the run of the country. Only the shores of Provence and Italy remained exposed to surprise attack and even this was becoming less frequent. The onslaught of the Northmen lasted longer. There was a pause in the Scandinavian raids between 930 and the 980s but then they picked up again with renewed vigour as the Danes subjected the whole of England to their rule. Trading centres in Frisia and along the Atlantic coast of Gaul were once more devastated during the first fifteen years of the eleventh century, and the danger in coastal districts did not subside before the beginning of the twelfth. Nevertheless, the big plundering expeditions came to an end after 1015. The great upheavals that had hurled successive waves of rapacious conquerors against western Europe for almost a millennium died down. It was the supreme advantage of this part of the world to be spared thereafter from invasion. Such immunity accounts for the economic development and steady progress of which it was now the focal point.

III POLES OF DEVELOPMENT

The most serious losses were sustained by cultural institutions, particularly the monasteries. This is why the period is so poor in written evidence and why we are so ill-equipped for finding out about the history of the countryside. The real break between the

Carolingian renaissance and the eleventh-century revival occurs with respect to the documentary sources. For all that, archaeological discoveries throw some light on economic life, especially in connection with towns and coins. In regions that prior to the great Scandinavian raids were on the periphery of christianized and relatively civilized Europe, these discoveries enable us to discern an economic system similar to that operating in the Christian West of the seventh and eighth centuries. Under the combined influences of profit, pillage and slow political maturation this system appears to have been developing quite rapidly in the course of the Dark Ages.

(*a*) BARBARIAN EUROPE. The best evidence of progress is shown by the countries from which the Vikings came. Thinly populated, they were dominated by a landed aristocracy and it was in this class that the adventurers had their origins. Based in large measure on animal husbandry, but leaving some room for cereal cultivation, their farming rested upon slavery. It is probable that agrarian colonization was stimulated by the influx of captives. From the ninth century villages in Denmark were extremely populous and new foci of settlement, the *torpe*, were on the increase. Slowly during the tenth century the main features of a state took shape, centred on the king as war-leader. This phase of political evolution reached its apogee with three contemporaneous developments: the introduction of Christianity as the millennium approached; the formation round the prince of an armed following, the *hirð*, presumably modelled on an experiment in the Danelaw of England; and the initiation of a system of royal taxation for which the basis in Denmark was the dwelling unit or *bol*, equivalent to the *mansus* of the Carolingian Empire. With the strengthening of kingship, the first permanent towns comparable with those in Gaul – Roskilde, Lund, Ribe – were founded. Hence urbanization, the consolidation of royal authority on the ruins of tribal structures, the infiltration of Christian beliefs and the expansion of the rural economy advanced together.

The initial impulse came from warfare. In the lives of the most prosperous free men, war was closely interwoven with hunting expeditions and farm management. Rounding up slaves and levying tribute on tribes subjugated by force of arms, along with trapping animals for their fur, stockraising and growing barley, formed the inseparable elements of a subsistence and profit-making economy.

Let us cite the case of the Norwegian Ohthere (Ottar), dwelling to the north of the Lofoten Islands on the frontiers of Scandinavian settlement. He is known to us from the account of his travels which he composed in 870–90 and which King Alfred the Great passed on to posterity. Whale hunter, keeper of cows, sheep and swine and rent collector, he himself also farmed an estate. Neighbouring Lapp communities purchased their security from him with periodic liveries of skins and reindeer antlers. Every now and then he loaded a ship with their tribute, taking it to trading centres in southern Norway, Denmark and England.

From their adventures in Anglo-Saxon and Frankish territory, the Vikings brought back more slaves than they could use on their own lands. These they turned into an article of commerce, sending them over in companies to English markets. They also brought home gold and silver, of which the Norse colonies in Iceland appear to have had an abundance in the tenth century. The accumulation of booty of southern provenance and the need to convert it into cash enriched those centres where shipping lanes crossed, and which were outlets for the eastward flow of traffic towards central Asia and Constantinople being developed by the Varangians. Specialists in trade who were usually not Scandinavians but foreigners, especially Christian Frisians, did well out of it, dealing mainly in slaves and furs. The most active of these emporia, apart from Birka in Sweden, on an island in Lake Mälar, was Hedeby (Haithabu) in Denmark. Adam of Bremen, who at the close of the eleventh century wrote down his recollections of a voyage in the Baltic, could still recall the days when it had been a busy place, though by his time it had ceased to exist as an important centre. Germans and Danes had disputed for control of it, Norwegians had wrecked it shortly after the year 1000, and the Wends sacked it once more in 1066. We know of it chiefly from the *Vita Anskarii*, the tale of a Carolingian proselytizing mission in these northern lands about the middle of the ninth century, which shows it to have been in regular contact with Duurstede. It is first referred to by name in 804 and its prosperity reached a peak *c.* 900 in the heyday of the Viking raids. Such centres seem to have remained isolated from the surrounding world, as mere outgrowths raised up by the fortunes of war and disappearing with them. The same was true of the pirates' nest (in the Baltic as in the North Sea there was no line of demarcation between piracy and orderly trade) inhabited by Slavs, Greeks and 'barbarians' perhaps ruled over by Viking exiles, which was mentioned both by Adam of Bremen and *c.* 968 by the Jewish merchant, Ibrahim ibn Yaqub, and should probably be identified with Wollin near the mouth of the Oder.

Close parallels exist between the economic development of Scandinavia and that of the Slav and Hungarian borderlands. Although Slav development took place rather later than Scandinavian, it involved the same connections between the birth of the state, missionary activity, the foundation of towns and slow advances in rural production. Upon the primitive basis of shifting agriculture, which a widely scattered population attempted on light soils in the middle of forests and grasslands, there came about during the tenth century, first in Bohemia, then in Poland and finally in Hungary, the dissolution of existing tribal structures and the concentration of power in the hands of a prince. Once again the change seems to have been the outcome of war. Overlords would gather round them a body of warriors – the *drużyna*, corresponding to the Scandinavian *hirð* – bound to them by moral obligation and the expectation of a share in the plunder. They would then be able to compel recognition by force, break or absorb tribal aristocracies, exploit the native peasantry and launch against neighbouring peoples marauding expeditions for booty or tribute. Similar were the ventures of Hungarian horsemen in the West, though on a far larger scale. All these prizes guaranteed the upkeep of the *trustis dominica*, the household of armed vassals living together with the prince. They provided foodstuffs, furs, honey, wax and slaves, which could be exchanged for pieces of jewellery in less economically backward lands to the west and south. It was the tiny élite of the lord's cronies, his right-hand men-in-power, who benefited from this circulation of luxury goods. But little by little, because the elements of effective authority were being consolidated at the same rate in near-by tribes, pillaging expeditions became more difficult and less successful. Around the year 1000, princes began to dissolve their military companies, keeping close at hand only a small number of household warriors as their personal bodyguards. By exercising their absolute right to exploit the subjects of their states, to make, in the words of Cosmas of Prague, 'slaves of some, peasants of others, tribute-payers of yet others; . . . cooks of some, bakers or millers of others', they granted to those of their companions whom they were disbanding, as also to surviving members of tribal aristocracies, the right to profit in their stead from charges laid upon the toil of the masses. This is how a social hierarchy was formed, dependent on the services due to princes, dominated by their narrow circle of 'friends', owners of *praedia* or great estates, and resting on the massive foundations of slavery. The institution of rural lordship, coupled with diminishing returns from warfare, may have given rise to an expansion of production, sustained by a slow increase in population. It created conditions for agriculture to stay put. In the late tenth century, well before the first colonists arrived from Germany, tribes of Obodrite Slavs north of the Elbe were already practising settled cultivation of heavy soils and making headway with permanent fields at the expense of the forest.

The foundation of towns seems to have been closely bound up with the consolidation of princely authority and the formation of groups of professional warriors around their overlords. Even in the tribal period, *grody* – enclosures of earth and timber – had been built near aristocratic residences, and remains of these have been uncovered dating from the seventh century. These strongholds were reconstructed by princes, who commanded greater resources, at the close of the ninth and during the first half of the tenth century, when the great Scandinavian emporia were already flourishing. On to this initial enclosure was later grafted a second defensive system embracing the *suburbium*, where the first places of Christian worship were erected. Inside these ramparts excavations have brought to light a few dozen dwellings, whose floor-levels concealed weapons and silver ornaments. These were homes for members of the military group, while the huts inhabited by peasants lay outside the defences. There were several dozen of these pre-urban nuclei in Poland before the year 1000. All the spoils from plundering forays and what little wealth the surrounding rural population could generate were concentrated in them. Within a radius of about ten kilometres of these towns, place-name studies disclose the presence in the tenth century of a circle of villages, whose inhabitants were obliged to hand over craft products for the prince's use. These communities consisted mainly of bee-keepers (especially in Poland) and smiths (in Hungary), and the injection of their labour into the rural world is indicative of the burden of a state created by force and based on the enslavement of subjugated tribes. The lord could do as he wished with his subjects. With warriors as overseers, artisan-peasants were compelled to come and work when required in workshops attached to the *gród*. This explains the co-existence of villages of specialized workers with a handicraft centre located inside the *suburbium* and devoted to the manufacture of those armaments and ornaments which could not be procured through pillage or long-distance trade.

Certain *castra*, notably in Moravia and later in Hungary, remained simple bases of operations for an established military aristocracy and an evolving ecclesiastical organization. Many others were flanked by an open space a short distance away where commercial transactions would periodically take place. Some of these markets, because they were centrally situated in the chief political groupings, became focal points of major trade routes. Ibn Yaqub, who visited Cracow *c.* 966, estimated the armed militia dwelling there at three thousand members, all of whom had to be supplied with items of distant provenance. He describes Prague as a town built of stone and frequented by Varangian, Jewish and Hungarian slave-traders: Europe's great slave market. While the maturing of political institutions limited the role of warfare in economic processes and substituted the exploitation of the native peasantry for profits from plundering raids, the urban network born of the establishment of royal power was thus available to support regular commercial ties. The pause in the great Scandinavian expeditions to western Europe between 930 and the closing decades of the tenth century, like the simultaneous decline of such trading stations as Hedeby, was perhaps not unrelated to the development of a commercial system of this kind. It stimulated boat traffic on the Polish rivers and by degrees familiarized the inhabitants of barbarian Europe with the use of money.

Only in the north and east of Europe have archaeologists discovered hoards in any quantity dating from the ninth, tenth and first half of the eleventh centuries. The long survival of heathenism in this part of the West explains to some extent why the practice of hoarding was kept up for so long. In these regions the dead still took with them into the grave the possessions they had accumulated in life, and only very gradually did the Church's teaching succeed in diverting these treasures towards the sacristies of places of worship. But though barbarian Europe's economic development continued to lag two or three centuries behind that of the christianized West, it was none the less unfolding in similar successive phases.

The hiding-places that have been brought to light concealed diverse collections of objects: metal bars (in Poland down to the beginning of the tenth century, before improvements in metallurgy caused it to be replaced by silver, iron was regarded as a sufficiently valuable material to be hoarded), pieces of jewellery, sometimes broken, and the coins that enable us to date the finds approximately. As time went by the number of coins gradually increased: in Polish districts it was after 915 that they became common.

Around the Baltic littoral almost all coins of the period from the ninth to mid-tenth century are of Moslem origin. These are silver *dirhams*, for this region was the terminal point of an extensive exchange network that brought coins struck in Moslem parts of Asia nearer and nearer the centres of European trade through the agency of piracy, as wages paid to mercenaries and as profits of trafficking in slaves and furs. In due course these coins accumulated in the native lands of Scandinavian adventurers, in the vicinity of the great emporia where seafarers congregated. The coins were lodged there in successive deposits, for there was no use for them save as ornaments and tokens of power. The surprising feature is that during this period, which saw the great Danish raids directed against the West, Scandinavian graves and hoards yield so few Western coins. Are we therefore to suppose that coins seized at random in raids on England and Gaul, as well as those collected for the payment of tribute to the Northmen, were melted down by northern silversmiths? Why should they alone have been subjected to this treatment, and not the *dirhams*? It is much more likely that these coins were employed on the spot to acquire lands, wine and other good things of life: trading and recourse to money were customary practices in England and Gaul as early as the ninth century, but were still unknown in the more uncivilized lands to the north and east. It may also be argued that the accumulation of large unused stocks of Arab silver on the shores of the Baltic was encouraging Western traders to extend their enterprises in that direction. This was the case with the Frisians whom the author of the *Vita Anskarii* encountered at Birka. They gradually took their chances in a world made less foreign to Latin Christendom by the Viking attacks, purchasing *dirhams* with offers of tempting commodities in exchange. Thus they succeeded in attracting towards western Europe some of the hoarded silver. This probably facilitated commercial expansion along the Christian shores of the North Sea from the ninth century; and little by little accustomed Norse and Slav tribes to regard money as a medium of exchange. From the early tenth century, Baltic hoards contain *dirhams* cut up into smaller pieces to serve more usefully in day-to-day transactions.

Already common near the coast, coin hoards in Poland became more numerous in the interior of the country close by the strongholds that underpinned the foundations of the new-born states. The pattern of continental trading activity, with the principal markets at intervals, was gradually taking shape during the same period. From the middle of the tenth century, Arab coins disappear. They were becoming scarce among the tribes of western Slavs from 960, in Poland and Scandinavia from the 980s, and in the Baltic lands about the year 1000. The latest *dirhams* in Scandinavian hoards come from mints no longer situated in the eastern but in the western parts of the Moslem world; they had probably arrived, not as in earlier times by routes across the Russian plains controlled by Varangians, but through central Europe via the staging post at Prague. Conversely, the number of coins struck in the West increases. We do not find any from Gaul, except some from mints along the Meuse at Huy, Dinant, Liège, Namur and Maastricht, and few of Italian provenance. The majority were issued in England, Frisia, Bavaria, the Rhineland and above all in Saxony, where mintage was just beginning. This penetration of the *denarius* into Scandinavian territory and beyond the Elbe is of great significance. It marks a new stage in familiarization with the economic uses of money. Lighter than the *dirham* and therefore more adaptable, the *denarius* was accepted as a stable measure of value, causing a decline in the use of the normal heavy coins. Its progress in the late tenth century also marks the development of relations between yet uncivilized parts of Europe and the West, through an intermediary zone of political contact extending from England (where Danish rule was imposed) to Magdeburg and Regensburg. In Saxony, coinage answered the needs of the contemporary internal market much less than it served the policy of prestige and magnificence pursued by its ruler, who was anxious to impress the princes of the northern and eastern borders. The change that substituted coins issued by authorities in the West for those of Islamic origin is finally indicative of the slow integration of Scandinavia, Poland, Bohemia and Hungary into the economic orbit of Latin Christendom at a time when these countries were also being incorporated in its religious and political system.

No less significant at a later stage seems to have been the progressive disappearance of coin hoards. The first signs of this date from the end of the tenth century. In Poland substantial hoards were still being concealed in subsequent decades but after *c.* 1050 their size and quality rapidly decline. The 1070s – a turning-point to remember – signalled the end of this method of accumulating valuables (a method that corresponds to a stage in economic development characteristic of primitive societies) by which pillagers could normally find no use for coins stolen from the outside world as an aid to exchanges: their value as legal tender was too high to enable them to serve effectively in local, everyday transactions. When he visited the Prague market *c.* 966, Ibrahim ibn Yaqub was struck by the maladjustment of the monetary system: he reports that for a single *denarius* one could buy about ten chickens, wheat or rye enough to sustain a man for one month, barley rations to feed a pack-horse for forty days. People were using linen squares worth one-tenth of a *denarius* as smaller units of exchange. We can therefore assume that coin hoards were released when the velocity of monetary circulation and the volume of commercial traffic, along with the rise in local production, were capable of reducing the purchasing power of coins sufficiently to make them convenient to handle. The growing scarcity of hoards bears witness to the gradual emergence of a more flexible economy.

This scarcity was accompanied by changes that were bringing the institutions of state to maturity. In the period when principalities were still in formation, rulers wanted to be seen in the midst of a dazzling display of precious metals. Cosmas of Prague speaks of the cross of fine gold which Mieszko, founder of the Polish monarchy, commissioned, and which weighed three times as much as his own body. In princely hoards silver was surpassed by gold seized as booty from defeated enemies: in 1019 and 1068 Bolesław the Brave and Bolesław the Bold laid their hands on the treasures of Kiev, whereas in 1039 Bratislav of Bohemia sacked Gniezno. These treasures were meant for ostentation and the rituals of hospitality. The monarch would share them out in lots among churches and his vassals. Gallus Anonymus tells us that in the days of Bolesław the Brave Polish magnates and their wives were bowed down beneath the weight of enormous gold necklaces. Items received by way of royal favour are not found in hoards at all. They remained decorative in purpose and were displayed in churches and aristocratic residences as expressions of the power of God and the nobility, not hidden away or bartered for other valuables. But attitudes to precious metals were changing. The consolidation of princely authority and the attendant growth of monetary circulation encouraged rulers to issue coins, after the fashion of western monarchs. The decrease in the number of coin hoards and the development of mintage kept in step with one another exactly in barbarian Europe. In Poland, Sweden and Denmark, as also in the small Slav principalities of Pomerania and Polabia to the west, mintage did not become active to the extent of driving foreign coins away until after 1070, and this stage was not reached in Bohemia before the opening decades of the twelfth century. The point at which the regular issue of coins began in all these regions was when commercial activities had become brisk enough for princes to anticipate a profit from mintage. Currency was at once an affirmation of political prestige and the first instrument of princely taxation: for the benefit of a state that was approaching maturity, the prince would impose a levy on the precious metal. Money long remained the preserve of rulers; the coins came back into their hands through the agency of judicial fines and tolls charged at markets and river crossings. Yet some of these coins were also given up in exchange for wax and other commodities, whose export was organized by the prince near mints or in those marts for which taverns served in contemporary Poland. In this way, the *renovatio monetae* made its contribution to economic growth, principally during the last quarter of the eleventh century.

(*b*) THE NORTH SEA AREA. This growth, focused as it then was on the northern and eastern frontiers of Latin Christendom, may be studied in close association with that taking place in an area bordering directly upon this region and connecting it with the heart of Carolingian Europe. We are here referring to the countries round the North Sea littoral. One of the outstanding features of medieval economic history is the development of this area between the ninth and eleventh centuries, a development comparable with that centred on the Mediterranean.

As the prime objective of Scandinavian expeditions, England presents a picture of vitality that is vouched for in the first instance by the size of the tributary payments imposed by her assailants. In 991 the Vikings demanded £10,000, in 994 £16,000, in 1002 £24,000, in 1007 £36,000 and in 1012 £48,000. These exactions were followed by levies made by Anglo-Saxon kings, who needed the money to pay the Scandinavian mercenaries they were taking into their service. Then Norman warriors led by William the Conqueror threw themselves into the onslaught on the island's wealth, which they knew to be considerable. The lasting impression is one of evident prosperity, long maintained no doubt by the presence of the Danes, by the liquidation of their spoils of war, by the slave trade that Archbishop Lanfranc was still entreating King William to abolish, as well as by agricultural expansion which lack of evidence prevents us from measuring satisfactorily. We can at least detect the amount of money in circulation. Attempts have been made to calculate the number of dies whose stamp is borne by the coins. We can count up to roughly two thousand dies used to strike the *Long Cross* pennies of King Æthelred at the end of the tenth century. If we bear in mind that one die might serve to mint approximately fifteen thousand coins, the value of these issues can be estimated at some £120,000. This possibly corresponds to the total amount of money then in circulation, since coins were reminted at regular intervals. From the valuations and renders recorded in Domesday Book and the many signs of purchases and sales contained in other documents, a picture unfolds of a country stirred into activity by the use of money and the practice of exchange.

This internal trade was linked to a network of commercial relations with a far wider community – chiefly in Scandinavia but also in mainland Europe. English types served as models for the first coinages of the northern lands. Rulers were careful to ensure the safety of English traders. By the terms of an agreement concluded with Æthelred in 991, the Vikings undertook not to attack merchant ships in the estuaries of English rivers and to leave in peace English traders who might fall into their hands on the Continent. In 1027 Cnut secured privileges from the German Emperor and king of Burgundy in favour of Anglo-Saxon *mercatores* trading in Italy. The *Colloquy* of Ælfric Grammaticus, composed just before the year 1000, refers to those adventurers who 'load their wares aboard their ships, put out to sea, sell their cargoes and buy commodities that are not to be found in England.' We know that some of them became rich. An Anglo-Saxon treatise dating from the same period implies that after three voyages overseas a merchant would prosper as a *thegn*, that is to say, a lord of middle rank. The main intersection for all this traffic was London, where a judicial assembly, the *husting*, would meet each week to regulate disputes between native and foreign traders. We catch a glimpse of the latter in the text of toll regulations issued by Æthelred in the year 1000: this singles out the 'Emperor's subjects', meaning Rhineland merchants, who are to enjoy the same privileges as Londoners and are coming to buy wool in particular; the 'men of Huy, Liège and Nivelles', who are permitted to enter the town before paying toll; the merchants of Rouen, described as purveyors of wine; those from Flanders, Ponthieu and 'France'; and lastly Danes and Norwegians, who are allowed to reside in London for one year.

Such an expanding economy promoted the urbanization of England. Before the ninth century there were no true towns except in the south-east – London, Winchester and Canterbury. The most active mints were still located in these places in the year 1000. But primarily for strategic reasons Alfred the Great and his successors at the turn of the ninth and beginning of the tenth century founded a number of strong-points surrounded by palisades and ramparts, the *byrig* which were similar to the *grody* of Slav countries. Some of these were built on sites already serving as commercial interchanges, and *hagae* (tenements enclosed within their defences) were granted by the king to traders in return for a money rent. The most favourably situated of these fortified places were given a mint; they are referred to in documents as *portus*, or special locations for trading. In the Scandinavian-occupied Danelaw, other settlements grew in size: York, for example, where mintage was developed in the tenth century and whose area doubled with the growth outside the Roman walls of a merchant and artisan quarter; or Norwich, a large village which became a minting centre in 920, was a real town a century later, and reckoned twenty-five churches in 1086. In the England of Domesday Book, where up to one-twelfth of the population may have been living in settlements of an urban character, the network of towns was already as close-knit as it was to be in the fourteenth century.

In Germany, which took over the lion's share of the Carolingian political and cultural inheritance during the tenth century, comparable changes occurred, but at a much slower pace. Here the countryside was wilder and the Frankish conquest had merely laid the basic foundations of a less primitive economy. Great estates already existed around the headquarters of counts, bishops and monasteries. But there were no proper towns, except in the Rhineland and those Danubian districts where traces of the Roman imprint survived. There were no mints. A few trackways led slave-trading adventurers towards the Slav borderlands: we can see them passing through the toll-bar at Raffelstetten on the Danube in the early tenth century, taking with them salt, weapons, ornaments and bringing back wax, horses and slaves. In the impenetrable gloom of this undocumented age we may suspect that agriculture was slowly expanding in response to new seigneurial exactions and the spread of a traditional diet of Western origin. This presumably caused the population to increase further. Germany suffered little damage from the Vikings, although she bore the brunt of Hungarian raids along the entire length of her southern boundary over a period of fifty years. None the less, towards the east and north she bordered on countries which, as we have observed, were undergoing continuous development during this period, and after the middle of the tenth century, resolutely delivered from the Hungarian peril, it was the German kingdom that served as the basis for the West's most solid political conformation. Princes from Saxony set out to reconstruct Charlemagne's Empire even if they found themselves directed towards Scandinavia and the Slav world rather than the Carolingian south. The newly restored Emperors wished to extend their sway over the Slav principalities taking shape beyond the Elbe, and Saxon warriors led by King Henry the Fowler had already seized control of the emporium of Hedeby by 934.

We have seen how often political acts had profound repercussions on the economy of this period, at least with respect to the circulation of wealth. It is in the field of political action that we must place the intense monetary activity that spread through Saxony between 970 and 1030. It was based on the mineral resources of the Harz Mountains, at Rammelsberg near Goslar. When he extolled Otto the Great's magnificence, the historian, Widukind of Corvey, omitted to mention his accession to the Empire, yet he praises him for having 'opened up the silver-bearing veins of the Saxon land'. It was an acute observation. Saxon *denarii* were infiltrating the Baltic and Polish region. There they advertised in the first instance the presence of the Emperor whose name they bore and whose glory they affirmed. But these standardized pieces of silver were also a medium of exchange, and the spread of German currency had an appreciable effect. It enlivened the trade-routes terminating in Germany from the east and north, and gradually extended the area of commercial activity and monetary circulation in these countries. Thus a demonstration of power indirectly furthered economic development. The creation of markets was the outcome of the same intentions and had similar effects. Like Charlemagne, the Ottonian Emperors wanted to control commercial operations and thereby bring them within a stable political framework. Accordingly they established markets in a land that knew little of such institutions. From extant documents we know of twenty-nine of these foundations belonging to the period 936–1002. In conformity with Carolingian tradition, they were initially institutions of law and order intended to facilitate, under cover of the judicial system the Emperor was focusing on his person, the journeys and meetings of those unruly, disquieting and vulnerable individuals who were specialists in long-distance trade. Granting a *mercatus publicus* to the monastery at Corvey in 946, Otto I bade holders of royal authority keep 'the peace with a firm hand among those who come and go, and among those who dwell here'. Traders set up their warehouses and, in the intervals between their seasonal expeditions, their homes on these sites. They therefore placed themselves under the Emperor's protection (the charter by which the ruler authorized the bishop of Hamburg to establish a market at Bremen in 965 makes this point explicitly) and this protection would accompany them on their travels. They became the 'Emperor's men' and by virtue of this enjoyed toll concessions in London. In return for the safe-conduct guaranteed by the imperial *bannum, negociatores* were expected to make periodic tributary payments to the court, as in the Carolingian period. In 1018 Tiel merchants called upon the Emperor to defend them more effectively: if they could not carry on trading with England they would no longer be able to present their *vectigalia*, obligatory gifts expressing their attachment to the imperial household. Hence commercial centres were founded primarily not to serve the needs of local trade but to channel long-distance traffic. In 947 the king created at the request of the abbot of St Gall a market at Rorschach 'for the convenience of travellers to Italy and Rome' and he confirmed his predecessors' foundation so that 'traders, craftsmen and Frisians might come' to Worms.

Mintage encouraged mining; the establishment of markets entailed the protection and control of itinerant traders. Both were acts closely bound up with the restoration of the state and came to be involved in a natural movement of growth, which in turn they strengthened. Little by little commercial practice and use of silver coins spread into the rural hinterland of each new market. 'Money and a market,' we read in an imperial Act establishing a market at Selz in 993, 'are necessary not only for the multitudes of folk thronging here, but also for the monks and people who dwell here'. The creation of a *mercatus* would be accompanied by that of a mint, so that any site set aside for commercial dealings might regularly be supplied with coins. The Emperor granted these minting rights to local potentates: counts, bishops and moneyers. Scattered throughout the land, they helped currency to enter districts where it had hitherto been rarely employed. Thus silver coins, which in the early days of Saxon coinage had served mainly for the essentially political relations with border tribes, were utilized more and more for the internal market. This gradually absorbed the bulk of the coins struck. The progressive withdrawal of German currency within the confines of the Empire prompted Scandinavian and Slav princes to issue their own coins during the last third of the eleventh century. The appearance of mints beyond the eastern and northern frontiers of the German lands signalled the moment when the use of money had been firmly established in the German regions themselves.

Finally, like England, these regions became urbanized. In the Rhineland and Bavaria we can detect the continued growth of townships (*bourgades*) cheek by jowl with the ruins of Roman cities. An Arab traveller passing through Mainz *c.* 973 observed that only a small part of the ancient urban area was inhabited at that time, but the *wik* that had grown up outside the former walls was nevertheless expanding. At Cologne in the days of Otto the Great there was already a long street built up on both sides, which was being widened to form a rectangular market-place. Fortified in 917, the *pagus mercatorum* at Regensburg covered thirty-six hectares. About the year 1000 the bishop of Worms encompassed within a single fortified enclosure the town centre, the market and mint, and the Jewish quarter. In the middle of the eleventh century the cluster of little houses that had been formed near the ancient ruins at Cologne encircled eleven communities of canons, two Benedictine monasteries and four parish churches, besides the archiepiscopal headquarters. The growth of towns with roots reaching back into antiquity was matched by the birth of new settlements in northern and central Germany. These were the direct outcome of princely initiative. Thus at Magdeburg, next to a river-crossing used by commercial and slave-trading pioneers striking into Slav territory, Otto the Great founded simultaneously the monastery of St Maurice and a *wik* for the use 'of Jews and other traders', enclosing them within a single complex of palisades and earthworks. In this way a secure relay station was provided for traffic which, according to a privilege conceded in 975 to merchants settled there, was developing both towards the Rhine and 'in heathen parts'. The area occupied by the township increased from seven to thirty-five hectares during the reign of the first German emperor. Of the twenty-nine locations where tenth-century kings and emperors founded markets, twelve became towns. None the less, pre-eminence in contemporary Germany went to settlements in which rulers chose to establish their courts. Nearly all were in romanized districts: Cologne, Mainz, Trier, Speyer, Worms, Salzburg, Augsburg and Regensburg. In spite of the increase in trade, towns remained primarily focal points of political power and religious life. Their economic vitality was sustained chiefly by exchange mechanisms that were not strictly speaking dependent on trade. They functioned as centres for collecting surplus produce from near-by country estates owned by king and churches, proceeds of requisitions for entertaining the prince and his retinue for the night (*gîte*), and *denarii* demanded by way of taxes and judicial fines. Urban prosperity was due especially to the permanent or periodic concentration of a sizeable group of lay or ecclesiastical consumers and to the presence of a body of *ministeriales*, or servants, some of whom would do a little occasional private business to satisfy the needs of their lords and for their own personal gain.

Through the Rhineland, the Germanic world was making contact with one of the regions which had suffered serious losses at the hands of Scandinavian freebooters but which now was emerging reinvigorated from these raids. During the tenth century and first half of the eleventh, Flanders and the Meuse valley experienced a period of brisk economic development, comparable with what probably took place in England but which is there largely obscured by the shortage of documentary evidence. Vikings had fallen upon the small townships and some they had destroyed. The old Roman town of Tongres was completely abandoned by its inhabitants. Duurstede, systematically pillaged in 834–7, disappears after the middle of the ninth century. But most of the devastated settlements recovered a few decades after the storm. Sometimes, as at Tournai or Valenciennes, they were refounded a short distance away from their early sites. Similarly, the *portus* of Ghent, twice destroyed, revived *c.* 900 on another site, close by a strong castle. The commercial functions of Duurstede were soon taken over by Utrecht,

Deventer (whose coins were widespread in Scandinavia in the second half of the tenth century) and Tiel on the Waal. Many towns on the other hand resisted all attacks and generated their own momentum in the enforced struggle against the plunderers. Inside the fortified citadel at Saint-Omer, booty seized from the Northmen was shared out between 'the nobles, people of middle rank and the poor'. May not this share in the spoils have supplied some initial capital for the traders we can see leaving for Rome in the company of Englishmen in the tenth century? At all events, the Meuse valley witnessed the growth of an inland waterway at this time. Along it were riverside moorings at Huy and Namur, Dinant where fairs were held, and Maastricht where the king of Germany, and later the bishop, charged tolls 'on the ships, at the harbour and in the market-place'. This traffic was in the hands of native merchants, whom we know to have been enjoying favourable concessions in the port of London in the year 1000. Near the Roman ramparts enclosing eight hectares at Arras a new settlement was expanding. In the ninth century a *vicus*, the 'old' *burgus*, had been formed at the monastery gate of St Vaast, while a 'new' *burgus* appears near St Gery in the tenth century. Eleventh-century sources reveal the presence of a large and a small market-place, and these successive extensions occupied about fifteen hectares. A toll-list drawn up for St Vaast in 1036 shows not only food supplies, brought by cart from the surrounding countryside, and products of local craftsmen being sold there, but also 'cloth and wholesale goods', as well as gold. The area of Tournai trebled during this period. The existence of annual fairs, with the coming and going of merchant caravans, is attested for Toul in 927 and Metz in 948 (two towns that had not suffered attacks by Northmen) and for Douai in 987–8.

We can detect other signs of commercial buoyancy and the prosperity it brought to certain sections of society. Through trade men acquired enough wealth to found churches, as at Ghent or Saint-Omer. The town population gathered sufficient strength to stand up to lords who monopolized power. Between 951 and 971 the inhabitants of Liège rebelled against episcopal authority, while in 958 the *cives* of Cambrai (were they all the townsmen or just the military garrison?) pledged themselves under oath to deny the bishop access to the town. In 1066 the townsfolk of Huy won privileges from their lord, who exempted them from certain taxes. Among those town-dwellers who controlled trade and profited from it, we can observe the birth of associations for mutual defence, like the 'charity' at Valenciennes whose statutes were drawn up in the mid-eleventh century. Bishop Alpert of Metz described the customs of Tiel merchants in 1021–4 only to condemn them, admittedly without understanding them. As he saw it, their customs 'are different from those of other men. . . . They are hard-hearted, dishonest folk for whom adultery is not sinful; they settle disputes among themselves not in accordance with the law but by virtue of their freedom' (meaning they had secured judicial autonomy through a privilege awarded by the Emperor). On appointed days they would meet not only to drink together but also to get drunk. Drinking bouts formed one of the chief rituals, for members evidently felt a sense of belonging to a family in these sworn associations and guilds, which were similar to those which Carolingian capitularies had been intended to abolish and whose convivial wassailing Archbishop Hincmar of Reims had censured in 852.

Most of the signs of growth concern trade and towns, but sparks of vitality spread from urban communities to rural ones. This was the case along the River Meuse. A collection of the *Miracles* of St Hubert made in the middle of the tenth century shows that, near the monastery where the miracle-worker's relics were kept, a fair was held in November lasting at least two days and frequented by foreigners. Other periodic gatherings took place at Bastogne, Fosses and Visé – small peasant communities where country people could sell livestock, wool and metal (like the rustic featured in the *Miracles* who presented the abbey with two bars of iron smelted by himself). Here some of the wares carried by river-traders were arriving by cart. The activity of the *portus*, where boatmen stopped overnight, was now accompanied by the rise of up-country townships, such as Nivelles, and of rural production to which the extension of clearings bears witness.

Perhaps Normandy should be regarded as the region most thoroughly infused with new blood by the dynamic nature of the Viking raids. Like York, the town of Rouen became the capital of an overlordship founded by invaders who set themselves up on country estates in place of the native aristocracy. They did not abandon the life of adventure but continued to participate in the numerous transfers of wealth occasioned by Norman pillaging expeditions. In close touch with England and the northern seas, the market at Rouen was favourably placed to dispose of booty, sell slaves and buy commodities taken down the Seine by boat – wine especially. Warriors based in Normandy brought back enormous quantities of movable goods when raiding the English coast in the tenth century; from southern Italy, where they ventured next; and finally from the whole kingdom of England which their overlord seized in 1066. Since the late tenth century there had possibly been no part of Europe where precious metals circulated more plentifully than in the vicinity of the lower Seine. Evidence of this lies in the composition of the treasure belonging to the monastery of Fécamp, the policy of land purchase that its Abbot John pursued in 1050, and the generosity of laymen who offered the small, recently-founded collegiate church of Aumale one chalice of gold, two of silver, a cross, and gilt candlesticks. Still clearer evidence is to be seen in the inception of large building sites where so many new churches were constructed. War-leaders who had tried their luck in Campánia and Apúlia provided funds for raising cathedrals at Sées and Coutances; and Duke William helped pay for the two great monasteries at Caen with spoils from the conquest of England. By means of the wages paid to quarrymen, carters and masons, these building projects caused large amounts of cash to filter down to the rank and file of local society. Preparations for distant adventures were likewise increasing demand for currency, familiarizing people with the uses of *denarii*, and mobilizing wealth by the practice of borrowing on the strength of land given in pledge. Thus an aristocracy of money, much concerned with trade, was formed within the entourage of dukes and great ecclesiastical lords. The rapid circulation of goods, further enlivened by the conquest of England, was reflected in the rise in revenue derived from the toll at Saint-Lô: in 1049 it was estimated at fifteen *librae*, in 1093 two hundred and twenty *librae*. It is also revealed in urban growth. Dieppe, Caen, Falaise and Valognes became towns during this period, while the countryside saw an increase in the number of settlements whose activities were not purely agricultural and which, because of this, are called *burgi*.

Norman prosperity brought new life to surrounding regions and its most powerful impulses were felt upstream along the Seine. They gave rise to an extension of the Paris wine district for another fair was founded at St Denis in the middle of the eleventh century. The instance of Picardy, lying between the two poles of development formed by Normandy and Flanders, well illustrates the various features of this revival. Greater reliance on hard currency represents its most progressive aspect. According to decrees by King Charles the Bald, a single mint at Quentovic should have sufficed to supply this region with coins. Yet we can identify eighteen mints in the second half of the eleventh century and four new ones in the following century. They were located along the coast and the valleys of the Scheldt, Scarpe and Somme. Cash payments seem to have become commoner in the countryside after *c.* 950: perhaps by selling woollen fabrics and certainly by disposing of agricultural surpluses, even the peasantry were now in a position to raise sums of money.

Coins, still so rare in Carolingian times, were thus the immediate cause of changes whose origins should be sought in the waging of aggressive warfare and in political action. These changes spread during the Dark Ages from a few centres where spoils of war and proceeds of tribute were collected together, and were taking place in Picardy, England, the Meuse valley, Germany, the wild borderlands where Christianity was making headway, and probably in central Gaul whose inner history for this period is virtually unknown.

(*c*) MEDITERRANEAN EUROPE. Another distinct development area was to be found in the south along the 'frontier', the unbroken perimeter of hostility and mistrust that witnessed the confrontation between Latin Christendom and the Islamic and Byzantine spheres of influence. In this southern half of Europe – and herein lies the chief contrast between this and the northern half – the sources of attack or harassment were advanced, go-ahead and prosperous countries. Across the water, the Latin world's position was still that of a prey, exposed at sea to piracy and far inland to strikes by slave-traders. In some areas such conditions were of long duration and no signs of a decisive uplift in economic activity can be detected until the late eleventh century. In Provence, even many decades after the local aristocracy had driven the Saracens out from their mountain and coastal lairs, the countryside along the seaboard remained unpopulated and apparently unproductive, while townsfolk cowered behind the walls where they had taken refuge from danger. Only Marseilles shows any indication of early urban expansion. Progressively busier roads leading into Spain may have given rise sooner to an awakening of towns in the Narbonnaise, a focal point of trade in salt from the coastal lagoons, and whose Jewish quarters served as relay stations for traffic in exotic commodities. But during the eleventh and a good part of the twelfth century the regions lying on either side of the Rhône *seem* to have been situated in a dead corner bypassed by the great dynamic forces generating rapid growth (though this impression is possibly due to the particularly serious lack of evidence). These forces had their origins farther west and east, on the Spanish and Italian borders, where the military situation had been reversed by the tenth century. Overland in the Iberian peninsula and by sea along the shores of Italy, Christians observing the Latin rite had taken the initiative in warfare. The technical means they had hammered out for self-defence proved powerful enough to permit a counter-attack in the form of joint expeditions: part plundering forays launched against infidels, part commercial ventures. While the bulk of western Europe saw the danger from external attack slowly fade away, complex activities evolved on these two fronts. Yet here as in Normandy – whose warriors were soon to descend upon the southern end of the Italian peninsula – open or private warfare continued to be the mainspring of economic growth.

On the flanks of Moslem Spain were two quite distinct poles of development. After the Arab conquest Christian refugees had taken shelter in the mountains. Here they remained for a long time, standing their ground and cut off from the Carolingian world by a barrier formed across the western passes over the Pyrenees by Basque tribes – those same tribes which had defeated the Frankish army at Roncevaux in the late eighth century. The slow domestication of savage tribes, which were simultaneously christianized and civilized, established connections between Gaul on the one hand and León, the Asturias, and the mountains of Navarre and Aragon on the other. These were symbolized by the initiation and rapid success of the pilgrimage to St James of Compostella during the last third of the tenth century. Along roads leading towards the western extremity of Galicia came ever greater numbers of prelates, lords of principalities in Aquitaine with their retinues of clerics and warriors, and lesser folk. The passage of companies of pilgrims (most of whom had provided themselves with money by mortgaging their land or setting aside part of their treasure in order to consecrate it to God) acted as a stimulant to the numerous stopping-places on these pious journeys. Among those travelling to Compostella, members of the lay aristocracy whose vocation was fighting, and their priestly brothers who had by no means forgotten how to wield a sword, also made available to local overlords the support of their military power. For decades these overlords had been waging war against the infidel, and the alternating phases of success and setback would sometimes take them beyond the no-man's-land constituting the frontier into those prosperous regions full of things to steal that were part of Islam's hegemony. Assisted by warriors from the other side of the Pyrenees, they could pursue these lightning raids (*algaradas*) deeper into enemy territory, coming back loaded with booty. They soon succeeded in imposing tributary payments (*parias*) on Moslem princes, who were independent but isolated from one another by the decline of the caliphate of Cordoba. This steady income in gold currency enriched every Christian ruler of Spain in the eleventh century. Echoes of this increasingly successful war resounded in epic legends of the West long afterwards and kept alive fascinated nostalgia for those marvellous pillaging expeditions. They channelled towards the little mountain states captives (like the Moslem slaves who 'barked like dogs' and were ridiculed by the people of the Limousin when pilgrim knights brought such curiosities back over the Pyrenees) or delicate objects fashioned by Mozarabic craftsmen, of which a few examples are preserved to this day among the treasures in French churches. For Christendom this war may have been a more plentiful source of precious metals than the mines of Saxony. It supplied silver, like that which was garnered from the bodies on a battlefield by a band of victorious warriors and offered to the abbey of Cluny: hence Abbot Odilo's decorations for the sanctuary altars in the first half of the eleventh century. It supplied gold, too, and in such quantities that fifty years later the king of Castile was able to institute an enormous annuity assessed in Moslem currency in favour of the Cluniac community, which Abbot Hugh used for reconstructing the abbey church on a grandiose scale.

A large part of these spoils was eventually taken to the heartland of western Europe, whence many of the warriors came. What was left enlivened the immediate neighbourhood, which slowly became accustomed to a money economy. Native mintage began *c.* 1030 in Navarre, at the close of the eleventh century in Aragon, and a little later in León and the Asturias, where coins issued by Islamic mints were circulating in larger numbers. Meanwhile, as the danger from Saracen raids subsided, the country was being populated. Transhumance of flocks became possible on the southern flank of the mountains, which military successes had made more secure. Pioneers, some of them returning from Gaul, settled down in liberated zones. As the frontier moved southwards, a unique society of peasant-soldiers took shape, holding their land freely and grouping their homesteads together to form substantial settlements akin to towns. In this land of Roman traditions and piecemeal expansion through conquest of islamized territory, all material activities were focused on a town, the defensive base of operations for men living constantly on the alert and the permanent market for exchanging surplus agricultural and pastoral produce. At León, capital of one of these kingdoms, a market was held outside the walls on Wednesdays: farm surpluses and ordinary craft products in leather, wood, pottery and metal, regularly brought in from nearby localities, were there assembled for sale. Trade in more exotic commodities sought shelter within the town, inside a kind of covered market (*souk*) whose riches royal authorities guarded more jealously.

At the other end of the Pyrenees, Carolingian enterprise had succeeded in creating and extending as far as the Ebro a bulwark of military defence, the march of Catalonia. This advanced post of Christendom, along with neighbouring Septimania, had since the ninth century welcomed refugees fleeing from districts subject to Islam. Rulers protected these immigrants and granted them, on favourable terms, lands depopulated during earlier Moslem incursions and the vicissitudes of reconquest. This practice of accepting outsiders explains the exceptional density of settlement, which is found particularly in mountain valleys at the beginning of the tenth century. Such wealth in men and women, unaffected by the onslaughts of Moslem plunderers that continued until after the year 1000, was one of the foundations of an economic boom, strongly marked by cultural vitality. Fifty years before the great building sites for church construction were opened up in Normandy, architectural experiments (from which Romanesque art was to emerge) had already been conducted in this area. Here, too, proximity to a war-front kept the impulses of growth in full vigour.

A remarkable study[1] based on unusually plentiful and hitherto little-used documents from Barcelona, permits close observation of the development of one village adjacent to the principal town during the years immediately before and after the millennium. This

[1] P. Bonnassie, 'Une famille de la campagne barcelonaise et ses activités économiques aux alentours de l'an mil', *Annales du Midi*, lxxvi (1964), pp. 261–303.

was a time of violent military confrontation, culminating in the raids of Al-Mansur and the holding to ransom of captives. The village was inhabited by fishermen and market-gardeners whose agricultural practices were already enlightened and based on horticulture, irrigation and wine production. A smith was in business making tools that were certainly less primitive than those being used by the majority of European peasants at that time. A number of its rustic inhabitants knew how to read, a further sign of a higher level of civilization than that existing in many areas. This explains the widespread use of written records and the abundance of documentary sources. The farmers provided the neighbouring town with food. There sizeable groups of consumers, notably the cathedral clergy owning large but distant estates, preferred to buy in their supplies and pay for them in cash. In this way money poured into the village. It was soon employed for purchasing land, made easier by legal conditions and the ubiquity of allods (landed property free from all dependence). Out of the seventy-three transactions that constitute the basis of these observations, only five involved a payment in kind. Broadly speaking, acquisitions were being paid for in cash with the balance made up in cereal crops. Up to 990, coins were silver ones of local provenance; next with the spread of dinars issued at Cordoba came the *mancus*, a gold coin; then imitations of these struck by the counts of Barcelona after 1018. This currency inflow, sustained by the monetary instability begotten of warfare and its after-effects, caused a speedy reduction in the price of land. Everyday use of money and the resultant flexibility in the land market quickened social mobility. We can see the new-rich rising, thereby making their less fortunate fellows envious.

For one family group we can follow the stages on the way up the social scale. In 987 the forebear was a substantial peasant, owner of two yokes of oxen and seventy sheep; yet he already possessed some military equipment, for at least the élite of the rural population collaborated with professional warriors. This man had inaugurated a policy of acquiring real estate, which his successors continued. In the 1020s there are numerous signs that his descendants were bettering themselves: ownership of a stone dwelling, participation in the pilgrimage to Compostella, successful marriages into the upper ranks of the aristocracy, so that the finery of the womenfolk bore 'the clearest possible traces of economic progress'. In 1053 one daughter's dowry was worth twenty-five ounces of gold, another's forty 'both in clothing and other personal effects', that is, as much as four war-horses. Thus upstarts from a peasant background succeeded in becoming members of the group of 'judges' (*iudices*), wealthy individuals residing in the town and owing their management of the urban community's affairs to material success. As big dealers in gold, they made handsome profits out of the movement of capital for the payment of ransoms and the redemption of captives from one end of the frontier to the other. The prosperity of the countryside, due alike to the density of settlement, to less rudimentary techniques imported from adjacent Islamic borderlands and to the proximity of the town, was closely linked here to the rapid circulation of coins stimulated by the disruptions born of almost incessant warfare.

Some of the exquisite jewellery made in Byzantium used to find its way into the Carolingian world through Italy, and especially through outlets from the Paduan plain to the Adriatic. For a long time Ravenna and other coastal towns maintained their political attachment to the Eastern Empire, serving as essential intermediaries. Among these towns Venice, which concluded an agreement with the Emperor Lothar in 840, gradually took the lead, outstripping Ferrara and Comácchio. But in the first half of the ninth century Byzantine naval power weakened, leaving the field clear for Moslem shipping. This retreat aroused the seaboard towns and forced them to strengthen their fleets in order to defend alone the connections they still retained with the Orient. The new risks and consequent stiffening of resolve, the necessary resort to privateering, the obligation to negotiate with princes in the Islamic world, all prompted seamen along the Italian shoreline to take the initiative. During the second half of the ninth century and the early years of the tenth, when Saracen enterprises placed the centre of the Tyrrhenian Sea out of bounds, two ports kept alive contacts between Latin Christendom and the eastern Mediterranean. These were Venice and Amalfi.

The inhabitants of the Venetian lagoon produced salt for sale in the interior of the country. But they were deep-sea sailors too and, despite prohibitions by the emperors of Constantinople, were venturing as far as the entrepôts of Moslem Egypt. In 829 they brought back from there the relics of St Mark. They offered in return the weapons and ship-building timber from the forests of Istria and Dalmatia in which Islamic arsenals were lacking. They also sold slaves, some captured among southern Slavs occupying the ill-defined borders between the Frankish and Byzantine spheres of influence, others brought under armed guard from central Europe across the Alps. In the eleventh century the bishop of Chur was levying a tax on these at two *denarii* a head. Possibly these Venetians were also taking corn from Lombardy to Byzantium. In the mid-tenth century customs officials at Constantinople reported to Bishop Liutprand of Cremona, Otto the Great's envoy, that Venetian traders were bartering food supplies for silken fabrics. Such trafficking was made easier by the exemptions from customs dues granted them by the Eastern Emperor in 922. Round about the same time, we know that their boats were sailing up the River Po, laden with merchandise. These varied activities steadily enriched an aristocracy who used part of their profits to acquire estates on islands in the lagoon and on the mainland, but who never ceased to risk substantial amounts of liquid capital in overseas adventures.

Like Venice, Amalfi was shielded from danger on the landward side, though by unscalable rock-faces rather than lagoons. Hence she escaped the political disorders fostered by rivalries between barbarian and Greek overlords that eventually ruined Naples. Amalfi also benefited from the distant protection of Byzantium, winning for her sailors the right to trade in Constantinople as freely as the Venetians. They too would bring home precious materials to serve for processional and liturgical ceremonial and hang on the walls of churches and palaces. In Rome these were being offered to prospective buyers at higher prices than those demanded by traders from the Adriatic. The biographer of St Gerald of Aurillac relates that his hero, who was a count and lived in the second half of the ninth century, was coming back from Rome one day bringing oriental fabrics with him; at Pavia he met with some Venetian merchants who thought they were worth less than he had paid for them. When the Eastern Emperor awarded privileges to the Venetians, he took care not to infringe those of the Amalfitans trading at Constantinople. By then the Amalfitans had already extensively developed their relations with ports in the Islamic world, and these were so close that, notwithstanding the political ties attaching Amalfi to Byzantium, a gold coin of Arab manufacture, the *tarin*, and its local imitations circulated in the town, as they did in neighbouring Salerno. Certainly, in no other corner of Latin Christendom was specialization in trade so far advanced as on this secluded water-front between the sea and the rocky heights. Out of such profitable business came prodigious fortunes for adventurers like the Pantaleoni, who bequeathed enormous riches to religious foundations at Rome, St Michael of Monte Gargano, Antioch and Jerusalem in the last quarter of the eleventh century. The distribution of these alms reflects the extent of Amalfi's horizons. They were dotted with trading colonies which the citizens of the Tyrrhenian town planted on every coastline. Such colonies were numerous and populous. At Cairo, not yet a commercial centre of prime importance, over one hundred Amalfitans perished in a riot in 996. How many able-bodied men were then left in Amalfi? Could a place so physically isolated have been anything more than a port of call, a refuge and a resting place for their dead, for so many traders scattered from the Bosporus and Durazzo to the Maghreb? As soon as they were old enough, young men would make straight for the risks and rewards of the sea and a life of trade. Like the shores of Frisia in the eighth century, like Upper Engadin in the fifteenth, like the commercial ports of the Levant at all times, Amalfi was a place to thrust men irresistibly into far-off adventures. The boldest left and returned, perhaps, only as casual visitors. Their energies were applied elsewhere and for the benefit of potential rivals. The town of their birth hardly profited at all from the capital accumulated through their enterprise, as the pious donations of the Pantaleoni clearly demonstrate.

In the end Amalfi could not resist the expansion of Norman power that had been built up at her gates, and she was forced to submit in 1077. Her whole prosperity had been based on an exceptional political situation that had allowed her to trade freely with infidels. As part of a state whose interests lay elsewhere, she declined very rapidly. Her role was partly taken over by Bari, where most tenth-century travellers to Constantinople or the Holy Land embarked, and whose 'Jewish and Lombard' traders were placed on the same footing as those from Amalfi by the commercial agreement concluded between Venice and Byzantium in 992. Amalfi's great days drew to a close in 1138, when Pisan landing craft arrived to sack the town.

The commercial development of Pisa and Genoa was more closely, and more violently, bound up with the aggressive forces that launched Western Christians on a counter-offensive as soon as they possessed the means to confront Saracen pirates effectively. The influence on economic growth of the idea of a holy war, then slowly coming to maturity on the 'frontiers' of the Iberian peninsula, is here very much in evidence. Venetians and Amalfitans had based on peaceful trading agreements their activities in entrepôts on Moslem territory, their warehouses protected like those of the Jews. But sailors from the northern part of the Tyrrhenian Sea built their ships primarily for privateering warfare, galleys equipped for attacking and slipping away quickly. Pisans in the van, they set out on the offensive as pillagers and soldiers of Christ, like warriors in Spain, or those younger sons of great Norman families who that same generation came to seek their fortunes in southern Italy. Spoils brought back from military expeditions accumulated over a long period of time the capital that was later to bear fruit in business activity.

When Pisa was ruled by Lombard kings a small colony of 'Romans' (that is subjects of the Greek Emperor) had survived for a while under royal protection. Nevertheless, as at Venice, it was presumably the exploitation of the salt marshes that kept the decayed township afloat during the Dark Ages. The diversion of the main road to Rome through Lucca started the revival of Pisa. By 975 Pisan ships were mingling with those of the Byzantines and threatening Messina. But the great pillaging expeditions began in the early eleventh century. Conducted initially on the shores of Corsica, then on those of Sardinia held by Saracens, they were gradually extended to the Balearic Islands, the coasts of Spain, to Sicily and the Maghreb. In 1072 Pisan pirates supported the Normans who were gaining a foothold in Sicily. By then plundering had amassed riches in the Arno river-port on a scale that was duly reflected in the construction of an imposing cathedral. After some delay Genoa followed suit. The Lombard conquest had dealt her a sharper blow. She had long suffered from the diversion of the routes across the Ligurian Apennines. From their 'Riviera' lairs, her nobles joined with Pisan pirates in their forays against Saracens on the islands, and Genoese maritime activity developed rapidly after the middle of the eleventh century. When the First Crusade was launched, seafaring warriors from the two towns had just sacked Mahdia; they were already in control of the ports of the lower Rhône and the Narbonnaise; now they were ready to pursue their depredations as far as the prosperous shores of the eastern Mediterranean. It would not be long before they were transmitting through the medium of peaceable commercial practices the greed for gain, the taste for rapine, the assumption that the principal forms of wealth were movable and could be reckoned up in cash. These mental traits were quite foreign to the rustic civilization of western Europe, but would thenceforth characterize the outlook of merchants. Such mental attitudes had nevertheless been formed in an environment imbued with the adventurous spirit of warfare exhibited by the Vikings and their successors, whose aggressiveness their raids had aroused.

In the Italian interior, tenacious survivals of ancient culture were still making the towns the focal points for all activities. At a time when towns beyond the mountains were nothing but ruins, or were only just coming into existence, in most parts of Italy they remained the focus of social relations. This was not as outgrowths with exclusively religious and military functions, isolated in the midst of an entirely peasant economy: rather it was the countryside that gravitated round Italian towns. In the course of the tenth century, after the slump following the Lombard conquests, then those of the Carolingians, manorial surpluses once more reached town market-places. And as town markets recovered, rural markets gradually declined. As elsewhere, the most powerful impulses of economic vitality came from fields, gardens, vineyards and pastures. But for the most part landlords were town-dwellers. They exploited their possessions from a distance. This state of affairs maintained the exceptional buoyancy of commercial activities, inviting constant recourse to the monetary medium.

Mintage was such a necessary function here that the most spectacular family successes of the age were founded upon it. At the close of the tenth century and up to the middle of the eleventh, supervisors of mints were in a high-ranking position among the town's inhabitants. They would sit in the courts alongside the Emperor's representatives, lend money to monasteries, and give their support to Church reformers. One of these moneyers paid 124 *librae* (in *denarii*) to acquire a quarter-share in a castle in 1036. From *c.* 970, the more intensive circulation of coins was causing prices to rise in Lombardy, and the growing shortage of means for making payment led the mints of Pavia, Lucca and Milan in the mid-eleventh century to issue lighter coins, which were therefore better suited to local commerce.

Throughout the tenth century, changes centred on the towns were slowly disengaging the economic machinery from the great estates as revealed in Carolingian polyptyques. Gangs of household slaves were first to be detached, while labour services imposed on tenants disappeared almost completely. After the year 1000, as the surplus product of the peasantry came on the urban market through the agency of professional traders from the towns, and the monetary medium became more flexible and widely diffused, farmers came to accept cash payments instead of delivering their produce direct to market. Contractual agreements of limited duration (*livelli*) replaced former customary ties attaching country workers to the landowner; and since these involved written records, a group of professional scribes became necessary, the notaries, increasingly prosperous men who acted as moneylenders as well. By means of similarly specific contracts the vast landed wealth of the Church was granted away piecemeal, for ridiculously low annual rents, to clerical or lay townsmen who exploited it more actively. This break-up of the Church's patrimony to the advantage of town-based entrepreneurs was taken so far that all the property of the monastery of Bóbbio, for example, had been alienated in this fashion by the end of the tenth century when the abbot begged the Emperor to intervene. The process at the same time extended urban control over the economy of the adjacent countryside and made for more intensive cultivation. But it also hastened the entry into the rural environment of the wealth in precious metals that had been concentrated in the towns. This capital stimulated the extension of vineyards and olive groves, likewise fresh conquests from tracts of wasteland. Thus Italy presents a picture of an altogether unique course of development: the growth of peasant production was initiated as soon as the last Saracen and Hungarian raids stopped by massive investment of the silver reserves accumulated by the townspeople. The flurry of economic activity stemming from urban wealth in this form was undoubtedly the most effective means of supporting a growing population, which seems to have continued to expand without serious interruption since Carolingian times. In Latium demographic expansion commenced early in the ninth century, if not sooner. It was accompanied to begin with by the spread of new agricultural undertakings, then by the foundation during the tenth century and the first half of the eleventh of fortified nucleated settlements, the *castra*.

Growing familiarity with the uses of money introduced forms of behaviour among the townsfolk (many of whom belonged to the nobility and bore arms) that were very different from those revealed in contemporary documents drawn up beyond the Alps. Townspeople knew how to count, to assess material values and to translate them into monetary units. They had acquired a feeling for the profit that might be made by investing their money in productive enterprises in the countryside, or by manipulating it in the world of commerce. And anxieties began to show themselves about these profits that were not solely the outcome of military conquest or a war-leader's generosity. Such mental attitudes were not unrelated to the early diffusion, among the lay inhabitants of Italian towns, of religious aspirations that ranked poverty and ascetic practices with the major virtues. At a time when no one in the rest of Latin Christendom was yet denying the Church the right to display her worldly power and accumulate precious metals in her sanctuaries to magnify the glory of God, Italian townsmen were first in wishing to despoil her. Because to them money had become an instrument, and wealth was no longer simply a reward for heroic deeds but had lost its moral virtue, these townsmen could instead see perfection in destitution.

It was because of these new economic features that this background was to be the point of departure for every attempt to recall Western churchmen to that life of poverty for which the Byzantine Church in the south of peninsula was offering models from another quarter. These forms of behaviour and the partial success of the reform movements also had immediate repercussions on the economy. The propensity for ostentation and wastefulness in the aristocracy's way of life diminished. Though their desire to consecrate part of their wealth to God remained steadfast, it gradually seemed less edifying to use gold and silver to decorate altars than to share it out among the poor or to provide for charitable institutions: in short, movable goods came increasingly to be redistributed and the proportion of riches locked away in the coffers of nobles or religious foundations was probably lowest in the Italian towns. Hence the greater part of the bullion reserves being transferred from the countryside to the towns remained on hand for commercial transactions.

The flow of long-distance trade was percolating into the towns of the interior from the sea-shores, primarily from those of the Adriatic by means of the river network centred on the Po. These towns had never been without at least some *negociantes* among their inhabitants: that is to say, moneyed individuals who would give credit and dabble in commerce now and then. The pilgrims' *tonta* made them wealthy. At stopping-places along every overland route to Rome, and farther on towards the Holy Land, it was even more profitable than in Spain. Penitents returning home sanctified might allow themselves to be tempted by the beautiful and strange objects that they were shown. Had not Count Gerald of Aurillac, that hero of lay holiness who lavishly gave away *denarii* to the poor and professed scorn for luxury, nevertheless purchased fine materials at Rome? As soon as a rich pilgrim reached the towns of the Lombard plain, merchants rushed out offering silk mantles and spices to the mighty lord and high-ranking personages in his train, before they again submerged themselves in barbarism over the mountains. Throughout the tenth century these traders' business, which had been brisk even in Charlemagne's day, expanded. Trade was by far the most intense at Pavia, because she was the principal seat of royal authority – yet another instance of the importance of political factors. Pavia built a new defensive enclosure at this time. Her mint was more active than all the others in the kingdom and long remained so. The *denarii* it issued competed with those struck at Rome in the course of the eleventh century. After the millennium, they sustained the continuous expansion of a money economy all over northern Italy. Following the collapse of the Carolingian dynasty, the 'most honourable and very wealthy' merchants of Pavia were still attached to the ruler's household, of which they formed one of the *ministeria* or special departments. This brought them an essential concession – that traders from other towns could not compete against them in any market. The public authorities were anxious for the exchange of the most valuable commodities to be centred in Pavia under their control, hence a royal *diploma* dating from 1009–26 for instance forbids Venetians to sell silken fabrics elsewhere than at two fairs of a fortnight's duration, one during Holy Week, the other at St Martin's in November. But in the early eleventh century, the further weakening of royal power caused Pavia to lose her commercial pre-eminence. She gave way to Milan, where the line of descent of leading merchant families can be traced well back into the ninth century. The richest of these were buying houses inside the walls and lands outside. Similar developments took place at Cremona, whose merchant-boatmen rose up in revolt against the bishop's authority in 924 and which the Emperor took under his protection by a special grant in 991. And Piacenza became another intersection of major importance at the crossing of the River Po and three overland routes – the Emilian Way, the road leading from Milan to Genoa, and that over the Apennines heading for Lucca. Lucca continued to be the chief centre in the Tuscan interior. Meanwhile at Florence and Siena the second half of the tenth century saw the origins of the great families that were to dominate the economy of both towns and their rural surroundings for a long time to come.

As soon as the expulsion of the Saracens made it possible to restore the monasteries serving as posting stations along mountain routes over the Alps (about the year 1000), relations, which brigandage had never broken off completely, grew closer between the Lombard centres of communications and countries to the north. At a time when there was a growing attraction for the great places of pilgrimage in Christendom, for churches in Rome and more distant ones in the East, these passes became busier. Something of the connections they provided can be detected in a record dating from 1010–27 but which actually refers to an earlier period, the *Honoranciae Civitatis Papiae* of the 920s. It demonstrates the variety and scale of the traffic converging on Pavia, of which the king of Italy's court intended to take advantage. The heaviest traffic was undoubtedly coming from the Adriatic and the south:

> For every year the doge of Venice and his Venetians are to bring fifty *librae* in Venetian *denarii* . . . to the palace and for the master of the treasury a silk scarf of the highest quality. . . . These folk do not plough or sow or gather grapes. They call this money-payment a 'pact' [*pactum*], and the reason for this is that the Venetian people can buy wheat and wine in every commercial centre, paying for them in Pavia without experiencing any difficulty. Traditionally, many rich Venetian merchants used to come to Pavia with their wares. Out of their trading profits they would give one *solidus* in forty to the monastery of St Martin, which is called 'Without-the-Walls'. The Venetians [or at least the wealthy ones] each have to give the master of the treasury every year on arrival in Pavia one large pound [*maiorem unam libram*] of pepper, one of cinnamon, one of galingale and also one pound of ginger; the treasury master's wife is to be given an ivory comb, a mirror and a dressing-case, or else twenty *solidi* in good Pavian coin. Similarly, the men of Salerno, Gaeta and Amalfi were accustomed to bring great quantities of merchandise to Pavia, giving every fortieth *solidus* to the treasury in the royal palace and, like the Venetians, spices and a dressing-case each to the treasurer's wife.

But merchants from across the mountains also reached the royal town.

> On their entry into the kingdom, they would pay one-tenth of all their wares at customs posts and on highways belonging to the king. Here is a list of these customs posts: the first is at Susa [at the entrance

to the Mont Genèvre Pass, which opens the way to Provence, Aquitaine and Spain via the River Durance]; the second at Bard [at the foot of the Great St Bernard]; the third at Bellinzona [commanding the Lukmanter Pass]; the fourth at Chiavenna; the fifth at Bolzano [on the descent from the Brenner]; the sixth at Velarno [by the River Ádige on the way to Verona]; the seventh at Treviso; the eighth at Zúglio on the route from Monte Croce; the ninth near Aquiléia and the tenth at Cividale del Friuli. Every person coming into Lombardy from over the mountains shall pay the tithe on horses, male and female slaves, woollen and linen cloth, hempen cloth, tin and spices. . . . But all that pilgrims to Rome and St Peter's carry with them for their expenses shall not be subject to any dues. . . . Every three years, Angles and Saxons . . . and the people of those nations are to send to the palace at Pavia and to the royal treasury fifty pounds of blanched silver, two large greyhounds, . . . two best-quality shields, two lances similarly and two well-proven swords; they shall present the master of the treasury with two large fur coats and two pounds of blanched silver; they shall then receive from him the seal that will protect them from being molested on the journey there and back.[1]

Reading between these lines, we can discern both the presence of numerous professional traders and the main directions of trade. No mention is made of Byzantines, nor of Jews. There is a distinct contrast between merchants coming from the Mediterranean area with spices, high-quality craft products and cash, and those passing over the Alps with slaves, ordinary cloth, tin from the British Isles, Frankish weapons and silver bullion. The market-place at Pavia indeed lay at the intersection of two worlds. Stress is placed on relations with England: the original ties between the Church in that country and Rome had led to a special relationship that already appears to have been intimate in the days of Alcuin and Charlemagne. But Anglo-Saxons were not alone in crossing the Alps and it is simply because of the immunity they enjoyed in the early eleventh century that the record pays particular attention to them. The extension throughout south-eastern Gaul of the monastic estate of St Michael of Chiusa, near Susa, during the first half of the eleventh century clearly shows that the flow of traffic in this period developed on a broad front in that direction as well. On the other hand Italian merchants were just beginning to take their chances beyond the Alps in the opposite direction. They took with them those silver coins of which they had a better supply than

[1] *Monumenta Germaniae Historica, Scriptores*, vol. xxx, part 2 (Leipzig 1934), pp. 1,451–3.

anyone else: a number of them are known to have been robbed on the roads of France in 1017. They also took with them their heretical doctrines, that is to say, the emphasis on poverty that had first been revealed in the parvenu circles of Italian towns. Italians had settled at Arras by *c.* 1025 and traders from Asti are known to have used the Mont Cenis Pass in 1034.

Such men formed the vanguard of those groups of adventurers who were leaving the Lombard pole of development in increasing numbers as the eleventh century progressed and were forging links with its northern counterpart in the North Sea area. They ventured deep into the interior of Gaul, but avoided the frontiers where pillage, warfare and the ensuing exchanges were stimulating the commercial economy and sometimes transforming the rural economy too. The economic vitality still being generated by warfare on the confines of Christendom hardly affected the country districts through which these men were passing. Nevertheless, with the help of the new political order now dawning, the countryside of western Europe was already discovering within itself the seeds of growth.

Part Three
Peasant Conquests

(MIDDLE OF THE ELEVENTH TO THE END OF THE TWELFTH CENTURY)

6 *The Age of Feudalism*

We have seen that on the frontiers of Latin Christendom, and progressively farther east and south, the pursuit and intensification of warfare revitalized an economy based on forcible capture and pillage, facilitated the transfer of wealth, and thereby created conditions favourable to growth. Yet at the same time, during the decades before and after the first millennium, we can observe within the main body of Europe the features of a new ordering of human relations. This ordering historians are in the habit of calling 'the feudal system'. Basically, these features represented the surface appearance of a large-scale change which had been precipitated by the invasions of the ninth and tenth centuries, but which had also had its starting-point as far back as the Carolingian period. In the most advanced regions, that is to say in Gaul, feudalism reached maturity during the closing decades of the eleventh century; but it affected newly formed Germany only after a time-lag of about one hundred years. And at the Mediterranean end of Christendom on the other hand, notably in Italy, feudal institutions dissolved on contact with more ancient ones resting on urban vitality and the earlier revival of monetary circulation.

Such a change in political and social organization was no doubt partly a response to changes in the agrarian economy. This was controlled by an aristocracy whose military adventures had strengthened their position. But the aristocracy reacted in their turn and created a new environment, the benefits of which acted decisively on the internal development of the European economy.

I FIRST SIGNS OF EXPANSION

The symptoms of this development were slow in coming forward. It is very noticeable that chroniclers writing in Gaul during the first half of the eleventh century – men such as Adémar of Chabannes or Raoul Glaber – give no clear hint that they were aware of any progress in the material civilization round about them. Of course, these men had all been schooled in monasteries and many had never been outside their gates. Moreover, the world of the flesh did not merit serious attention, for the real elements of the world were spiritual. History as conceived by these monks was concerned with mankind's moral destiny, the march towards the end of time and the celestial city. We cannot therefore expect them to be informative witnesses in economic matters. All the same, their silence does indicate that changes in the economy were taking place slowly and were not of a disruptive nature. And some features of these changes have been brought into relief by Church writers because they could see in them signs of God's intentions.

They were especially aware of two kinds of phenomenon. On the one hand were the disasters which they interpreted as expressions either of Divine wrath or of the evil forces retarding man's advancement towards the light. Thus they depicted the great epidemics sweeping across the Western countryside which could be stemmed only by prayers, acts of collective penitence and recourse to the protective power of relics. No doubt the spread of disease, and notably of ergotism (*mal des ardents*), was furthered by deficiencies in diet. One such writer, moreover, points to a distinct connection between the epidemic raging through northern France in 1045 and the shortage of food: 'A mortal fire began to devour countless victims. . . . At the same time, the population of almost the entire world endured a famine resulting from the scarcity of wine and grain.'[1] The people described in these accounts seem to have been living under constant threat of starvation. Now and then the chronic malnutrition worsened, causing catastrophic mortality; hence the 'penitential scourge' which, if we can believe Raoul Glaber, lashed Europe for three years *c.* 1033.

There is nothing however to prevent us from seeing real signs of expansion in this permanent hunger, and in the periodic crises

[1] Raoul Glaber, *Les cinq livres de son histoire*, book V, §1, ed. M. Prou (Paris 1886), p. 127.

that left heaps of bodies unburied at cross-roads and drove men and women to eat anything – earth and even human flesh. They surely represent a temporary imbalance between the level of production, the technical shortcomings of a subsistence agriculture still highly vulnerable to bad weather ('continual rains had saturated the whole land to the point where, for three years, it was impossible to open up furrows capable of receiving the seed'), and the number of consumers which rose with the population. In any case, the tragic picture drawn of the 1033 famine in Raoul Glaber's account shows that these disasters were taking place in an economic climate that was already singularly volatile. The acts of cannibalism he condemns occurred in a country where travellers moved along trackways and made stops at inns; where meat was habitually sold in market-places; where money was normally used for procuring food ('then ornaments were stripped from churches to be sold for the benefit of the poor'); and speculators took advantage of the common misery.[1] This was a changing world, and the calamities afflicting it were in reality the price of demographic expansion which was possibly too rapid and at all events unregulated, but which may be regarded as one of the first fruits of economic growth.

On the other hand chroniclers were struck by certain innovations. They interpreted all of them in the light of a story centred on the salvation of mankind, but they themselves considered them as unmistakable marks of progress. After the millennium of Christ's Passion, Raoul Glaber records manifestations of what seemed to him like a new alliance, a new springtime for the world, whose efflorescence was the outcome of Divine clemency. Among the signs that impressed him, there are three that apparently involved the play of economic forces. First he lays stress on the unusual amount of traffic on the roads. The only travellers to whom this churchman refers specifically are pilgrims, but to him they seemed more numerous then than ever before:

> . . . no one could have foreseen such a multitude: to begin with there were members of the lower classes; next persons of middle rank; then all the very greatest, whether kings or counts, marquises or prelates; finally, something that had never happened before, many womenfolk, the noblest with the poorest, were making their way to Jerusalem.[2]

[1] Glaber, *Les cinq livres*, book IV, §§4, 5, ed. Prou, pp. 99–106.
[2] Glaber, *Les cinq livres*, book IV, §6, ed. Prou, p. 106.

Even if it really is necessary to explain the increase in these pious journeys by an underlying change in religious attitudes, as contemporary historians suggest, it cannot be doubted that the process was facilitated by the growing mobility of wealth; nor that it in turn contributed to that mobility. For in order to start off on their travels, pilgrims had to raise cash, use it and distribute it. People of any rank might take advantage of free board and lodging at religious houses, but they could not so benefit at every stopping-place. And whilst on pilgrimage they did not as a rule secure their food supplies by pillaging, so long as they remained on Christian soil. They had to buy food and equipment. They would thus leave behind them a trail of *denarii*, to be picked up by producers and middlemen, which acted as a stimulus from every cross-roads right into the countryside. In addition, these journeys often took them to the turbulent borderlands of Christendom, where there would be no lack of opportunity for profitable looting at the expense of infidels, and many pilgrims did not come back empty-handed.

A second innovation noticed by contemporary historians and likewise depicted as spiritual progress, was the rebuilding of churches.

> As the third year following the millennium was drawing nigh, you could see church basilicas being renovated over almost the entire face of the Earth, but especially in Italy and Gaul. Although most of these had no need of it, being of sound construction, rivalry would drive each Christian community to have one more sumptuous than its neighbours. It was as if the very world had bestirred herself and, casting aside her decrepitude, had been reclad all over with a white robe of churches. At that time nearly all the churches of episcopal seats, monastic sanctuaries dedicated to divers saints, and even little village oratories were rendered more beautiful by the faithful.[1]

It is plain that these building programmes deprived the rural hinterland of some of its productive forces for the quarrying, transportation and processing of materials. Some workmen may have been the dependants of ecclesiastical lordships, compelled to put in a day's work without payment, but certainly many were free labourers. They would have to be fed when working on building sites and, since normal surpluses from manorial production were unable to support this additional quota of consumers, extra provisions would have to be brought in from outside. It would also be neces-

[1] Glaber, *Les cinq livres*, book III, §4, ed. Prou, p. 62.

sary to pay out wages in *denarii*. Thus the restoration of ecclesiastical buildings too was promoted by the progressive easing of monetary circulation. It helped to mobilize the precious metals that had slowly been accumulating in the coffers of churches, as well as in those of magnates who were creating sumptuous interiors for the Divine office through their alms in gold and silver. Scattered clues in contemporary records indicate a tendency for hoarded wealth to be released. In their accounts of improvements to religious buildings, chroniclers refer to the discovery and immediate dispersion of hidden treasure, frequently by presenting it as a miracle. Turning to the reconstruction of Orléans Cathedral, Raoul Glaber writes as follows:

> While the bishop and all his associates were busily pressing on with the work that had been started, so as to complete it magnificently and as quickly as possible, he was visibly blessed with Divine encouragement. One day, when masons were testing the firmness of the ground to select a site for the basilica's foundations, they came across a considerable quantity of gold. They estimated that there would certainly be enough to carry out all the work of restoration on the basilica, despite its size. They picked up the gold discovered by chance and conveyed the whole of it to the bishop. He gave thanks to almighty God for the gift He had bestown upon him, took it and consigned it to those in charge of the work, telling them to spend it all on building the church. . . . Thus it was that not only the cathedral buildings but also, on the bishop's advice, other decaying churches in that same town – basilicas raised in memory of various saints – were reconstructed more elegantly than their predecessors. . . . Shortly afterwards, the town itself was filled with houses . . .

Helgaud of St Benoît-sur-Loire, biographer of King Robert the Pious of France, relates that after her husband's death Queen Constance 'had the seven pounds of gold ornamentation with which the monarch had covered the altar of St Peter in Orléans Cathedral removed' and offered them to 'make it possible to repair the church roof'.[1]

Signs of yet a third kind of renewal recorded by chroniclers of the early eleventh century bear witness to the founding of a new order: the establishment of feudal institutions.

[1] Glaber, *Les cinq livres*, book II, §5, ed. Prou, p. 36; Helgaud, *Epitoma Vitae Regis Roberti Pii*, §22 in J. P. Migne (ed.), *Patrologia Latina*, vol. cxli (Paris 1853), cols. 925–6.

II THE FEUDAL ORDER

The usage of the word 'feudalism' (*féodalisme*) adopted by Marxist historians to define one of the principal phases of economic and social evolution is justified by the part played by 'feudalism' (*féodalité*) (in its very broad sense of the forms clothing the exercise of power in Western Europe as from the first millennium) in arranging new relations between productive forces and those who profited from them. Accordingly, it is essential to examine carefully this major alteration to political structures.

Feudalism was characterized in the first instance by the decay of royal authority, and we have seen that the inability of Carolingian kings to contain attacks by outsiders had hastened the dispersion of their power in the course of the ninth century. Defence of the land – the original function of kingship – passed rapidly and irreversibly into the hands of local princes. The latter subsumed the royal rights that had been delegated to them and incorporated them in the patrimony of a dynasty whose foundations were laid as part of the same process. Afterwards, most of the great principalities themselves disintegrated little by little, like the kingdoms. Overlords of middle rank – counts to begin with, then, towards the year 1000, commanders of individual strongholds – won their independence from the princes. These developments occupied the whole tenth century in Gaul, affected the English monarchy, and penetrated Italy, though deviating somewhat here because of the strength of the towns. They were slow to reach Germany, where Carolingian political institutions survived until the dawn of the twelfth century. This subdivision between smaller and smaller territorial units of the right to command and punish, to ensure peace and justice, constituted an adjustment to the concrete possibilities of exercising effective authority in a rural and barbaric world where it was difficult to communicate over any distance. Political organization was being adapted to the ordering of material life. But it is important to stress that this change was accomplished just when the memory of seasonal wars of pillage, formerly conducted by the whole body of free men against external tribal enemies, was fading from the peasant mentality. It coincided with the adoption of a new type of warfare and with the creation of a new concept of peace.

The development of the 'Peace of God' ideology went hand in

hand with the last phases of feudalization. It was expressed for the first time shortly before the year 1000 in southern Gaul, the region where the collapse of royal authority had come about earliest. By slow degrees this ideology acquired a measure of consistency, though it spread through the whole of Latin Christendom in various guises. Its principles were quite straightforward: God had deputed to anointed kings the task of maintaining peace and justice; kings were no longer capable of so doing; God therefore took back His power of command into His own hands and vested it in those of His servants, the bishops, with the support of local princes. Thus councils summoned by prelates met together in each district, and magnates and their warriors took part. These assemblies, falling back on constraints of a moral and spiritual nature, aimed to curb violence and to lay down rules of conduct for those who bore arms: by means of a collective oath, all professional fighters had to undertake to respect certain prohibitions under pain of excommunication. Such a system proved to be only relatively effective. Throughout the eleventh and twelfth centuries, the Western countryside was constantly devastated by unruly bands of warriors. Even so, the institution of the Peace of God had profound repercussions on men's behaviour and on the most basic elements of economic life.

To begin with, it laid down a coherent morality of warfare for the first time. In early medieval society fighting had been regarded as a normal activity and one in which legal freedom had attained its highest expression. No gains had been considered more just than those from war. In future, according to the precepts of peace councils, it would no longer be permissible to fight – any more than to handle money or to indulge in sexual intercourse – except within precise limits. Fields of action were defined wherein the clash of arms was condemned as evil, contrary to God's designs and the right ordering of the world. All military violence was forbidden inside certain areas (near places of worship, marked by crosses erected on the roads), during certain periods corresponding to the most sacred occasions in the liturgical calendar, and against certain social groups deemed to be vulnerable (churchmen and the 'poor' or common masses). These moral principles had all existed in embryonic form in the regulations for peace and justice that kings of Carolingian times had striven to get accepted. But because the Latin Church assumed responsibility for them and amalgamated them into a unified code, valid for all followers of Christ, they were imposed much more effectively on the Christian community as a whole, and this at the very moment when the great states recently carved out by conquest were disintegrating into a multitude of small competing powers. Europe's fragmentation into countless political units might have created conditions for military confrontations to increase, for new strength to be lent to tribal warfare, and for economic organization based largely on incessant plundering to be restored in the European heartland. The injunctions of the Peace of God deflected the aggressive forces harboured by feudal society away from the Christian world. Against the enemies of God, the 'infidels', it was not only permissible but eminently salutary to bear arms. Men of war were therefore invited to practise their own special form of activity outside Christendom. The crusading spirit, emanating directly from the new peace ideology, guided them towards external war-fronts, towards the prosperous borderlands where fighting acted as a powerful stimulant to the circulation of wealth.

The seizure of the goods of churches and rustics through military violence against God's own people was thus seen more and more clearly, by those whose vocation was fighting, as a danger to the salvation of their souls. None the less, the acquisition of riches could be achieved by other means, provided these were 'peaceful' – and these were afforded by the institution of lordship. Condemning the spoils of violence, the ethic of the Peace of God by way of compensation legitimized seigneurial exploitation. This was presented as the price that had to be paid for the security offered to working men and women by the new regime.

Seigneurial exploitation conformed to a sociological pattern that was eventually brought closely into line with the reality of economic relations, and at the same time gave the latter greater solidity. As the year 1000 passed by, prohibitions laid down in peace councils brought to fruition the theory of the three orders that was being slowly nurtured by a narrow circle of intellectuals: since the Creation, God had assigned specific tasks among men; some were commissioned to pray for the salvation of all, others were pledged to fight to protect the mass of the people; it was up to members of the third order, by far the most numerous, to provide for the men of religion and men of war by their labour. This design, which impressed itself very quickly on the collective consciousness, presented a simple picture in conformity with the Divine plan, thereby sanctioning social inequalities and all forms of economic exploitation. Within so rigid and clear-cut a mental framework could freely exist the various dependent relations which had long since been established between peasant workers and landowners, and which governed the machinery of an economic system that can essentially be called 'feudal'.

(*a*) THE THREE ORDERS. In this ideological model constructed by intellectuals, all members of the Church in those days, the specialists in prayer were obviously to be placed at the apex of the hierarchy of orders. Not only were they to be exempt from the many exactions to which powerful men could subject their dependencies through pillage or taxation, but they were also to be awarded a substantial share of all produce, this to be offered up to God through their intercession. People were thus induced to give preference to economic activities relating to consecration and sacrifice. This penetration of the collective consciousness coincided with the moment when the flood of pious donations in favour of religious houses reached its highest point; never in the history of the Christian Church in the West were the laity's bequests so bountiful as during the five or six decades overlapping the year 1000. The faithful gave from day to day in order to redeem such sins as they had just committed and which they knew would place their souls in jeopardy. They gave still more generously on their death-beds – at the risk of leaving their heirs in straitened circumstances – for their burials and to earn the support of guardian saints before the day of judgement. They gave what they could: principally land since it was then regarded as the most valuable form of wealth, especially when provided with peasant workers to farm it. All contemporary written sources available to historians come from ecclesiastical archives: they are for the most part deeds guaranteeing acquisitions by churches, so shedding particular light on this phenomenon and running the risk of exaggerating its scale. Nevertheless, this enormous transfer of landed property – of which Benedictine abbeys were the greatest beneficiaries, with episcopal churches in second place – was the most dynamic change affecting the European economy at this time. It established the Western Church in a paramount temporal position. From those endeavouring to understand the Gospel message better, it soon drew forth criticism, and by the middle of the eleventh century a desire to disengage God's servants from preoccupations that were too material was already being widely expressed. The Church's enormously increased wealth fostered a restlessness that acted as a breeding ground for heretical propaganda and a starting-point for successive attempts at reform. It also caused the number of monks and clerks to rise constantly during the eleventh and twelfth centuries.

These men were not totally removed from productive processes. The rural clergy remained, by and large, on a par with the peasantry whose origins and customs they shared. Country churches and chapels were served by priests who followed the plough themselves and with their families (many indeed were married) farmed the plots of land granted to them by lords of the manor for their services. Communities of monks and reformed canons, which became widespread from the end of the eleventh century, enjoined manual labour on their members. This harsh asceticism fell especially on those who, recruited among base-born rustics, could not participate fully in the liturgical office. In their drudgery and material circumstances these 'lay brothers' (*conversi*) thus resembled the peasantry. Many of the richest churchmen, however, as recipients of the most substantial offerings, were pure consumers. Residents in the vicinity of cathedral churches enjoyed standards approaching those of the most powerful laymen. It did not occur to them that their role of serving God could be fulfilled without ostentation. Of the riches they naturally acquired in plenty, they undoubtedly devoted part to assisting the poor. Their hospitality was on a large scale. Paupers received food or money at church doors and these ritual alms would be extended in times of calamity. This function of redistribution, carefully defined in the financial arrangements of great monastic foundations, was certainly not negligible; it made an effective contribution to keeping destitution within bounds in a society that was still so underdeveloped and harboured deep down an ingrained and growing mass of poverty-stricken and rootless men. Yet charity retained second place behind the age-old requirement of celebrating Divine office in the most dazzling sumptuousness. The best uses to which heads of monasteries and cathedral churches could think of putting their wealth were dutifully to embellish, rebuild and decorate the place of prayer, and to accumulate round the altar and saints' relics the most glittering splendour. Assured of resources that the generosity of the faithful kept on increasing, they had but one economic attitude: to spend for the glory of God.

This outlook was shared by members of the second order of society, the specialists in warfare. They too would spend, but in the interests of their own glory and the pleasures of life. Supplying the Church with all her administrators, monopolizing the force of arms and using it harshly notwithstanding prohibitions laid down by the Peace of God ethic, this social category constituted the ruling class, despite the overriding value attributed to the priestly calling, despite the wealth and undoubted numerical superiority of churchmen. It was in terms of the power and conduct of these laymen that the theory of the three orders was constructed and that peace-making institutions of a sort were framed. It was their position and behaviour that governed the whole feudal economy of the eleventh and twelfth centuries. They held the land, apart from that portion which fears of an untimely death made them surrender to God, His saints and those who served Him. They lived in idleness and looked upon productive tasks as unworthy of their rank and of that lofty freedom to which they claimed to reserve a preferential right for themselves. Because the decay of royal authority had ended by establishing members of this order in a position of independence and had bequeathed them mental attitudes worthy of kings, they accepted no constraint, no service except what they had freely chosen to give and which, by not taking the form of material dues, did not seem dishonourable. They therefore withheld all payment to which they had not consented and condescended to part with their possessions only by way of free gifts and acts of mutual generosity. Their vocation was war, and the prime purpose of their wealth was to acquire the most effective means of fighting, through the physical training to which they devoted much of their time and those investments from which they expected one sole return – greater military strength. In the household economy of men in this category, a significant proportion of their incomes, and one that appears to have risen throughout the eleventh and twelfth centuries, was assigned to perfecting the equipment of the warriors, improving the qualities of the horse, and procuring the best offensive and defensive weapons. The horse became the fighting man's principal arm and the symbol of his superiority; now it was that these warriors became accustomed to describing themselves as 'mounted knights' (*milites*). At the close of the eleventh century, the mail shirt had already become so intricate that it equalled the price of a good farm. The urge to improve armour lay behind the steady development of iron-working. Rapid progress in military architecture during the twelfth century led to the opening up of further building sites for castles, often near those of churches. There was one other occasion for spending by members of this social group, who were ruled by the spirit of competitiveness and among whom individual worth was measured not only in terms of bravery and skill in handling weapons but also in terms of finery, display and extravagance. In the *ethos* to which these aristocrats were dedicated, one of the time-honoured virtues was largess, the pleasure of being spendthrift. Like kings of former times, the knight had always to be open-handed, showering riches all around him. Feasting and carousing at gatherings where the fruits of the earth were collectively destroyed amid revelry and ostentatious rivalry formed, along with warfare, the mainstay of the aristocratic way of life. The economic outlook that the knightly order represented in contemporary society was one of plunder by professional calling and consumption by customary practice.

There remains the third order, the workers, the bottom layer made up of the vast majority of the population, each of whom was persuaded that he or she had to supply the two élites of *oratores* and *bellatores*, those who prayed and those who fought, with the means to sustain their sloth and prodigality. Their specific function which, following the dictates of Providence, doomed them inescapably to a life of reputedly degrading manual labour, deprived them of full liberty. While the last elements of slavery faded away (the word *servus* disappears from most parts of France in the early twelfth century), the peasantry as a whole, weighed down by increased pressure from those who monopolized power, appear to have succumbed to the exploitation of others because of their very situation. Some won salvation for them through prayer; others were responsible, in theory, for defending them against aggressors. As the price of these favours, their capacity to produce was totally subordinated to lordship.

(*b*) LORDSHIP. Economically, feudalism was characterized not only by the hierarchy of social conditions that the schematic arrangement of the three orders was intended to represent; it was also characterized by the institution of lordship. This was not new, but had slowly been modified by the development of political power.

Despite the rationalized social structure whose simplicity compelled recognition after the first millennium, the barrier separating workers from churchmen and warriors did not coincide exactly with that which placed the lords on one side and those subject to seigneurial exploitation on the other. Many priests, as we have seen, formed part of the manorial staff. Under orders from a lord who made use of their professional expertise, they performed services analogous to those of a miller or the holder of a bread-oven. Down to the end of the twelfth century many knights, particularly in Germany and countries bordering on the North Sea, remained in the position of household dependants in the home of a patron who would employ and maintain them. Owning no land they would share in the profits of lordship, though without exercising any authority. Conversely, there were peasants who had managed to acquire more land than they themselves could farm and who might grant the surplus to less well-endowed neighbours, in return for a manorial-type rent. Among those servants of humble origins whom overlords had made responsible for running their estates, many were doing well for themselves – and rapidly too. Appropriating some of the powers bestowed upon them, they were able to exploit underlings so as to create out of their master's lordship a network of dues, the proceeds of which they would keep entirely for themselves and which would virtually amount to their own personal lordship. Nevertheless feudal society was arranged in two classes, one of which, the lords, comprised both clerics and knights. To them it seemed scandalous, if not sinful, that a worker might haul himself up from his station in life to the point of sharing in the privileges of priests and warriors, of living in idleness thanks to the labour of others. During the period when feudal institutions were attaining maturity, that is in the years following the millennium, tensions within the social fabric led to a consolidation of the seigneurial position of the clerical and knightly orders, and to a widening of the gulf separating them from the common people in the field of economic relations. This process of consolidation took place on two distinct levels.

First, the unity of aristocratic estates was reinforced. Those belonging to laymen were threatened with dissolution through the action of two practices – pious gifts and partible inheritance. Their combined effect was most powerful whenever the patrimony passed from one generation to another: one part, which the deceased's generosity tended to magnify, would fall into the hands of the Church; the remainder, according to customs bequeathed by Germanic cultures, would be subdivided into equal portions among the sons and daughters due to succeed to their father's inheritance. By an instinctive defensive reaction, and taking advantage of the flexibility of customary regulations in the absence of any written code, the lay aristocracy tried to ward off the double danger represented by the progressive diminution and fragmentation of their basic landed reserves. They used their power and the many ties of kinship and mutual aid attaching them to the heads of great religious foundations to obtain compensatory grants out of ecclesiastical property. Often the latter would by far and away exceed the needs of communities of monks and canons, especially after that great outburst of piety *c.* 1000. To ensure favourable treatment for themselves at the hands of powerful contemporaries abbots, bishops and deans of chapters did not hesitate to confer upon their kinsmen or friends the usufruct of some of the land offered to the patron saints of their churches. This would normally be on a temporary basis, but it was difficult to recover from the first beneficiary's heirs property that had actually been incorporated for many years in the family patrimony. In due course a grant of this nature might become indistinguishable from the family's allodial holdings, and all the more so because it would involve virtually no material obligation, whether it were a fief requiring simply the performance of homage and services of mutual assistance, or a precarial contract, or, as in Italy, a *livello* stipulating a purely symbolic money payment. Such grants were being restricted in the late eleventh century. They gave way before the sustained though usually vain efforts by administrators of ecclesiastical temporalities to recover rights that had formerly been misappropriated in this fashion. None the less, the practice had lasted long enough to reduce partially the imbalance between the landed wealth of Church and lay aristocracy. Further, what brought this practice to an end were the twin facts that not only did the spirit of Gregorian reform condemn the dependence of spiritual upon temporal powers, but also the flood of benefactions in the form of real estate was steadily subsiding. The contents of ecclesiastical archives clearly show a gradual decrease in the number of deeds of gift, starting from the middle of the eleventh century, and their replacement by title deeds subject to payment. This phenomenon was connected with slow changes in religious sentiment, a retreat from formalism, an ever keener awareness that one's soul could be saved by means other than the purchase of Divine forgiveness with a gift. But it seems to have been still more directly affected by the growth of a money economy, which made it possible to offer valuables considered less precious than land, and by the desire of families to ensure better protection for their possessions. Cartularies of religious houses leave an impression that members of the aristocracy in the twelfth century sometimes gave away less than they reclaimed doggedly from the benefactions of their ancestors. A litigious age was dawning, marked by complicated bargaining in which money played an increasingly decisive role and dictated what may have been a more deliberate policy of consolidating landed inheritances.

The unity of aristocratic estates was also promoted by slow modifications in kinship. Still little investigated by scholars, these appear to have accompanied in many parts of Europe the implantation of a network of feudal relations. In the upper levels of society, family ties were being arranged within a rigid framework calculated to safeguard the unity of the inheritance – in a word, lineage. For each family there would be one line of male descent. On succeeding his father, the eldest son would exercise control over the common property handed down from his forebears, as a guarantee that the family might maintain its ascendancy. Against this relatively clear cut background, the wish to counter the effects of partible inheritance imposed limits on collateral descent. The family would permit only one son – the eldest, or two at the most – to be party to a legitimate marriage; as far as possible, the others would be secured high-ranking positions in the upper clergy or in monasteries; in other words, they would rely on the Church's resources to avoid relegation. This same desire led to the practice of giving a dowry in movable goods to daughters who were about to marry, depriving them of any claim on the landed inheritance. It slowly brought acceptance of the idea that the eldest son should enjoy preferential treatment by receiving the lion's share, if not the whole, of his father's estate. Practices of this kind, which crept into customary usage unnoticed, seem effectively to have restrained the various forces causing lay inheritances to dwindle in an age of widespread population growth. Add to this the irresistible pressure of social constraints, compelling magnates to 'find homes for' (*casare*) most of the knights still being supported in their households; to enable them to marry by granting them fiefs, whose hereditary character was quickly accepted because of the strength of family ties; and so to provide them with personal lordships. The aristocracy thus became more firmly rooted in their landed estates during this period. The greater part of the twelfth century was apparently a time of relative stability for the estates of both Church and knightly aristocracy. Even petty knights maintained themselves in an economic position distinctly superior to the peasants' standard of living.

On a second level, the process of consolidation was furthered by the development of a fiscal system, the burden of which was borne entirely by the 'poor' or 'workers'. Such taxation was not new but was organized differently. It descended in a direct line from the authority (*bannum*) wielded by early medieval kings. Yet two major changes can be detected.

First, whereas all free men had once been subject to the royal *bannum*, the division of society into three orders introduced a fundamental cleavage within the mass of the population. A new notion of freedom, hereafter conceived of as a privilege, that of avoiding humiliating constraints and notably fiscal exactions, came to withdraw churchmen and knights completely from the economic pressure exerted by those in authority. Conversely, it placed in a subordinate position anyone who did not belong to the two privileged orders. It combined on a single farm men whose ancestors were free-born with the descendants of slaves. It gathered up one and all into a homogeneous class, liable to identical services. In this class the characteristics of erstwhile slavery were quickly assimilated.

Second, the exercise of the *bannum* and the collection of dues sanctioned by it were now confined to a restricted area, a *districtus* (the term comes from a word meaning 'to distrain') whose outer limits were rarely more than half a day's ride from some central point, invariably a fortified place. The commander of the castle garrison would take upon himself responsibility for peace and justice over the whole territory – in other words, the precise functions of kingship. In that part of Christian Europe where the foundations of kingdoms and principalities had retained greater strength – in England and the north-west of the Continent – the castellan would still be dependent on a lord, acting in his name and handing over to him a portion of the income derived from the exercise of power. Elsewhere, he might be independent and behave like a law unto himself. Everywhere, he would claim jurisdiction over anyone living in the neighbourhood of the stronghold who was neither a cleric, monk, nor knight. He would impose fines on them and, in cases of grave offence, confiscate their goods and chattels. His judicial and police action were looked on as forceful and shrewd to the extent that they were lucrative in actual practice. He could compel farmers to labour on the upkeep of works of fortification and supply the castle's soldiers and horsemen with fresh provisions. He could exact payment from strangers crossing the castellany – merchants, pilgrims, and anyone frequenting markets – for the temporary protection he afforded them. Like kings in the recent past, he was guarantor of weights and measures. He might well mint coins. Through all manner of expedients he would make use of the authority at his command, so that in the end the *bannum* assumed the form of a network of exactions imposed in various ways on the surpluses from peasant output and on the profits from trade.

The local commander would be first to dip into the workers' savings, since he wielded the military power. He would also appropriate the biggest share for himself. But nearly all the inhabitants of the castellany would find themselves also in a position of economic dependence on other lords whose land they cultivated or to whom they were personally subject because they were descended from slaves or had voluntarily submitted. These private lords strove to remove their tenants and dependants from the power of whoever held the *bannum*. The taxes he levied, called 'exactions' (*exactiones*) or 'customs' (*consuetudines*) in contemporary records, drew on reserves of wealth and labour that these other lords wished to appropriate for their own exclusive use. Usually they failed and had to share economic power over peasants on their estates or in their servile households (*familiae*) with the master of peace and justice. Some did succeed in having their monopoly recognized, however, and the district comprising the castellany was normally interspersed with enclaves, sometimes tiny ones limited to a knight's household, sometimes larger ones the size of a village, especially when a religious house had managed to secure recognition of the ancient privilege of immunity it once held from the Carolingians. Yet the inhabitants of these enclaves would by no means evade taxation. They were exposed to similar demands by the owner of their land or their persons, who would himself claim the right to judge them and to extort protection money from them, just as the 'banal'[1] lord did elsewhere.

In short, banal power, whether intact or fragmented, was established on uniform lines and acted as a determining factor in economic processes in two special ways. First, the exercise of such power made it necessary to rely on numerous assistants, like the 'sergeants' (*servientes*) who kept order on manors, the reeves or

[1] Since the *Oxford English Dictionary* gives as the first meaning of the adjective 'banal': 'Of or belonging to compulsory feudal service', there seems to be every justification for resurrecting this useful term. On the other hand, the word 'ban' has never acquired the full significance of the medieval Latin *bannum*, which has therefore been preferred as the noun to represent the French *ban*. (Translator's note.)

'provosts' (*prepositi*) who presided over village assemblies, the 'foresters' (*forestarii*) who pursued offenders against customary rights in woods or on common land, and the tax gatherers stationed in market-places and at major river-crossings. All these *ministeriales*, as records call them, especially in Germany, would be recruited by lords among those of their servants who were most closely attached to them. The problem was to keep them firmly under control. Because these assistants would share directly in the profits of 'customs' and get their rake-off from the taxes and fines they collected, they naturally showed themselves to be the most ruthless agents in exploiting the rights of the *bannum*. They increased the burden as much as they could, craftily amassing their own fortunes out of the income it provided. Second, this form of exploitation could be highly effective when pushed to the utmost, though presumably it was not unlimited. As their names suggest, these taxes levied on the pretext of maintaining peace and justice were 'customs'; that is to say, the collective memory set limits on their assessment. It would also be necessary to take particular account of the resistance of peasant households, of fraud, evasion and all manner of delaying tactics. Even so, custom was malleable. It offered feeble resistance to pressure from those who wielded authority. Agents of banal taxation were ubiquitous, avaricious, and well equipped with reinforcements. To whom could victims of their malpractices complain? That is why this fiscal machinery worked well. It was able to mulct the peasantry of most of what they produced and in excess of their subsistence needs. It therefore retarded considerably any tendency towards higher living standards for the poor. It narrowed the gap between tenants and independent farmers. It stabilized peasant circumstances. But it reduced them and, as a result, widened beyond recall the gulf separating the working from the seigneurial class.

The seigneurial class was far from being homogeneous: lords were not all social equals, nor were they able to take advantage of other people's labour in the same way. Intricate, inextricably mixed up with one another, and confused in the minds of contemporaries, there were really three distinct forms of seigneurial exploitation. Because it was often associated with what then was designated by the word *familia* – the household surrounding anyone who had a modicum of power – one of these forms might be described as 'domestic lordship' (*seigneurie domestique*). By this we mean that transference of rights which put the body of one human being at the disposal of another. It was the tenacious residue of slavery. Under pressure from banal power, bondage of the ancient type had generally been reduced, though here and there it had been reimposed. Elsewhere, it had made inroads at the expense of the erstwhile free population through 'commendation' (*commendatio*), through necessity that drove so many weak and poor men to avoid starvation, oppression by the castellan's sergeants, or even fear of the world to come, by placing themselves in the patronage of a protector. These bonds had not been undone; rather they had become those of what is commonly called 'serfdom'. In most villages of Europe there were peasants whom a lord referred to as 'his men' (*homines proprii*). Their numbers varied: sometimes the entire village community was in this category. They were really his from birth and their descendants belonged to him; he could sell them or give them away; he could punish them; in theory, they would owe him everything. It was primarily their labour of which he took advantage, in his house and fields, and the 'service' (*obsequium*) he expected from them knew no bounds. They made available to the domestic economy a permanent labour force whose cost was solely that of its upkeep. This form of dependence could also be a source of revenue. In practice not all the individuals subject to it would live in their master's residence. Far removed from his reach, having settled on land belonging to him or someone else, they would still remain attached to their lord. This tie was represented not only by the labour services that custom and distance were tending to curtail, but also by three kinds of payment: an annual rent in cash, a fine to purchase the right to take a spouse not of the lord's household, and a deduction made by the lord from the inheritance. Down to the end of the twelfth century, the farming of estates of every size relied on this type of lordship, which was widespread and commonly shared by all members of aristocracy as well as a few rich peasants. It considerably limited recourse to wage-labour. Through the pool of workers that it provided, domestic lordship constituted one of the two fundamental bases of economic power.

The other was what may be termed 'landlordship' (*seigneurie foncière*), because it stemmed from possession not of people but of land. Its characteristics were a continuation of those which Carolingian polyptyques have already made familiar. Rare indeed was it for the rich to exploit all the land in their possession by means of the labour of their personal dependants. Often they would grant a substantial part of it to tenants, who might be 'their men', or the 'men' of others, or perhaps live completely free of bodily subjection. To grant land was to acquire power – the power to fasten upon the resources of tenant households. Strictly speaking these exactions were not unlimited like those representing serfdom. They were precisely defined, either by the terms of an agreement in countries such as Italy where the use of writing had been better preserved, or by equally binding customary rules. They would always, or nearly always, involve a levy on what the holding produced, paid either in agricultural produce or in cash. Frequently, they would also involve a levy on the working capacities of the peasant family, whose members were compelled to perform a given number of labour services (*corvées*).

The third form of seigneurial exploitation arose, as we have seen, from the exercise of rights derived from the *bannum* (*seigneurie banale*). Banal lordship might authorize its beneficiaries to take everything that could be removed from peasant households: cash, crops, livestock, even labour (through requisitions for rebuilding the castle or the carriage of provisions). It was really a kind of legitimized and organized pillage, tempered only by the resistance of village communities. This form of economic exploitation coincided with the other two and frequently overshadowed them. But it was much more exclusive, since only a small number of lords benefited from its advantages.

The unequal distribution of banal authority created the chief economic division within the seigneurial class. On the one hand were those whom documents describe as 'magnates' (*optimates, principes*) in the eleventh century and 'rich men' (*ric oms*) in the twelfth. Individually, the title of 'lord' (*dominus*) accompanies their names in written deeds. They really were the master class; that is why they were the richest. Whether they happened to be high ecclesiastical dignitaries (bishops, abbots of monasteries) or men who wielded military power – territorial princes, counts, 'barons' (*barones*) – commanders of castles who exploited the prerogatives attached to these corner-stones of public order were more or less well provided for. Their domestic lordship and landlordship extended far and wide over the territory they controlled. As heirs to regalian rights, they could lay their hands on vast uncultivated areas formerly dependent on the supreme landlord, the king himself. Yet their very wealth and the functions they fulfilled kept them remote from the soil and the peasants who cultivated it. Lords like these looked down on them from too great a height. Between such lords and working people, therefore, came middlemen who acted as interpreters of their commands and held the actual levers of economic power. The magnates themselves were generally *rentiers*. Caring only to be supplied regularly with what was necessary for their ostentatious display and family reputation, they surrendered a substantial part of their power into the hands of those they had made responsible for exercising it in their names.

On the other hand were countless other lords – plain knights, canons holding as 'prebends' (*prebendae*) a portion of the endowment of a cathedral church, monks put in charge of a country priory – as well as representatives of the magnates. They too enjoyed varied living standards, but had in common direct control over the day-to-day running of a compact estate whose size did not overtax their managerial ability. They were the neighbours of the peasants; they knew them by name; they shared their anxieties; they were aware of what they produced and of how much could be extorted from them. Striving to model their behaviour on that of the 'rich men' whose courts they frequented, they tried to maximize the profits of lordship. And since they lived in immediate contact with the land and the working masses, they can be regarded as the most active agents of economic vitality, and of the growth that is revealed so strikingly by twelfth-century documents.

III SEEDS OF GROWTH

In the last analysis, the impetus behind the internal expansion now experienced by the European economy must have originated in pressure exerted by seigneurial power on productive forces. This growing pressure arose from the desire shared by churchmen and warriors to realize more fully an ideal of consumption in the service of God or for their own self-esteem. In the eleventh and twelfth centuries, the limits of this desire broadened constantly as Latin Christendom's enterprises in the Mediterranean were pursued farther afield. For the fascination that models of Roman antiquity had held for aristocrats in the early Middle Ages was substituted that of souvenirs brought home by adventurers from Spain and southern Italy, after the capture of Barbastro or Toledo, Palermo or Bari, or acquired by pilgrims to the Holy Land passing through Constantinople or Antioch. These mementoes implanted in the seigneurial mentality a fixed determination to reject country ways and attain the lifestyle led by southern town-dwellers. This desire was gaining ground as lords emerged from their isolation, as opportunities for meeting one another grew, and as the attractions of princely courts increased. At these fashionable gatherings, models of noble behaviour were exemplified and riches brought back from the Orient displayed. In far distant barbarian Europe, Slav princes dreamt of aping the manners of German princes, who in their turn heard the call for greater refinement from Gaul and Italy. The predisposition towards high living became everywhere more pronounced.

To satisfy increasingly fastidious tastes, it was essential to indulge in more pillaging. This could still be done by violent means on Christendom's war-torn frontiers, but law and order of a sort had been established in feudal Europe, restricting the scope of military adventure as power structures were consolidated. The prime need was to raise income from seigneurial exploitation, but two limitations stood in the way. The first was created by custom. From his personal dependants the lord could in theory demand anything, and from villagers dwelling in the castellany the holder of the *bannum* was in a position to take nearly everything. Villagers were harried for the slightest misdemeanours or exploited through the lord's right to hospitality (*droit de gîte*). Economic power conferred by the various forms of lordship was all the more effective when allied to judicial authority. Ordinary landlords themselves presided over the courts that settled disputes about tenurial burdens and penalized the tenants' failings. Decisions of these courts were usually without appeal. All lords, then, judged cases in which their own interests were at stake. Yet every judicial assembly in the lordship was composed of the workers themselves; on their advice the judge passed sentence. Facing him, common people would feel at one with each other and form a bulwark out of customary usages. No man could go against custom. They were its joint trustees; it was imperative to call upon their witness by conducting an inquiry, and, should the lord use his seigneurial power to bring into customary rules innovations favourable to himself, he would come up against the stubborn, hide-bound popular conscience, whose selective memory knew how to cast any intolerable change into oblivion. The second limitation was strictly economic. No man could exploit the workers excessively without seeing their productivity fall, or forcing them to take flight in a world where there was still plenty of room for emigrants. That is why the desire to raise profits from seigneurial exploitation gradually formulated in the minds of lords and their agents the idea of 'ameliorating' output from dependent peasants, and the Latin word *meliorare* is often encountered in contemporary economic documents. Peasants were either encouraged to beget more children, or given an opportunity to expand their productive capacities. Part conscious, part countered by other influences and unsophisticated mental attitudes, this aim stimulated further progress within the new feudal milieu.

Symptoms of such progress can be discerned as early as 1000, but these become much more evident from *c.* 1075. Collectively the sources suggest that this point in time marked a vital stage in a chronology that still remains highly imprecise, because of the terse, extremely fragmentary, and always indirect nature of the documentation. This is the period when hoards were put to use and small currency spread in eastern Europe. Farther west, the pace of change had unmistakably gathered momentum. During the last three decades of the eleventh century sites for new churches were opened up, far more numerous and extensive than before. Western knights hastened to embark on more ambitious acts of aggression, culminating in the launching of the First Crusade in 1095. New monastic communities flourished, and recruited countless members from various social classes, all activated by the yearning for asceticism and the condemnation of wealth. This can be explained only by the realization, in a less static economic environment, of a reputedly perverse yet positive desire for economic growth – in other words, the discovery of the first attacks of the profit-motive disease. In addition, we can see commercial activities infiltrating country districts during the same period. Thus, for example, the respective values of different coins begin to be specified in charters of the Mâconnais region from 1080, indicating the growing influence of money in the rural world, the diversification of mintage, and the conception of a new notion – the exchange rate. At the same time, banal lords determined to take advantage of the more frequent passage of traders carrying precious wares. Hereafter there are more references to tolls, a type of exaction now multiplying rapidly: the Pope secured exemption for merchants of Asti crossing the Ile de France from taxes King Philip I was about to impose on them; the abbot of Cluny chided a neighbouring castellan for detaining a merchant caravan from Langres and attempting to compel the traders to pay him protection money. Toll regulations laid down by the monks of St Aubin of Angers in 1080–2 show clearly that trade was not solely the concern of professionals. Peasants bought and sold livestock; they concluded stock-raising agreements with outsiders; they took wax, honey, pork meat, hides and wool to be disposed of in near-by markets, 'carrying them round their necks'. They even entered into partnerships to operate over longer distances, initially by loading their pack-animals with food supplies and occasionally 'foreign and high-priced goods' as well. About 1075 the abbot of Reichenau granted to all the 'peasants' (*rustici*) in one of his villages 'the right to trade . . . so that they themselves and their descendants might be merchants'. In these years an infectious vitality becomes apparent for the first time. Its cause lay in the fact that men were slowly familiarizing themselves with coins, which were being minted more plentifully and regularly. Deep in the heart of the Western countryside, the circulation of money stimulated activities whose growth had been barely perceptible during the previous century, except on the borders of Christendom where warfare kept wealth mobile. The commercial and monetary buoyancy observable henceforth in the West arose from the vitality of more basic elements in the economy. This new buoyancy was its outward sign, but the elements were themselves combining to generate still greater vitality. In the last three decades of the eleventh century we may discern the opening of a fresh phase in European economic history: that of a broad, sustained and rapid development, whose various features we must now analyse.

7 *Peasants*

The intensification of agricultural endeavour lay at the root of this new vitality. It stemmed largely from pressure by lords anxious to see the surplus product from the labour of their personal dependants grow, so that they might appropriate it for themselves. But the way had been prepared over a long period by two interrelated changes. First, there seems to have been an improvement in ecological conditions, since there are indications that the European countryside had for several centuries enjoyed a milder and drier climate, more favourable to successful farming. Second, there was the unquestionable factor of population growth.

I THE HUMAN FACTOR

Here we refer to an undercurrent which is virtually impossible to observe but which we may guess had long been active in Germany and England. In Gaul, however, it had been temporarily retarded by the rigidity of Carolingian manorial structures. The tendency for population to rise is apparent from the moment when feudal institutions were first established and throughout the eleventh and twelfth centuries. The nature of the documentary evidence precludes any attempt to measure the scale of this change. True enough, for the bulk of England during the last third of the eleventh century, Domesday Book provides statistical data of exceptional value, if hard to interpret. But this source is unique. For comparable figures later on we have to wait until taxation methods had been improved sufficiently to produce systematic surveys. Again these are of England: for a few villages dependent upon ecclesiastical estates they were conducted with special care in the late twelfth century, and for the whole kingdom in the fourteenth. All that can reasonably be ascertained is that the English population more than trebled between 1086 and 1346, though it has not proved possible to follow in detail the fluctuations of this growth. We therefore have to fall back on scattered clues that relate mainly to the upper levels of the social hierarchy. The scope of military undertakings in this period, as well as the rapid proliferation of new religious houses, cannot be explained without postulating a steady rise in membership of the knightly aristocracy. Proof of this lies in the genealogies that can be constructed with some precision for a few aristocratic pedigrees. The desire on the part of these families to avoid a dissolution of the patrimony would prompt each generation to restrict the number of male children getting married; yet, with every generation, couples who were not childless often had numerous sons, many of whom attained adulthood. For Picardy an attempt has been made to calculate the rate of population increase on the basis of information of this kind: the average number of grown-up sons per couple with children comes to 2·53 for 1075–1100, 2·26 for 1100–25, 2·35 for 1125–50, 2·46 for 1150–75 and 2·70 for 1175–1200. The resulting hypothesis is an annual growth rate of 0·28 per cent during the third quarter of the twelfth century and 0·72 per cent during the final quarter. Such dynamism was probably favoured by an average life expectation of between forty and fifty years and intensified by a high birth rate, which the effects of infant mortality and the sizeable proportion (perhaps one-third) of childless couples only modified. Nor is there any reason to suppose that this tendency was exclusive to aristocratic circles, who were presumably better fed but also more exposed to the dangers of a military career than the rest of the population. The great pressures that impelled crowds of paupers along the roads leading to Jerusalem or in the wake of wandering preachers at the close of the eleventh century, or the influx of lay brothers of peasant origin into the new monasteries of the twelfth, denote a vitality among the working masses akin to that which simultaneously launched so many sons of the nobility on expeditions far and wide and on careers as monks or canons. In the few families of servile status about whom details are known from legal documents relating to their personal dependence, boys appear to have been no less numerous than in aristocratic ones. Unquestionably, the tide of demographic expansion was the main stimulus for the fragmentation and multiplication of agricultural holdings, and for the pronounced mobility of the rural population that was becoming more marked as the twelfth century progressed.

What were the origins of this expansion and what decisive factors lay behind it? We cannot leave out of account the waning of destructive raids and the creation of the feudal order and its peace-making institutions. Yet it would probably be wrong to over-emphasize the effects of these, for seasonal warfare, inflamed by constant squabbling between owners of rival castles, remained rife in all parts of Christendom. In defiance of every interdict, the community of professional soldiers, whose family trees show so many sons killed in skirmishes or by accident while on military training, were not the only ones to suffer physical harm as a result. More decisive, without a shadow of doubt, was the continued rise of subsistence production, itself a direct outcome of the increase in numbers of the work force. The extra food available for the masses, however, hardly brought about better nutritional standards in the majority of peasant households: famine remained an abiding threat and malnutrition and other diseases continued to spread. (Hospitals and charitable institutions were also proliferating, as attitudes towards Christian piety adapted to encompass good works.) On the contrary, the main effect of agricultural expansion was to lower obstacles to the segmentation of family groupings and to enable a greater number of individuals to survive, in circumstances as straitened as those of their forebears.

Finally, it seems that legal changes affecting the peasantry also had a decisive part to play. The most profound repercussions on the growth of population and productivity arose from the development of unfree status. As long as young men and women remained members of a gang of household slaves in a master's dwelling, without legal possession of goods, homes or even their own bodies (and we have seen that such gangs might well have been maintained at full strength on big seventh-century estates in Gaul), a whole section of the rural population languished in conditions most unfavourable for human reproduction. Children exposed to the dangers of childbirth and infancy in slave gangs had least chance of survival. When masters gradually allowed such gangs to disperse and decided to settle their slaves as couples on farms managed by themselves, not only did they stimulate the productive capacities of these workers; they placed them in a much better position to beget children and bring them up into the adult world. From this progeny they continued to recruit the servants necessary for running their households, but many sons and daughters of slave tenants were still available for setting up new homes. And when the establishment of banal lordship came to smooth over distinctions between free and unfree peasants, making peasant status more uniform, mixed marriages became more usual, joining together, with the master's consent, children of slaves with those of other villagers, now subject to the same customs. Such marriages had already been common among tenants of the abbey of St Germain-des-Prés in the early ninth century. Matrimonial segregation soon disappeared between two groups within the peasantry who, until recently, were kept apart by the legal criteria of ancient slavery, and this fusion was precipitated by the mobility of the rural population promoted in turn by demographic expansion. A document from the abbey of Cluny instances an eleventh-century free-born immigrant who settled in a village on the banks of the Saône; he took as his wife a woman of servile status from a near-by settlement and branches of the family they started soon spread through the neighbouring countryside. As far as we can see, to the extent that it brought about the disbandment of teams of domestic slaves and an increase in autonomous units of production, the transition from slavery to serfdom provided the most powerful incentive for ordinary country people to have more children. In my view this change, which may also have given rise to a higher expectation of life, was the mainspring behind the steady growth of population. Way back in the early Middle Ages, it looks as if demographic vitality was already more marked in Germania and in England, that is to say, in those parts of the West where the bonds of slavery were less precisely defined. At any rate, the first visible signs of settlement expansion come to the surface just when the disruptions consequent upon the last invasions rapidly loosened these bonds in Gaul, and when the common subjection of farmers to the authority of castle lords caused the words *mancipium* and *servus* to be abandoned one after the other (in Dauphiné, after 957 and 1117 respectively) as the final, conscious expressions of the ancient notion of servitude.

Associated changes affecting other legal usages reinforced this fundamental transformation. Everything, or almost everything, we can ascertain about family customs in this period concerns the aristocracy: before the close of the twelfth century, direct participation by peasants in property transactions was too rare to leave traces of any rules for passing on their inheritances. We may suspect, however, that the cohesion of the family group among tenants was powerful enough for the principle of hereditary succession to holdings to be accepted tacitly, with the possible exception of Italy, where normal recourse to written deeds through the agency of notaries maintained a thriving market in leasehold contracts for a term of years. Yet it is quite likely (as has recently been suggested in the context of Picardy) that peasant families were branching outwards at the same time as knightly lineages were becoming more close-knit. This loosening of kinship ties and the slow advance of the rights of the married pair at the expense of those of a more extended family grouping, would clearly have favoured the permanent residence of young couples and consequently an increase in the number of settlement nuclei. The tendency was to some extent counteracted by the lords' wish not to allow the agrarian units, on which the assessment of dues and services was based, to disintegrate: holdings remained indivisible on many estates. But the strength of manorial custom did not succeed in curbing the desire of young men who were not due for a share in the family property to find themselves a farm. It drove them to leave their homelands. It therefore kept some villages in a state of demographic stagnation, while supplying pioneer frontiers with the manpower to press on with the agrarian conquest. Broadly speaking the move towards expanding and dispersing the family apparently broke down seigneurial reticence. Landowners were forced to admit that a holding could legitimately be divided among the heirs, though they did insist that their permission was sought and a fine was paid. Thus a process of partitioning the ancient units of peasant farming commenced slowly, then accelerated in the twelfth century. To measure its extent it will suffice to compare the *censiers* (lists of tenements and their burdens drawn up in France towards the end of that century) with the inventories made by ninth- and tenth-century administrators. In the former, the description of dues is subdivided to correspond to the innumerable parcels of land shared by different peasant households and forming highly unstable groupings. The flexibility thereby introduced into the distribution of peasant land made the task of farm-managers more complicated. And it caused the family trees of ordinary folk to segment and production units to multiply. In this way it reinforced the effects of a growing money economy. While stimulating the peasant land market by making landlords accept the idea that holdings could not only be subject to partible inheritance but also dismembered by the alienation of plots of ground on payment of transfer charges, the more decisive influence of cash was fostering individual gain, encouraging economic initiative, and permitting capital formation. It provided the most enterprising peasants with the means to give their children a better start in life and to marry well outside the immediate family circle. The astonishing growth of peasant exogamy is revealed by many a fleeting sign in the records. It is one further indication of the intensity of that zest for life released by the relaxation of the legal restraint that throughout the early medieval period had limited the expansive powers of the rural population within the confines of slavery and manorial institutions.

Of the three factors affecting rural production, one had been superabundant in the seventh and eighth centuries: everywhere, even in districts such as southern Burgundy where the pattern of rural settlement laid down by the Romans had been largely preserved, land was available for all-comers. In many regions it formed an immense reserve on the margins of each patch of settlement, open to various types of farming. Development was held up solely by deficiencies in the other two factors: manpower and equipment. These impediments gave way during the obscure period separating Carolingian times from the eleventh century. The economic growth that now recommenced was rooted in the slow and protracted break-up of the great estates based on slavery. It was dependent upon the rising population of the countryside, which was itself closely associated with improvements in agrarian techniques.

II THE TECHNICAL FACTOR

The history of techniques, as I have already remarked, is the most difficult of all to trace, for want of explicit documentary evidence. Work, the tools used, and the way in which they were handled belonged to the most run-of-the-mill department of daily life, about which little was said and still less written. Who would have been concerned in those days to observe the procedures for farming the land, apart from the surveyors commissioned by lords to record peasant obligations and evaluate manorial profits? And even they never describe them in detail. We can gain some insight into agrarian practices when such officials wrote down for an individual manor the nature of the labour services required from the tenements and the time of year they were to be performed. We can also venture to measure the yield from agricultural endeavour with estimates, albeit rough-and-ready ones, of sowings and harvests. But our knowledge of twelfth-century implements, like those of the ninth, is restricted to words, which means that we know nothing about them. We have to fall back on hypotheses, most of which will for ever remain unverifiable.

The first relates to the highly obscure problem of dietary customs. It may well be that the Roman model, disseminated by the Benedictine rule in particular, continued to win acceptance during this phase of European history and that, as a result, the part played by bread in the human diet did likewise. This part was undoubtedly larger than ever at the end of the twelfth century, before the pursuit of material progress and gradual popularization of aristocratic modes of behaviour enlarged the scope of the *companagium*, fancy foodstuffs eaten to 'accompany' the bread. The surest sign of a rise in bread consumption during the eleventh and twelfth centuries is the increasing role performed by the watermill in the rural economy. By the Carolingian period, mills had become exceedingly profitable manorial installations, providing the garnerer of the monastery at Corbie, for example, with much of his supplies. But they still remained extremely rare: no more than a dozen were to be found in the thirty-odd villages comprising the endowment of the abbey of St Riquier. Now Domesday Book records about six thousand mills, so that by 1086 there was already an average of one per forty-six peasant households in England. Later their number rose steadily, notably in underdeveloped regions like Devon. Painstaking research enables us to detect the pace of progress in Picardy, where forty new mills are mentioned between the mid-ninth century and 1080; a further forty appear within a markedly shorter space of time, between 1080 and 1125; then the growth rate becomes faster still, for the number of mills known to us from the records reaches two hundred and forty-five inside fifty years. Nevertheless the process of building a watermill necessitated substantial resources, particularly to acquire the millstones and pieces of iron essential for making the apparatus work properly. We can therefore assume that lords took the initiative on most occasions. In so doing, they would be thinking in terms of ensuring new sources of profit for themselves. Dictated by the lords' own interests, mill construction may not always have catered for the real needs of the peasantry. It represents one of the forms of economic oppression practised by lords and there is no shortage of evidence showing peasants compelled by force to use these installations. Around 1015 a knight from the castle at Dreux was making tenants of the abbey of Bourgueil carry their grain to his mills, though situated three hours' walk away. Among the pressures causing greater resort to flour in the popular diet, the enforcement of seigneurial constraints was certainly not without effect. But if lords impetuously vied with one another in these costly undertakings, higher bread consumption was a further reason why their investments should bring in such handsome returns. Their hopes were not disappointed. Far more numerous than before, mills remained among the most lucrative sources of seigneurial income. Growing numbers of flour-merchants along inland waterways, even in the middle of barbarian Europe, and a corresponding rise in the number of bread-ovens (also a feature of the first quarter of the twelfth century in Picardy) reflect the continuing advance of bread-grains in Europe's farming system and the extension of permanent fields at the expense of unsown waste used for food gathering, hunting and primitive forms of animal husbandry.

This advance brought with it the choice of what kinds of grain should be sown. Some species, still bulking large in Carolingian granaries, were disappearing in the most developed regions after the year 1000. In Picardy this applies to spelt, which is no longer mentioned after the eleventh century. Landowners' requirements still impinged directly on this choice. They compelled workers on the land to hand over the varieties of corn that they themselves wanted, including oats to provision their stables. In this equestrian civilization, which was making horsemanship one of the distinctive signs of social superiority, the development of the cultivation of oats proceeded apace with the rise of knightly society and improvements in its military equipment. But the rich themselves preferred to eat white bread and so encouraged wheat production. We might expect that peasants continued to subsist on less exalted cereals. Yet records with information about what crops were grown (that is, descriptions of output from manorial estates and renders in kind delivered by tenants to their lord) bear witness to the triumph of wheat wherever natural conditions did not present an insuperable obstacle. In Picardy, barley and rye still represented 17 per cent of the grains mentioned in manorial documents between 1125 and 1150, excluding oats; afterwards, this proportion fell to 8 per cent, where it rested for a long time. Everything points to the conclusion that the dietary customs of the well-to-do were passed on unnoticed to the mass of the population. For twelfth-century men and women, the staple diet was bread, the best they could obtain. The agrarian expansion after the first millennium was strictly agricultural in the sense that it was based on increasingly widespread cultivation of bread-grains.

It may be doubted whether this extension of the cultivated area was accompanied by any marked improvement in agrarian practices. Those that can be reconstructed from twelfth-century records differed little from methods employed in Charlemagne's time on big monastic estates in the Paris region. In all probability these estates were by far the most advanced; more primitive methods were in force on many aristocratic farms and on the lands of the majority of peasant households. Progress consisted in disseminating these procedures; it appears not to have depended on improving them. There is no sign that the soil was being fertilized by greater deposits of manure. Everyone recognized the time-honoured benefits of this commodity, but it was in short supply and fetched high prices, for far too few cattle were as yet housed in byres. What little dung was picked up in these would mostly be devoted to the heavy demands of permanent tillage in horticultural and viticultural enclosures. As late as the thirteenth century leases arranged in the Paris area, where agriculture was almost certainly the most prosperous and technically advanced of the age, required the farmer to manure the cornfields 'only one year in nine, that being the fifth'. The sole improving agent whose usage seems to have been popularized in some regions was marl. In twelfth-century Picardy, land grants of medium duration normally included a clause obliging the lessee to raise the lime and phosphate content of the soil by adding marl to it. But there is little to suggest that farmers in those days thought it feasible to increase cereal production deliberately through more intensive recourse to manuring the ground.

As for crop rotation, its principles seem not to have undergone any profound modifications either. The practice of sowing in two phases – wheat and rye after the autumn ploughing, barley and oats after ploughing in March – was usual in all parts of the countryside subject to Atlantic Europe's unpredictable rainfall. It had the advantage of spreading the main agricultural tasks more evenly through the course of the year and of making better use of the domestic and domesticated work force, by dividing their ploughing into two seasons. This method of tillage was applied as early as the ninth century to fields belonging to great monasteries in northern

Gaul, cultivated by their household servants and the labour services of their tenants. But did the latter treat the arable attached to their tenements in the same fashion? There is no proof of this, but it may be that the slow diffusion of sowing in two 'seasons' on peasant holdings was one form of agricultural progress between the ninth and twelfth centuries. This diffusion was incomplete, for soil capabilities and climatic conditions, as well as the wish to produce grains especially suited to bread-making, presented formidable obstacles to any extension of spring sowings. These were still severely limited in the twelfth century, even on lords' demesnes and despite the development of fighting on horseback. Let us turn to the particulars of an exceptionally interesting document, a survey which the abbot of Cluny commissioned *c.* 1150 and which describes some of the manors close by this famous Burgundian monastery. For ten of these it is possible to estimate the area occupied in the lord's fields by spring and winter grains respectively. This area was equal on only two of these farms. On seven others the oats harvest represented two-thirds, a half, a third, even a quarter of the wheat and rye harvests. These last-mentioned grains comprised the total output from the tenth manor. The system was extremely flexible, entirely dictated as it was by the lord's needs and the suitability of the soil in each locality. This is where we encounter the problem of legumes, the basis of all soup dishes (*potages*) accompanying the bread, to judge by the regulations of hospitals and leper-houses in the late twelfth century. There is no denying that peas, vetches and beans were playing a significant role in peasant output and in the diet of the poor at least. But were they grown in the fields, and did their cultivation alternate with corn? Was it not an unusual step, necessitated by food shortage, that was taken by Charles the Good, count of Flanders, at the beginning of the twelfth century, when he decreed that 'every time two measures of land shall be put to seed, the second shall be sown . . . with beans and peas'? Galbert of Bruges explains this ruling as follows: '. . . these varieties of legume bear fruit quicker and earlier in fact, wherefore poor folk might subsist more readily should dearth, famine and want persist throughout the year.'[1] We have no proof that the agronomic benefits of these crops, which help soils exhausted by cereals to recover, had been grasped by contemporary farmers at this stage.

It is far more important to discover whether fallowing was

[1] Galbert of Bruges in J. P. Migne (ed.), *Patrologia Latina*, vol. clxvi (Paris 1854), col. 946.

restricted in this period, that is whether by improved methods of tillage farmers had succeeded in reducing the time during which fields had to be left untilled so as to restore their fertility by natural means, and consequently whether they had succeeded in extending the productive area. It is impossible to answer this fundamental question which, by posing the problem of how intensive was agrarian activity, brings into play the reality of technical progress. Contemporary records refer only to parcels of cultivated land and say nothing about the rest. A few pointers indicate that in regions as fertile as Picardy, on certain farms at least, three-course rotation of crops (leaving only one-third of the arable under grass each year) was in operation by the late twelfth century. An agreement drawn up between two lords in 1199 prescribes that the land must be sown with spring corn every three years, and that the tenant, whoever he is, will have to hand over wheat one year, oats the second and nothing at all the third year.[1] But even in populous and productive districts, such practices were probably still not common enough for collective restrictions on crop rotation to be adopted by whole agricultural communities. Nowhere are these expressly mentioned before the mid-thirteenth century. Until then, the arable was almost everywhere sufficiently plentiful for the farmer to preserve his freedom of choice as to which rotational system to apply to his crops, depending on his needs and technical means. No doubt most farmers were reluctant to subject their fields to too fast a cycle of cultivation, the immediate effect of which would be to lower appreciably the yield from each patch. It was preferable to leave the ground ample time for it to take heart, and meanwhile to fall back on other portions of a cultivation area that was still capable of being extended on a large scale. Everything suggests that until the close of the period under consideration, demographic growth and advances in settlement were not pushed far enough to deprive agriculture in most parts of Europe of its shifting character. Here are two pieces of evidence concerning the Ile de France, which was, let us repeat, one of the regions most affected by intense agricultural activity. In 1116 the king of France permitted villagers to cultivate former clearings in woods belonging to him, on condition 'that they till them and win crops from them for two harvests only; afterwards, they shall move on to other parts of the forest.'[2] The

[1] Archives nationales, Paris, S. 1412.

[2] M. Guérard (ed.), *Cartulaire de l'église Notre-Dame de Paris*, vol. i (Paris 1850), p. 259.

procedure hereby encouraged is the primitive one of periodic beat-burning, which leaves the ground lying under grass for much of the time. This method alone seemed capable of procuring a decent harvest from patently mediocre soils and of enabling the land-owner to realize any appreciable profit. The second document is from a century later. It is the measure of a certain amount of progress, since the lord is insisting on principle that the peasants he is allowing to clear his woodland should practise three-course rotation of crops. But he can foresee necessary departures from principle, giving the farmers permission to leave the ploughlands fallow for several years in succession, whether 'by reason of poverty' (meaning should they find themselves deprived temporarily of the vital team of draught animals that more intensive tillage was making indispensable) or 'in order to improve the land'.[1] This was a matter for regulation therefore: on the one hand, because the soil was fragile and it was essential not to exhaust it by excessive demands; on the other, because a reduction of the period under grass required high-quality equipment that was certainly not within reach of the 'poor'. This is where we come to the crux of the matter: if cereal cultivation in Europe was extended during the eleventh and twelfth centuries, it was mainly by dint of human toil and sweat. People devoted their energies in greater numbers to working the land, to turning over the soil so as to help it to recover more rapidly in the absence of manure. To this end, they used more effective ploughs. The agricultural achievements of this period depended principally on improvements in ploughing.

In the middle of the twelfth century, tenants on one manor belonging to the abbey of Cluny owed four ploughing services a year: one in March, before the sowing of barley and oats; the other three in autumn, preparing the fallow for winter grains by turning over the sod on three successive occasions. This marked an advance on the practices used on the most efficient farms in Carolingian times when the land was ploughed only thrice yearly. And it was a decisive advance, for the yield from wheat sown on this manor was two or three times higher than on its neighbours. It is further proof of the fundamental influence of ploughing on productivity. But this improvement remained very limited: on Cluny's other nine manors described in the same survey, ploughing still adhered to the Carolingian custom of three seasons. As far as can be seen from the

[1] Archives nationales, Paris, LL-1599. B.

records, a greater number of ploughings did not become general before the end of the twelfth century. If there was any improvement, it concerned the instrument itself, the chief weapon available to peasants for working the land, which contemporary writers still designate, no doubt interchangeably, by the two Latin words *aratrum* and *carruca*. Such an improvement is really the basic hypothesis needed to explain technological advance during this obscure period of agrarian history.

Even supposing that the numerical strength of the plough-team had been increased, it is quite impossible to know enough about the physical condition of plough-oxen, in the age both of Charlemagne and the Third Crusade, so as to compare their tractive effort. Further, there always were oxen of every sort, and those belonging to the peasantry were probably not so strong as others raised in the lord's byre on hay from the best meadows. We can at least postulate a rise in the number of draught beasts on the farm. We are well informed only about manorial demesnes, but this detailed evidence proves that contemporary farm-managers were busy assembling bigger plough-teams. On nine Ramsey Abbey manors in eastern England, draught animals increased by 20 to 30 per cent between the end of the eleventh and the mid-twelfth century. Just at this moment, surveyors entrusted by the abbot of Cluny with the preparation of a plan for expanding manorial production proposed to acquire more oxen to reinforce the demesne plough-teams, as the form of investment most likely to promote economic growth. Such preoccupations are telling signs of the value attributed to the plough as a tool by contemporaries: they regarded it as the prime factor of agricultural development. Behind this development, therefore, it is surely necessary to posit a more rational arrangement of the system of mixed farming. This would involve progress in raising horned cattle, and then the crucial choice of how far to concentrate on feeding the draught animals better in the expectation of more bountiful harvests and a more nourishing human diet: whether for instance to look after the hay-fields more carefully and assign to them a greater portion of the village arable. A scarcely distinguishable extension of meadow land and less rudimentary organization of grazing unquestionably lay in the background of every advance in cereal cultivation. In addition improved harnessing methods, such as the collar-harness for oxen, may well have been adopted in the course of the eleventh century, allowing for fuller utilization of the beasts' pulling power. Lastly, farmers in certain districts chose to substitute the horse for the ox in agricultural work. This change probably came about in the most fertile regions of the West during the second half of the twelfth century. References to labour services with horses become more plentiful in Picardy from 1160, while allusions to plough-oxen disappear almost completely from the documents in the early thirteenth century. On one manor belonging to Ramsey Abbey the number of oxen was halved and that of draught horses quadrupled between 1125 and 1160. The horse's advantage was its faster pace. To harness it to the plough meant that dressing the soil took up less time, so that the farmer was given the means both to increase the number of ploughings and to practise harrowing. Already, by the end of the eleventh century, the Bayeux Tapestry shows a harrow drawn by a horse. Even so, this improvement in ploughing equipment could make headway only in the most prosperous parts of the countryside. Indeed, 'the horse costs more than the ox', as Walter of Henley reminded English farmers in his thirteenth-century treatise on practical husbandry, for it had to be shod and fed on oats. It could be employed only by village communities with cash to spare and producing ample quantities of spring grains through regular triennial rotation. Thus the adoption of the draught horse appears as the most unmistakable sign of progress in the rural economy. A threshold had been crossed. It pinpoints both in time and space the arrival of a more highly productive agricultural system and the end of a long period of barely perceptible growth.

During this period the plough itself was probably improved as well, at least in the most thriving districts. Pieces of iron were added to the wood from which it was wholly constructed in the Carolingian age, reinforcing the action of its points of contact with the soil – coulter, share and mould-board. After the millennium, advances in metal-working are to be found all over Europe, stimulated primarily by the aristocracy's desire for more effective military equipment. And the use of metal, like that of the horse, was handed down from knightly residences to the peasantry in the course of the twelfth century. It may be that decisive technical improvements in iron smelting had already been made earlier, by the use of furnaces with a forced draught and the application of water-power to metal refining, for by 1086 English mills were burdened with dues in iron. In any case, references to trip-hammers are frequent in the Pyrenees, Alps and Massif Central at the beginning of the twelfth century. At the same time more references to iron ore occur. In his book, *De Miraculis*, Peter the Venerable mentions the miners in the Grenoble region, the risks they ran in the levels, and the profits they made from sales to smiths in the neighbourhood. More numerous still are allusions to forest workshops processing iron ore, such as those offered in alms by the count of Champagne to various Cistercian abbeys between 1156 and 1171. From then on, metal became much commoner. After *c.* 1160 Venetian sailors no longer hired iron anchors for each sea-passage; every vessel now had its own. Metal objects now produced in woodland areas, near the fuel supplies essential for smelting, had apparently been made in *urban* centres to begin with. At Arras, *c.* 1100, iron was still being used basically for the manufacture of cutting instruments – knives, sickles and spades. But it was soon employed for making ploughshares. This was so in the town of Metz in the twelfth century, where the seven 'ploughshare-makers' (*soccarii*) formed the most powerful craft guild. And smiths quickly gained a firm foothold in country districts, within easy reach of their peasant customers. By 1100 charcoal for smelting was being sold in villages of the Beauvaisis. The spread of these rural craftsmen has been examined in Picardy: no trace is to be found before the early twelfth century, but thirty *fabri* appear at random in the sources between 1125 and 1180. By then there was a smith at work in ten of the thirty villages belonging to the priory of Hesdin. This is an astonishing proportion, and it was presumably much lower in the many backward regions remaining faithful to the old wooden tools. It is nevertheless a mark of the scale of technological change taking place at the most unobtrusive level of rural activity before the end of the twelfth century. The appearance of the village smithy, though later than that of the mill, likewise introduced in the midst of a peasant society specialized workers, no doubt closely dependent on the local lord, their chief customer if not the owner of their bodies, yet enjoying a privileged position owing to their actual function. One of the causes of economic growth, the smithy was also its direct result, since it could not have existed without an appreciable rise in the standard of living of the peasantry. But simultaneously it upheld and raised that standard. If the implement fashioned by the smith was more expensive and people had to save up to acquire one, it proved far more efficient. For anyone who was not too impoverished to use it and provide it with a good team, it promised less mediocre harvests, profits therefore, and the means to consolidate his hold over the land and to give his children a better start in life.

Thus a sizeable number of straws in the wind point to the fact that western Europe passed through a critical stage in the history of the means of production between the first millennium and the last years of the twelfth century. The improvement of the plough and its team was central to economic progress and demographic growth in general. The 'plough', meaning the whole apparatus comprising the contraption itself, the draught animals and the man to lead them along, thereby assumed greater importance in the lifeblood of the rural economy. It tended to become the basic economic unit, which the manse had been in the early Middle Ages. It was in 'ploughlands' (*carrucatae*) that arable in Picardy began to be measured in the late eleventh century and in terms of ploughings that labour services were counted in twelfth-century manorial surveys, whether those of the abbey of Cluny or monasteries in England, at the precise moment when the 'oxherd' (*bovarius*), or driver of the team, appears to have been foremost among the domestic workforce farming the land. Technical advance brought about a crucial change – an increase in the value of equipment in relation to that of land. The factors behind these improvements, the iron parts and the livestock, were very expensive. A late-eleventh-century toll list for one village in the Angers region indicates the cost of these additions: an unshod animal was charged at the rate of one *denarius*, a shod one at twice that amount. And this shift in relative values immediately had a twofold effect upon peasant circumstances.

First, because the plough and its team were movable goods, less well protected than land by joint family responsibilities, and their ownership was more closely connected with monetary fluctuations, and above all because they could easily be seized, peasants became more vulnerable to exploitation by the rich. They were more subject to pressure from lords, who could keep a firmer hold over their men by lending them livestock or by threatening to confiscate the beasts they owned. They were more subject to pressure from those who had cash to spare, and from whom it could be borrowed. There is every reason to suppose that technical improvements played a conspicuous part in stimulating recourse to credit in the rural world.

Second, not all peasants were able to upgrade their equipment, either because they lacked the necessary capital, or because a contrivance that was too heavy might cause the soil they were cultivating to deteriorate. Thus in parts of the countryside with thin, flimsy soils, the light swing-plough continued in use, while everywhere the hoe and wooden tools formed the sole equipment of poor households. As a result, there was a growing gap in the twelfth century between regions like the Ile de France or Picardy, which were in a position to welcome any technical innovations and increase the pace of life, and others, notably the southern countries, which remained stagnant. At the same time, on each estate there was a further widening of the divide already apparent in the tenth century between 'those who do their work with oxen or with other beasts'[1] and those who had nothing but their own physical strength with which to work; between 'ploughmen' (*laboratores*, a term which may intimate the respect due to the men who were making a more effective contribution to the general welfare) and 'manual workers' (*manoperarii*). They were treated differently by lords. In certain areas the former alone would participate fully in the life of the village community. Within the ranks of a peasantry who were being reduced to the same social level by seigneurial exactions and where lines of demarcation based on personal dependence were scarcely visible any longer, new economic inequalities between inhabitants of the same village, or between those of adjoining districts, were introduced in the twelfth century as a concomitant to improved equipment.

Interesting as it would be to measure the effects of technical progress on returns from agricultural enterprise, the idea is hardly practicable. Before the late twelfth century, methods of manorial administration were crude; they afforded little scope to the use of writing and even less to statistics, so that the documents are more unforthcoming than those of the Carolingian period. Amid such a profound dearth of evidence, it is tempting to turn to whatever clues there are, especially those fairly precise but highly localized ones furnished by the mid-twelfth-century survey of manors belonging to the abbey of Cluny. Surveyors who visited these assessed both the sowings and harvests of winter grains on six of them. The particulars, like those supplied by the description of the royal manor of Annapes in the ninth century, permit us to hazard a guess at the yield from the seed. This varied a good deal from one manor to another. On one of these farms the harvest was worth six times as much as the sowing; on another the return reached 5 to 1 for

[1] M. C. Ragut (ed.), *Cartulaire de Saint-Vincent de Mâcon* (Mâcon 1864), no. 476, p. 274.

rye and 4 to 1 for wheat; it stood at between 2 to 1 and 2·5 to 1 on the last four manors. How feeble productivity seems to have been! On most of these large farms, whose equipment it was felt necessary to build up (the object of the survey) yet which probably already had above-average resources upon which to draw, the land remained extremely unproductive even midway through the twelfth century, when the broad movement of expansion that had been unfolding in the European countryside for at least two centuries was in full swing. Much toil and space were still prerequisite for feeding the population. None the less, two facts emerge from all this. If yields varied by as much as two- or threefold from farm to farm, this was probably owing to the quality of their soils but also partly to differences in the standard of their equipment; the manor on which harvests were by far the most bountiful had the best-stocked byres and the most numerous ploughs. Thus, to go by this particular document, rising yields seem to have been closely connected with more intensive ploughing. On the other hand we have to allow for the fact that the low level of output is accentuated in the Cluniac survey by unfavourable weather conditions; the surveyors noted that the year had been a bad one and that the bailiffs had estimated the shortfall at one-fifth of a normal harvest. If we make the necessary adjustments, we notice immediately that even on the least fertile and least thoroughly worked soils, seed returns were higher than those which can be ascertained from Carolingian sources. No doubt it is extremely rash to make comparisons between statistical data that are so isolated in time and space. But we can at least entertain the idea that between the ninth and thirteenth centuries (before Walter of Henley reckoned in his treatise that a plot of land brought in nothing if it did not yield more than three times the seed sown) productivity of the soil had risen, while technical advances were spreading imperceptibly and there was still enough room to enable farmers not to overtax the ground but to rest it adequately. The pace of development was painfully slow, but it became distinctly faster as soon as landowners buckled to the task of providing the agricultural conquest with more effective means. And this progress was certainly not negligible, for when the yield rose from 2 to 1 to 3 to 1, the portion of the harvest available for consumption doubled.

The effects of such a rise in productivity were felt throughout the rural economy. Whenever land placed under direct management bore more abundant harvests, lords, and those who administered their demesnes, could either sell the surplus (on one of their manors *c.* 1150, the monks of Cluny had had one-eighth of the cereal crop taken to market) or reduce the size of their farms in order to save themselves trouble. Because higher quality equipment was causing manual labour services to lose the best part of their value, lords with big estates became less demanding of their tenants. They were tempted to release them stage by stage from their obligation to work, and no longer to retain them on the demesne except during peak periods of activity. For the farms of dependent peasants, there ensued a crucial form of relief: they were nearer to acquiring full use of their equipment and manpower. The additional labour supply soon made returns from the land increase on peasant holdings more quickly than on the demesne, and by such a margin that the size of the old agrarian units was seen to be much too large for the needs of one household. Several homes could be accommodated comfortably on a former manse. The leasing of manorial demesnes and subdivision of tenements permitted greater density of settlement on many estates. At the same time the reduction of labour services, coupled with higher productivity from human endeavour, freed part of the work-force in each family unit for the agrarian conquest. The attack on wasteland and the extension of village arable made a twofold contribution to raising yields. They improved output both by enlarging the area where crop rotation could be put into practice, and by creating the necessary space (despite the greater density of settlement) for the ground to lie under grass, thus avoiding soil exhaustion. The influx of manpower to sites where land was cleared came from villages where more generous harvests were causing families to segment and the number of available hands to increase.

III LAND CLEARANCE

Breaking new ground was a normal and regular operation in the agrarian system of the early Middle Ages. Every year it was necessary to abandon some of the erstwhile fields that tillage had exhausted and open up new ones on part of the uncultivated area. The slow rotation of ploughlands around the arable, an enormous portion of which was temporarily given over to natural vegetation, made habitual pioneers of the peasantry. They so remained as long as the shortage of manure kept up the tradition of fallowing. In the properly organized system of mixed farming that was emerging at the close of the period under consideration, the first ploughing of the fallow represented the ultimate, residual form of seasonal assarting. Hence land clearance was firmly integrated into the group of practices associated with cereal-based agriculture. It was primarily a palliative against deterioration of the soil, an indispensable measure for maintaining it on a par with output.

This process took on quite another economic significance when it ceased to occur in the context of village farmland with stable boundaries, but moved outside them. It then assumed the aspect of a veritable conquest, resulting in a lasting extension to the food-producing area. This defeat of the wilderness was beyond question the great economic venture of the twelfth century in western Europe. Land clearance was brought on by demographic pressure and technical improvements. To farm uncultivated tracts of land, to clear away the natural vegetation and to control water-courses made it essential to have better tools. The heavy waterlogged soils of Schleswig could not have been profitably sown before it was possible to till them with ploughs that were sturdy enough to hollow out deep furrows between long ridges and so create some sort of drainage. It was essential for increasing numbers of workers to be induced to embark on arduous and uncertain schemes, overcoming the instinctive fears that wide-open spaces had once inspired in their ancestors. In other words, human settlement had become too dense on the ancient arable. The driving force behind agrarian expansion was shortage of food; its operatives were the poor, or surplus children from families whose capacity to produce had been enlarged by technical advances. It was also essential for owners of virgin soils, the lords, not to place obstacles in the way of settler initiative. Though these pioneers were sometimes able to carry on with their task in secret and, eluding the forester's vigilance, carve out parcels of land on the edges of wooded or marshy terrain over which they claimed full ownership (peasant allods in the twelfth century were nowhere commoner than on the fringes of vast, unguarded solitudes), the agricultural conquest was equally the concern of the rich, since any uncultivated land wholly belonged to them. Ecclesiastical lords and (very likely in greater numbers) lay lords yielded to pressure from poor men in search of a holding. They sanctioned colonizing ventures. They welcomed 'settlers' (*hospites*), and 'offered them hospitality' (*hospitaverunt*) as was said in those days. They went still further: they encouraged pioneers, they incurred expenses so as to attract them, they wrangled over them. In effect the territorial aristocracy were being compelled to change their ancestral economic behaviour. Keen huntsmen though they were, owners of wasteland chose to sacrifice some of the pleasures that forest, marsh and warren could offer. They saw that the colonization of deserted tracts, even if it cost them money to speed up the process, would be a source of extra income in the long run. They were alive to the necessity of increasing their resources and appreciated that a transformation of the landscape could be the opportunity of so doing. They became more conscious of the profit motive. As an integral part of an economic mentality dominated by the taste for spending and the habit of sacrifice, or 'largess', common to all contemporary lords, the operations involved in breaking new ground to enlarge the cultivable area and enhance the value of land were first to lend meaning to the word 'gain' (*gagner*). Semantics proves this, for were not new farms created from scratch in the middle of woods in twelfth-century Lorraine called *gainagia*? This major psychological readjustment is not the least interesting facet of the history of the great medieval land clearances. Unfortunately, the chronology of this history remains regrettably imprecise.

This lack of precision stems initially from the dearth of explicit source material. More serious is the fact that there were several species of land clearance, and they did not evolve at the same rate. First and simplest was the progressive extension of the village arable. It was also by far the commonest. It is virtually the only form of which traces are to be found in many regions, such as the Mâconnais or Périgord, where all agrarian units had been in existence since the Roman period. It has been estimated that five-sixths of the ground gained in Picardy were due to this type of clearance. But it was the achievement of countless individual enterprises, conducted year in and year out with meagre resources, and about which written documents have little to say. Highly unusual circumstances are needed before we can visualize them clearly. The tenacity of the Cistercian abbey of La Ferté-sur-Grosne in enlarging its estate through a patient policy of land purchase is reflected in the contents of a cartulary by new fields and meadows, many of them bearing the names of the peasants who planned them, which were nibbling away round the edge of a Burgundian forest during the course of the twelfth century. Again, the care put into recording their rights by the monks of Ramsey discloses a manor in the second half of the twelfth century with one hundred and forty hectares of assarted land held by thirty peasants. Or again, the desire of Suger, abbot of St Denis, to justify his administrative actions led him to describe in detail the improvements he had made to running the estate, and in particular to count the number of settlers he had welcomed in various manorial 'courts' (*curtes*) to farm the land more intensively. But generally we have to rely on less sure signs that are difficult to date: traces left behind in the layout of the present-day farmland and in country place-names by the labours of medieval peasants; references to dues which, like the *champart* or *tâche* in France, were specifically for holdings created by clearing operations; conflicts arising from the collection of tithes called *novales* on lands that had been unproductive until recently and from which crops were now being taken. We can also rely on what plant remains tell us, especially pollen grains from peat-bogs. The graph that can be drawn for certain favoured spots in Germany indicates a sharp rise in cereal cultivation at the turn of the eleventh century.

The drive that gradually pushed back the limits of cultivation seems to have been launched at a very early date. Had it even been interrupted in Germania since the seventh century? We can detect it in Normandy in the Cinglais forest as far back as the tenth century, and the first assarts to be mentioned in documents from the Mâconnais pre-date the year 1000. In those times it was often simply a question of beginning over again, of reconquering abandoned terrain, as in the Gâtine of Poitou where, throughout the eleventh century, agrarian expansion hardly involved any but former clearings that had been deserted. It was sometimes a question of temporary advance, too, of trial and error on deceptive soils. One deed of gift in Berry of *c.* 1075 gives us a glimpse of 'a patch of ground where brushwood is growing and where once were the assarts of a few peasants'. What is certain is that this process was accelerated in the last decades of the eleventh century; that from then on it occurred everywhere to some extent; and that (as statistical tables worked out for Picardy illustrate) it was continued throughout the twelfth century. The peak period of intense activity appears to lie between the years 1075 and 1180. It is difficult to state precisely its relation to demographic growth, for its chronology is just as hazy. An attempt has been made to do this for Picardy; and the hypothesis proposed is that the extension of the village arable was noticeably earlier than the great outburst making population rise still faster after *c.* 1125. Peasant households had been first to take advantage of this spontaneous, slow and stealthy movement, thereby avoiding headlong collision with seigneurial resistance. Nearly everywhere, cleared land was consigned to the production of grass. At an early stage assarting permitted the rearing of draught beasts to be developed and plough-teams to be strengthened. Next it would be sown, and play its part, with the former patches of infield, in providing human beings with sustenance from completely fresh ground where corn might thrive. But landlords took advantage of it as well, especially the lesser ones, who were living in the villages and managing their farms from close at hand. They too urged their domestic task-forces to clear land and so add new and less exhausted plots to their manorial demesnes. They allowed the wasteland to be whittled away piecemeal, deriving unforeseen profits from it. Accustomed as they were to observing the peasants, lords knew how to obtain lucrative dues from the parcels of land that had been laid out on the margins of the waste. These generally took the form of a proportion of the crop. Finally, since lords would often keep parochial tithes for themselves, they effected further inroads into the harvests from the assarts without much difficulty.

Land clearance assumed a second aspect when it gave rise to a new settlement, when pioneering activity took hold in the middle of an uncultivated area for an internal attack and gradual reduction. In many regions belts of wooded or boggy terrain were quite narrow. Extensions to former clearings sometimes eroded these to the point of destroying them completely and making the boundaries of neighbouring settlements come together to form one vast prairie. But there were also enormous stretches of wilderness which began to be settled after the first millennium. At first they were penetrated by men who had no desire to settle down permanently. Some would wander about the forest exploiting its natural resources, for which demand was rising with the slow refinement of material civilization: makers of iron or charcoal, for example, appear with growing frequency in twelfth-century records. Others might be religious spirits fleeing the world. Hermits, common in western parts of France from the eleventh century, were among the first to open up new clearings amid deserted tracts. Then daughter houses of religious Orders were founded – Cistercians, Carthusians, reformed canons – whose rules would prescribe strict isolation. Yet already by the end of the eleventh century peasant households were also establishing themselves on *bordae* or *bordagia* scattered among

● Places mentioned in written sources earlier than the twelfth century

○ Similar places which have now disappeared

□ Present-day place-names earlier than the twelfth century

△ Sites of Merovingian or Carolingian archaeological remains

• Places mentioned later than the twelfth century

Forest — Roman roads

Map 2 Settlement in the Middle Yonne Valley in the Eleventh Century

the woods and heaths of certain parts of Gaul, such as Anjou, Maine, Poitou and the Ile de France. Then *c.* 1175 we begin to discover traces in French documents of large-scale farms laid out by rich men alongside the existing arable. In this way new settlements were interspersed in empty spaces separating ancient villages. They were characterized by a pattern of dispersed dwelling units, each lying at the centre of a cluster of gardens, fields and meadows. These parcels were enclosed for protection against damage by wild animals, and the countryside was criss-crossed with hedges. It was a type of landscape known in western France as a *bocage*. This form of agricultural conquest, somewhat later than the first, seems to have taken place on a broader front in regions like Maine, where the early medieval *villa* had been less coherent and settlement always very tenuous. But it tended to spread everywhere in the late twelfth century, and apparently for two reasons. On the one hand improved peasant equipment was now enabling farmers to withdraw more easily from collective organizations and dispense with mutual assistance from the village community; and so venture forth alone to build up a farm less dependent upon neighbourhood constraints. Technical advances had therefore given free rein to agrarian individualism, held back in more anciently settled districts by restrictions that the intensification of arable farming made increasingly irksome. On the other hand farms located in a forest or pastoral environment were less deliberately geared towards cereal cultivation. The upkeep of trees and grass left less room for cornfields. Their system of production conformed to new tendencies in a less homespun consumer economy. In the closing decades of the twelfth century an ever larger section of European society was demanding less bread and more meat, wool, timber and leather. The dawn of systematic exploitation of the forest was breaking, bringing prosperity to butchers and graziers. The advance of *bocage*-type settlement went hand in hand with this change.

The assault on the untilled wilderness appeared in a third form, the creation of new tracts of arable. This aspect is by far the best illuminated by the documentation, for such creations were frequently mapped out by agreement, many of them written down. Here the chronology of the process becomes less vague. By the end of the eleventh century it appears to have started in Flanders, northern Italy (where great works were undertaken to contain the floodwaters of the Po in the neighbourhood of Mantua and Verona as well as in the river delta, and almost totally waste *latifundia* were parcelled out into new lands) in south-western England, Normandy, the Toulousain a few years later perhaps, in Germany and Brabant. It reached its zenith in the mid-twelfth century. Probably more often than it seems – for in this instance documentary sources are lacking, and with good reason – new villages were born of spontaneous migration from near-by farming areas. In this way a settlement comprising one hundred and fifteen peasant households took shape in the Weald of Kent *c.* 1100, inside less than forty years. Yet most pioneering ventures of this nature were instigated by seigneurial initiative, and in particular by the greatest lords who as masters of the *bannum* had inherited from kings their ownership of big tracts of wasteland. They were resolved to rescue these from the wild and make fields out of them. They paid the necessary price in order to increase the number of their subjects. In so doing, they were concerned less to realize strictly agricultural sources of income than to raise profits from taxation and justice and, with a view to securing a better hold over their territory, to create communities that could eventually co-operate in the defence of the land. To their way of thinking, it was primarily a fiscal and political operation.

In its economic repercussions, therefore, this last type of land clearance differed markedly from the second and very sharply from the first. To begin with, it entailed a formal decision on the part of the lord who was giving pioneers an opportunity to exploit the forest, marshland, or tracts from which the sea had retreated – hence an act of conscious reflection on the potential profitability of each undertaking and the sacrifices it might be worth. On the one hand it was more closely bound up with a money economy, for the lord intended to levy mainly cash payments on the new inhabitants of his land; on the other hand it was usually necessary to advance them some capital as an inducement to settle down. The transformation of a wilderness into farmland sometimes required people to be conveyed over enormous distances. Peasants of Flemish origin came to occupy marshlands in north-western Germany at the behest of episcopal lords – there to parcel out grazing-grounds, then cornfields – and their removal in the early years of the twelfth century was only the first wave of a large-scale migration. In the course of the century some two hundred thousand German colonists moved across the Elbe and Saale rivers on to fertile soils, only the lightest of which were being farmed by the Slav tribes, but which colonists could turn to account thanks to their superior tools.

To attract settlers, it was essential to promise them some advantages: to create a 'sanctuary' (*sanctuarium*) surrounded by crosses where they could escape from violent attack; to ensure, by means of a verbal agreement or preferably a written charter, their immunity from the heaviest exactions of seigneurial exploitation in their native villages:

> the inhabitants shall be exempt and free from *tolta* and *tallia* and from every unjust exaction. They shall not go on army service, whether on foot or on horseback, without returning home the same day, except in time of war. . . . In cases of misdemeanour, fines shall be five *solidi* for offences liable to a fine of sixty *solidi*, twelve *denarii* for those of five *solidi*, while any man who wishes to clear himself by taking an oath shall be free to do this and not pay anything.[1]

Such were the benefits that the French king in 1182 put before any peasants who would help to found a village in one of his forests. It was imperative that these privileges be made public; that they be broadcast in suitable districts where overpopulation was seen to be more serious and seigneurial exactions more stringent than elsewhere; and that the movable goods needed by the emigrants for their journey and the early stages of resettlement be placed at their disposal. Publicity and capital outlay were indispensable. Because owners of tracts to be colonized were often princes who were too eminent to take a personal interest in the operation or too impoverished to finance the undertaking alone, the creation of new farmland might be effected as a joint venture. Sometimes a lay lord, as owner of the land to be made productive, would come to an arrangement with a religious house by one of those contracts called *paragia* in France. The monastery's connections with others far distant could facilitate the recruitment of colonists and it would readily find in its treasury the necessary spare cash to invest. The two partners would promise to share the expected profits equally. Sometimes, as in Germany, the lord would draw up an agreement with a *locator*, a true entrepreneur (often an ecclesiastic or junior member of an aristocratic family) who would take the matter into his own hands and receive in return for his services a tenement in the new village and an interest in the seigneurial revenues:

> I have given Heribert a village named Pechau with all its appurtenant fields, meadows, woods and ponds, to cultivate and make fruitful

[1] H. F. Delaborde (ed.), *Recueil des actes de Philippe Auguste, roi de France*, vol. i (Paris 1916), no. 51, p. 69.

according to the agreement concluded between him and me. For the inhabitants he shall settle on these properties himself, I have instituted that jurisdiction which is called 'burgess law' (*ius burgense*) for all legal causes and proceedings. I have granted Heribert six manses in fief. . . . This same Heribert, and after him his heir, shall give judgement in all cases they shall have to settle between them. . . . Two-thirds of all profits of justice shall be handed over to me or my successor, the other third given for the use of Heribert or his heir.[1]

Such were the conditions of an agreement reached by the archbishop of Magdeburg in 1159 with one of these guiding spirits of the agrarian conquest. Here was a little group of entrepreneurs in the vanguard of that conquest, exemplifying all the energy and drive behind the twelfth-century economy. They remained close to the soil, yet they were well endowed with means and ambition; countrymen themselves they knew how to ensure that the profit motive, with which no one was more imbued than they, was shared with the great lords whose interests they were serving.

Slowly and at first hardly noticed, the process of land clearance seems to have commenced here and there by the tenth century, just when population was starting to increase. Then little by little its range was extended coincidentally with technical innovations and demographic pressure. Soon, decisions by lords and their agents directly intervened to enliven the whole process. In the period under consideration in this study, we can place its point of greatest intensity in the twelfth century and, perhaps, more precisely between 1140 and 1170. Its effects were manifold and complex. To begin with, it brought about profound changes in the appearance of the rural landscape, not only because it broke up the broad expanses of wilderness criss-crossing the European landmass in the early Middle Ages and acting as a barrier to communications, but also because it started to transform radically the layout of the farmland. This internal transformation of agrarian units can be traced only with difficulty. It probably occurred earlier in some regions than in others, but by and large the twelfth century marks only the beginning of a process that was to take place over a considerable length of time and constitutes a fundamental fact in the history of the rural economy. The colonists' efforts extended the pitifully small area of occupation from which each peasant

[1] R. Kötzschke, *Quellen zur Geschichte der ostdeutschen Kolonisation im 12. bis 14. Jahrhundert* (Leipzig and Berlin 1912), no. 15, pp. 33–4.

community derived its livelihood, while simultaneously population growth was tending to concentrate settlement at the centre of the expanding fields. And as long as field boundaries were receding steadily and new meadows for feeding more oxen in the byre (and producing more manure) were being created, the central parcels of arable land (those laid out furthest back in time, closer to the houses, stables and farmyards and so better provided with compost and dung) gradually became the scene of less extensive tillage and subject to more intensive systems of crop rotation, in which fallowing played a smaller part. This more demanding agricultural nucleus grew in line with the assarted area on the perimeter, that is, with more methodical organization of cattle farming. In the late twelfth century there remained enough room almost everywhere for the circle of land clearance to extend farther; and so for the necessary flexibility to last a little longer between, on the one hand, the *royes, soles* and *Gewannen* situated in the middle of the village arable and now threatened with exhaustion by more intensive methods of tillage and, on the other hand, the pioneer fringes that were less obstructed by collective constraints and benefited from the newness of virgin ground. Again, vast tracts were still on offer to welcome landless men, reducing pressure of population elsewhere. This state of affairs explains why it was possible for agricultural yields to increase and for famines, if not to disappear, at least to lose their tragic character in the twelfth century. Land clearance had promoted balanced growth of production and population.

Similar flexibility seems to have been introduced into peasant circumstances thanks to clearing operations. In the first place, colonization probably quickened the fragmentation of the ancient units of seigneurial exploitation. The manse finally disappeared in the Paris region in the twelfth century, while two new types of tenure, for rent and for crop-sharing payments (*à champart*), were becoming more usual on plots of land newly brought into cultivation on the margins of the existing arable. The annual rental was either fixed or proportionate to the harvest respectively. The latter was better suited to land where there was no way of estimating its yield until it had been cleared of scrub, but in both cases dues were levied on a piece of land which could pass readily from person to person; which could be incorporated in a particular farm, only to be detached from it; and which would generally exclude labour services. In the second place, the creation by the entrepreneurs of the agrarian conquest of free zones and 'sanctuaries' (where immigrants could be sure of enjoying clearly defined privileges, of being treated as 'burgesses' (*burgenses*), and of benefiting from tax-relief by virtue of living there) forced lords of ancient estates to relax their grip somewhat and to curtail their demands. Hence freedom of a sort gradually percolated through the rural world, starting from the pioneer frontiers where it was essential to make large promises to those involved in agricultural expansion. We can well imagine the penniless immigrant, whom hunger and the desire to set up home had induced to try his luck somewhere empty-handed, finding himself at the mercy of the landlord and the entrepreneurs, his official agents. There is no shortage of examples of personal dependence growing more burdensome in localities where assarting was forging ahead. Yet the evidence suggests that the assault on the waste had caused less ruthlessly exploited social groups to multiply among workers in the fields: the *Königsfreien* whom German kings helped to colonize their forests in the twelfth century; or the pioneer settlers (*hospites*) who were increasing in most parts of the French countryside during the same period. By the middle of the eleventh century, when the extension of the cultivable area was still in its hesitant beginnings, the *hospites* constituted a body of men who were quite distinct from the native group of villagers. Their arrival would meet with the lord's favour. He treated them less harshly. They escaped from the collective burdens imposed on ancient holdings. They were more free. Conceivably it was from their ranks that millers and smiths emerged. Their numbers grew as fast as technical advances enabled manorial lordships to absorb them. And the stage was reached when custom extended to them the privileges they used to enjoy within the village community as a whole. Demographic pressure, improved equipment and additional farmland seem to have assured the aristocracy of such affluence that, at the close of the twelfth century, they could easily afford to allow a slight though temporary relaxation of their economic stranglehold over the mass of the working population.

8 Lords

Europe in the twelfth century witnessed the age of peasant conquerors. The demands of their masters drove them forward and in order to satisfy them peasants would sow wheat, plant vines, and endeavour to amass a few *denarii* by selling their labour or agricultural produce on the market. Conversely yet complementarily, the independence gradually assumed by these peasants also provided them with an incentive. Consciously or otherwise, lords reduced partially their inroads into the resources of their men. It was their way of making an investment, by leaving the workers the wherewithal to develop the productive forces of their households, bring up more children, feed more draught animals, add necessary parts to the plough and gain ground at the expense of the untilled waste. Between 1075 and 1180 the main channel for investment and saving was through the relaxation of seigneurial burdens. This relaxation, which was undoubtedly the most active agent of growth, exhibits three distinct features.

First, the small allod, or independent peasant holding, was common enough in almost all regions. In 1090 the monks of Cluny purchased a whole stretch of farmland in the surrounding district piece by piece: fifteen of the vendors were peasants; six of these were part tenants, while the land relinquished by the others was entirely free from overlordship. Presumably the property of the poor was threatened, like that of the rich, by partible inheritance and by the practice of making pious gifts, as well as by pressure from neighbouring lords who were seeking to absorb it. Yet such property continued to be accumulated, either by means of those countless contracts which left the worker in full possession of half the manorial land he had been commissioned to plant with vines; by clandestine land clearance; or by guile, for the tenant could frequently contrive to shirk his obligations long enough for his farmland to appear free from any dues in customary law. In certain regions references to small allods become progressively fewer in the course of the twelfth century: their share of the land, as described in documents from Picardy, declined from 17 per cent in the first quarter of the century, to 4 per cent in the second, and to 2 per cent in the third. There were also countries like England where allodial property remained unknown. Where the allod was absent or in retreat, however, there was a corresponding increase in the number of tenements owing the landlord virtually nothing – so little indeed that their economic standing scarcely differed from that of allods. In fact, lords were allowing peasants to strengthen their hold over the land, relinquishing their farming profits to them almost completely. But although they were permitting them greater means to enrich themselves, they knew perfectly well how to siphon off an ample share of their savings by other channels.

Land tenure underwent a second change that made relations between workers on the land and their masters more flexible. The manse, as we have seen, had disintegrated. It maintained its cohesion in the countryside of southern Gaul, less profoundly shaken than elsewhere by the impact of technical advance; and in some other regions, such as north-western Germany, where custom strictly forbade the division of a holding among the heirs. But in the rest of Europe it disappeared. Traces had vanished in Normandy by the end of the eleventh century. In Picardy it was eventually replaced by what documents call a 'curtilage' (*curtilagium*), a smaller piece of land originating in the dismemberment of the manse. Of nineteen manses mentioned in the records of one Burgundian manor *c.* 1150, only three had not yet disintegrated completely. This process was precipitated by population growth, higher yields from the soil, and the extension of the cultivated area, which made it possible to build up new farms by combining patches of cleared land on the edge of the village arable with fragments of former manses. But the primary reason for the decomposition of the units that initially encompassed the seigneurial exploitation of peasant labour was that they no longer measured up to the new circumstances of the village economy. The peasant family could now have the advantage of greater freedom from restriction; while landlords benefited from exercising their rights no longer over households, but over multifarious parcels of land whose flexibility enabled manorial exactions to be brought more closely into line with the peasants' taxable capacity. The third aspect of the relaxation of seigneurial burdens is that peasants were gradually winning privileges. These might be established by means of an agreement between rival lords who were vying for power over them; by the grant of a charter of liberties; by one of those plantation charters anticipating the foundation of a new village; or simply by dint of those 'statements of rights' (*Weistümer*) whereby subordinates on German or Lotharingian lordships every now and then declared the customary law. Arbitrary action by the lord was brought to an end, customary usages were codified and drawn up in written form and the strongest bonds of servitude were loosened as customs were committed to writing. Lords consented to all this because such concessions helped to increase the number of peasant families subject to their authority and enabled the rural population to amass more cash. In the charters of liberties that spread through the French countryside during the second half of the twelfth century, clauses designed to stimulate commercial exchanges in the village are given a prominent position by virtue of their novelty.

These concessions did not abrogate the lords' fiscal powers, however. On the contrary they were being regularized and thereby becoming even more effective. In the economic boom of this period, workers did indeed achieve greater freedom of action, but their masters did not cease to appropriate most of the goods they produced. They seized them by other means, with an adaptability that markedly increased the velocity of monetary circulation. And, as lords had always done, they used the proceeds with a view to spending still more.

I THE MONASTIC EXAMPLE

Nothing affords us a clearer insight into the economic attitudes of lords than an examination of the great Benedictine monasteries. They represent medieval farming at its best. Efforts made in them since the late eleventh century to reform religious life led to the better defence and management of their patrimonies, and so to resistance against encroachments by laymen. Carefully preserving the contents of their archives and therewith the rights of the house concerned, they returned to the Carolingian tradition of writing things down, issued internal regulations as Abbot Adalard of

Corbie had done in the ninth century, and meticulously drafted manorial surveys: *censiers* (*censarii*) recording burdens on land, and 'customaries' (*consuetudinarii*) establishing lists of banal exactions. These documents are all that we have for analysing the manorial economy.

Basically this economy retained its spendthrift character. Anyone aiming to regulate it did so in terms of needs to be satisfied. *Constitutio Expensae* is the expressive title given to the project for a planned household economy drawn up by the abbot of Cluny *c.* 1150. What were the requirements for members of the community to lead the kind of life that suited them? Monks were not working men, nor middlemen; they were about God's service, and they fulfilled their office best to the extent that they were relieved of all worldly preoccupations. It was of prime importance therefore to ensure that the house was regularly supplied with victuals and cash. To avoid changing the lifestyle of the monastic family, it was essential to manage the collective endowment in such a way that the cellarer in charge of the *victus* and the chamberlain in charge of the *vestitus* were amply provided for.

The methods used in running the estate arose out of this overriding consideration. The estate was generally divided into farming units, responsibility for which was delegated to individual monks: that of St Emmeram at Regensburg was thus subdivided into thirty-three manorial centres *c.* 1030; that of the abbey of Cluny into about a score at the end of the eleventh century. It would fall to each of these centres to take upon itself the task of provisioning the monastery over a certain length of time. A rota system was drawn up between them – *mesaticum* in contemporary language. To feed the community attached to Ely Cathedral, the service was shared on a weekly basis between thirty-three manors, while 'the order according to which the manors should make farm' (*firmas facere debent*, i.e. bring in food) on Rochester estates subdivided the whole year into twenty-eight-day periods. For the method to work well it was important for the obligations imposed on each manor to equal its resources. This would necessitate periodic readjustment of the burden. As a rule the burden on each manor was less than its output, and the bailiff disposed of what was left as he thought fit. By selling any surplus crops, he strove to collect the money to be forwarded to the chamberlain. Such managerial principles would leave middlemen with wide powers of initiative. Their freedom of action became greater still as the practice of *mesaticum* gave way imperceptibly to that of 'farming'. This was the case in twelfth-century England. To save themselves further trouble, monasteries entrusted their manors to *firmarii*, who were not wardens chosen from the community but veritable entrepreneurs invested with full seigneurial powers by a life contract. The size of the 'farm' (*firma*) they were to hand over every year could be increased if output from the manor were rising appreciably; thus the yield from 'farms' charged by Ramsey Abbey doubled between 1086 and 1140. It seems that this procedure was also employed on the Continent, in the Rhineland especially and in the Ile de France, where Abbot Suger of St Denis considered it advantageous to put individual manors to farm by agreements renewable annually.

To ensure that goods were transferred between widely dispersed properties and the single centre for consumption formed by the monastery, it might be convenient to use money. And it was indeed the deeper penetration of silver currency into the machinery of the domestic economy that apparently brought about the most marked changes in the course of the twelfth century. It also gave rise to the most difficult problems of adjustment. As the market for agricultural produce became more buoyant, it might well have seemed preferable to sell surplus crops on the spot and forward a bag of *denarii*, rather than undertake long journeys with carts, such as had weighed so heavily upon the economy of great estates in the Carolingian period. The utilization of coins was thus assuming greater importance in the administration of monastic endowments. The role of the chamberlain grew while that of the cellarer declined. It is true that receipts in kind made some headway in English monasteries during the first half of the twelfth century; at the same time the number of monks was growing, so that the most pressing need was to feed the brethren and stock up the refectories. But after *c*. 1150 cash revenues tended for various reasons to prevail. At Canterbury a reduction in the number of consumers meant that renders in kind were no longer of any use and were converted into cash. On the other hand, at Ramsey there was an increase in purchasing from the outside world which led to a greater burden of debt. Faced with similar budgetary difficulties, administrators of Cluny's temporalities looked elsewhere for a remedy to curb expenditure and so built up stocks of grain and wine. The solutions were many but the problem was identical, posed as it was by the new function of money. Cluny represents a typical case, and one that is extremely well illuminated by the documentary evidence. It will bear close examination because it reveals seigneurial reactions in the face of economic development.

The interpretation placed by Cluny on St Benedict's rule was pushing up costs. It was imperative to magnify God's glory, and so to confer greater splendour upon the liturgy; to rebuild the sanctuaries and decorate them lavishly; to establish the monks in a degree of comfort that might make them perfectly fitted for the Divine office and clearly demonstrate their pre-eminence among the various 'estates' (*status*) of the world. They were given plentiful and choice food. Their wardrobe was renewed annually. The manual labour prescribed by the rule was reduced to entirely symbolic tasks about the kitchen. The monks lived like lords: when on his travels the abbot would appear in public escorted, like a ruler, by a sizeable retinue mounted on horseback. Cluny's success caused her reserves in precious metals to grow considerably during the last third of the eleventh century. The abbey exercised control over a vast congregation, whose daughter houses sent the mother house rents in cash: the fifteen priories in Provence alone supplied the chamberlain with the sum of approximately fifty *librae* a year. She received alms from the greatest princes in Christendom. Since her influence extended as far south as the Spanish frontiers with Islam, where warfare enlivened the circulation of precious metals, these gifts did not consist solely of land, but included gold and silver as well. In 1077 the king of Castile made over to the Burgundian abbey an annuity in gold worth four hundred *librae* in Cluny's own *denarii*, or more than the total cash income derived from the lordship. One portion of these riches was used by goldsmiths for embellishing the sanctuary; another for acquiring land, particularly by lending money to local knights who would set out for the Holy Land leaving their property to the abbey as security. But nearly all of it was spent. In 1088 a huge building site for the new basilica was opened up, the largest anywhere in Latin Christendom. Lapped in the life of ease enjoyed by the chamberlain's office, monastic administrators quickly came to neglect the estate. Inadequately supervised in many villages, *ministeriales* in the late eleventh century increased their personal profits enormously to the detriment of the lord. Yet plenty of cash was available. In order to stock up the refectories, more and more was bought. By 1122 Cluny was drawing no more than a quarter of her food supplies from her own lands. She was spending vast sums on bread and wine. Every year close on one thousand *librae*, or two hundred and forty thousand silver coins, were distributed among producers in the surrounding area and middlemen promoting the sale of crops. Hence the abbey's massive needs and the bias she had deliberately imparted to her economy were by the early twelfth century giving a tremendous boost to monetary circulation. They were causing money to filter through in smaller and smaller quantities into an essentially peasant environment, by way of the wages doled out to carriers, quarrymen and gangs of pieceworkers employed in building the church, and by purchases of provisions. It is hardly surprising that money payments could by now form a ready substitute for labour services on the monastic estate: the lord was severing his ties with the land, and the peasants could freely earn cash.

While cheerfully basing the whole of her expense economy on the use of money, Cluny was unwittingly exposing herself to difficulties that were to become chronic in the first quarter of the twelfth century. The sources of cash were drying up just when the velocity of monetary circulation was causing commodity prices to rise. It was now necessary to dip into reserves. Hoarded wealth dwindled. Abbot Peter the Venerable, who bore the brunt of the crisis, accused his predecessor, Pons of Melgueil, of having squandered the treasure. But the fact was that the chamberlain could no longer cover, with income from rents, the expenses that had become customary in the palmy days of the late eleventh century. For twenty-five years the abbot tried to find a cure for this economic malady. The brethren, despite their grumbles, were enjoined to tighten their belts a little. Yet it was impossible to travel far along the road to austerity: this would have been to deprive the monastic profession of the lordly bearing lent by the whole Cluniac tradition. There remained two feasible courses of action. The first was to fall back on a rational exploitation of the estate, so as to draw from it once more supplies of bread and wine for the refectories. For this it would be essential to restore orderly management: to pursue the policy undertaken at the turn of the eleventh century against lay stewards who had built up their own parasitic lordships to the detriment of the abbey's rights; to assess the income from each manor by making detailed surveys; to share out the *mesaticum* services more equitably; and to supervise the collection of dues. Above all it would be essential to develop direct exploitation: to increase the number of ploughs on every manor with a view to harvesting more corn; to plant new vines and assign a portion of the cash receipts to the hire of vineyard workers.

Thus difficulties forced the abbey's administrators to turn their attention to the domestic economy, to reckon up, to handle figures, to calculate profits and losses, to think about ways and means of expanding production, in short, to transform themselves into farmers even at the risk of betraying their special calling. We do not know whether the plan of reorganization worked out by Peter the Venerable bore fruit. The sources simply show that the abbot was nevertheless compelled to commit himself to the second course of action: borrowing. He was helped by one of his guests, the bishop of Winchester and brother of King Stephen of England, who had sought refuge at Cluny bringing with him his church's treasure. This prelate probably initiated the Cluniacs in more advanced English methods of manorial administration, placing at their disposal sizeable amounts of precious metals, though not without precautions and guarantees. His contribution was not enough however, and Peter the Venerable had to pawn valuables from the sacristy. The creditors were mainly Jews (which perhaps excited the anti-Semitism displayed by the abbot in some of his writings) but also Christian merchants who had settled near the abbey gates at a time when she was importing most of her supplies, and had thereby made their fortunes. Little by little the burden of debt grew heavier in the course of the twelfth century and it appeared increasingly normal to base the monastery's economy on credit, since she could not dispense with money.

The options revealed by the rich documentation left behind by Cluny do not seem to have been peculiar to that house. The overriding consideration was to enhance the splendour of the liturgical office. But the dissipation of reserves and deliberate recourse to borrowing typified a widespread economic outlook among contemporary heads of Benedictine monasteries of the old observance. When Norman monasteries were ceasing to advance money to the laity in the late twelfth century, was this really out of respect for interdicts recently launched by the Pope against loans secured by pledging land? Was it not rather because treasuries had been depleted? The new attention paid to the profitability of manorial farming was outstanding in Suger, Peter the Venerable's contemporary. Suger spared no means to make the basilica at St Denis the most splendid place of worship of his day, entering into enormous expense to adorn it for the glory of God. Even so, he added the treatise *De Rebus in Administratione sua Gestis* to the book that he compiled to relate (not without a degree of self-satisfaction) the story of his building and decorating schemes. As he saw it, the treatise was its necessary complement. All the work carried out on the site of the church did indeed depend on sound management of the estate. His account lays bare intentions similar to those of the abbot of Cluny: essentially, to develop direct exploitation in order to cut back sharply on the purchase of basic foodstuffs. At Saint-Lucien he invested twenty *librae* in creating a vineyard so that it would no longer be necessary to pawn the abbey's ornaments at the fairs of Lagny to buy wine. All the land at Guillerval was granted to tenants, for Suger came to the conclusion that the system based on the collection of fixed rents was not the most profitable. Instead a *champart* (payment proportionate to the harvest) was substituted, so that the abbey might take advantage of the peasants' greater resources. At great expense, three 'ploughlands' (*carrucatae*) were acquired: on one of these he installed a *ministerialis* charged with 'quelling the murmurs of the peasants and any opposition to changing customs'; with the other two he formed a manor, and in this way income rose from four to fifty *modii* of grain. At Vaucresson he 'founded a village, built a church and a house and had the wasteland cleared with the plough'; soon there were sixty *hospites* in residence, and many others asking to come. At Rouvray he turned down the agreement *in paragio* offered by the lord of the near-by castle, took charge of the manor himself, raised its yield from twenty to one hundred *librae*, and each year set aside the extra eighty for the construction of the basilica.

By the late eleventh century criticisms had been voiced against the age-old style of monastic life that Cluny had brought to perfection. The debate was conducted in terms of needful asceticism and a return to the text of the original rules. Critics condemned over-spending, but not the ownership of land or use of money. Such predilections gave rise to economic circumstances differing widely from those of long-established Benedictine abbeys. They can best be observed in the Cistercian Order, one of the new monastic congregations to meet with the greatest measure of success.

The Cistercians rejected Cluny's seigneurial attitudes. They refused to live off rents or the labour of others. They simply owned land – but not personal dependants, tenants, mills or tithes – and farmed it themselves. More firmly than the Cluniacs or Suger, they based their household economy on direct exploitation. Yet this choice had the effect of altering completely the monks' standing in relation to production, withdrawing them at least partially from a life of ceremonial idleness and making workers out of them. Did this amount to a thorough-going revolution? In reality farmwork remained a fringe occupation for choir monks, assuming importance only in the age of large-scale operations on the land. And in conformity with the spirit of St Benedict, work did not cease to be regarded as an instrument of bodily mortification. Nevertheless Cistercian communities made room for a second category of religious: those recruited from the order of workers, the lay brothers (*conversi*). For them, participation in prayer was limited and their role would be the creation of wealth. The farming of the estate fell mainly to them, working on soils for the most part uncultivated since Cistercian custom required monasteries to be founded in the 'desert' (*desertum*). Thus the profound division in lay society separating specialists in work from the rest was permeating the very soul of the monastic family.

The ensuing relationship established between land and productive forces, involving the employment of an enthusiastic, domestic and cheap labour supply supplemented only now and then by a few wage-earners (whose hire was sanctioned by the chapter general of Cîteaux as early as 1134), was preparing the way for a remarkable economic achievement. Cistercian abbeys had been founded on new and therefore fertile land. They soon came to harvest more corn and wine than was needed for their own sustenance. On the portion of their landed endowment that had not been cleared, they practised stockraising and exploited timber and iron ore resources on a large scale. The community did not eat meat or use heating, and it required very little leather and wool. With such huge surpluses at their disposal, the monks speedily devoted themselves to the task of selling. Those of Longpont had started to plant vines in 1145, thirteen years after the foundation of their abbey. Two years later they were beginning to crave exemption from tolls on routes leading to countries that imported wine; they installed a warehouse in the town of Noyon; they made every arrangement that could possibly facilitate the sale of their vintage. The part played by English Cistercian houses in the wool trade from the end of the twelfth century is well known. Because the rule of St Benedict, whose prescriptions they were following to the letter, had sanctioned the use of money, the monks of Cîteaux gathered in *denarii* without hesitation. But what did they do with them? They did not buy anything for home consumption. Their customs forbade them to hoard treasure or to embellish the sanctuary. Suger tells of the bargain he struck by purchasing a collection of precious stones from Cistercians who were at a loss to know how to dispose of them. Thus the ascetic bent was promoting economic growth; Benedictine monks of the new observance used their money basically to increase their capital. They pushed technical advances further than anyone else. The best plough-teams and implements were to be found on their farms. They bought land. Their 'granges' (*grangia*), subsidiary manorial centres on their estates, became more numerous everywhere. There was no deficit, strain or borrowing here. On the contrary widespread collective affluence stood in sharp contrast to the individual privation of members of the community. There was a keen awareness of business, so much so that the extensive liquid assets of the Cistercians ended by arousing the laity's distrust in the late twelfth century. To ordinary laymen they emerged from their seclusion only to buy lands coveted by themselves, or to talk about the state of the money market.

Documents emanating from monastic archives display two major economic attitudes. In the first place the domestic economy was deeply entrenched in direct exploitation of the landed estate. In the second (and one that seems to typify the twelfth century), buying, selling, lending and running up debts became commonplace: in other words, at varying rates and in varying degrees, an economy based chiefly on landownership was launched into the money market, which became lively enough appreciably to upset traditional channels for exchanging goods and services. These two attitudes were common to all twelfth-century lords. This is shown by an analysis of the income they derived from their rights over land on the one hand and their power over people on the other.

II EXPLOITATION

(*a*) GROUND RENT. Among the profits derived from landlordship, those coming from the tenements were now counting for less and less. Fixed by custom and in theory immutable, rates of payment do not appear to have altered much since Carolingian times:

On this manse dwells Guichard . . . who owes as his service: at Easter a lamb; at haymaking six *denarii*; at harvest time a meal [with several associates] and a measure of oats; at the grape harvest twelve *denarii*; at Christmas twelve *denarii*, three loaves and a half-measure of wine; at the beginning of Lent a capon; at Mid-Lent six *denarii*.[1]

Such were the liveries expected in southern Burgundy *c.* 1100 from one long-standing peasant holding, still not subdivided and therefore capable of keeping busy and alive several working men's households. For the peasants the burden was light but for the landlord the profit was meagre. By comparison with Carolingian prototypes, the only new feature in this document is perhaps the greater emphasis on cash payments, some of which, exacted at times of haymaking or grape-picking, were probably replacing former labour services. The spread of money payments among burdens attached to land is striking. In Picardy renders in kind had almost entirely disappeared by the eleventh century: at its close ten tenants of the priory of Hesdin were alone handing over uncoined silver to the annual value of six *librae*. Similarly the proportion of cash rents seems to have been very high in England. Yet this process was far from being general. In northern Italy in the twelfth century landlords strove to substitute renders in kind for money rents. These men were town-dwellers with business interests who intended to corner the market in sales of surplus produce from dependent farms. In short, it may well be that returns from customary tenements became relatively poor in nearly all parts of the European countryside in the twelfth century; lords obtained agricultural products from them, but in small quantities.

The weak hold of lordship over peasant land can be explained. Land clearance had relieved demographic pressure. There was plenty of room for field workers. The value of land was low. Yet the actual process that caused the structure of holdings to alter as the wastes retreated favoured the growth of manorial rent. As soon as fresh patches of ground were in full production, *champarts* (*campipartes*), *tâches* (*taschae*) and any due proportionate to the harvest laid upon newly created fields and vineyards, brought in to the lords' store-rooms far more than the old ones had done, even though the proportion demanded was small. This kind of levy declined in the mid-twelfth century; lords and peasants fixed money rents in their place; and the longer agreement was delayed, the heavier was the burden of cash payments. The lord received more and more money from assarted land. And there was another source

[1] M. C. Ragut (ed.), *Cartulaire de Saint-Vincent de Mâcon* (Mâcon 1864), no. 511, pp. 297–8.

of cash: the disintegration of former manses, the apportionment of dues among countless plots of land, and the scope left for tenants to alienate property and divide it between their heirs provided numerous opportunities to levy cash payments for conveyancing rights. The growing buoyancy of the land market made these increasingly lucrative.

Nevertheless, as every extant survey of manorial profits testifies, the most substantial rents enjoyed by landlords came from the exploitation of bread-ovens, mills and tithes. These still remained mostly in the hands of laymen. In the course of the eleventh century almost all the laity had handed back to monasteries and cathedral chapters the ownership of churches founded by their ancestors, but they had not relinquished tithes: they were too profitable. Their yield, like that from mills and ovens, continued to rise as long as the area under crop expanded, the use of bread became more widespread, and the population increased. Owners of these installations derived ample food supplies from them for the whole of their households, and sometimes money as well, whenever they had been put to 'farm'. They retained them as one of their steadiest sources of income. In the twelfth century these assets formed the principal object of lawsuits between lords, and the veritable heart of landlordship. On estates belonging to churches in Picardy the bulk of the revenue came from traditional dues on land up to *c.* 1080; afterwards, the balance tilted towards taxes levied on users of woods, mills, ovens and towards tithes.

Technical progress, land clearance and the advance of viticulture therefore enhanced the value of ground rent in the twelfth century. This explains the life of ease maintained by knights and churchmen, despite the fact that the granting of fiefs, the segmentation of lineages, and the founding of so many religious houses had considerably increased their numbers. Three comments are necessary here. First, that the rate of agrarian expansion was apparently fast enough for this rise in income to be accompanied by a reduction of the burden of landlordship on the peasantry. Second, that before *c.* 1180 the part played by money in this form of rent remained limited: each year, for example, the cathedral at Mâcon derived barely forty *solidi* (the price of a poor horse) from the seventy-two tenements it owned in one village, beyond bread and wine sufficient to provide for a single family of servants. Third, that the most profitable of these sources of income, consisting of levies on crops or charges on customary rights, would fetch high returns only if the lord were near and watchful. In order not to see them disappear it was essential on vast, scattered estates to have recourse to agents, who would keep a large share of the proceeds for themselves.

(*b*) DIRECT EXPLOITATION. This is why rent was of less consequence than direct exploitation to all contemporary landlords, with the possible exception of the most eminent. The bulk of their income came from their 'demesne' (*dominium*), land cultivated by their domestic staff and from which they took the whole crop for themselves. Allusions to the break-up and decay of manorial demesne can be found in the records. Pious gifts, partible inheritance and the provision of fiefs had frequently dismembered big farms, and the best solution was often to combine these scattered pieces and entrust their exploitation to tenants. More intensive farming and higher productivity from the land made it possible to reduce the size of the demesne with impunity. None the less, like Suger or Peter the Venerable, twelfth-century heads of aristocratic households were normally busy keeping their demesnes in good order, reconstructing and enlarging them by clearing new ground or planting vines. Everywhere the best closes and finest assarts were dependent upon the manorial demesne. In Picardy we come across lay lords whose demesnes extended over hundreds of hectares, as in Carolingian times. In Domesday Book there is hardly a manor without a demesne whose area surpasses that of the tenements and comprises the most fertile and best-worked lands.

Seigneurial households appear to have been amply provided with manpower. The permanent tasks always devolved upon a domestic staff consisting of about twenty or thirty individuals headed by the 'oxherds', who drove the ploughs. These folk 'lived by the bread of their masters', according to contemporary records. But custom would often allow them to consume this 'prebend' at home, surrounded by a garden granted to them close by the manorial 'court'. This smallholding enabled them to live as a household and raise children. It attached them more firmly to the farm, in an age when people were far scarcer than land and when peasant mobility was great. Peasants called 'bordars' (*bordarii*) or 'cottars' (*cottarii*) in English documents were in a position that was little different. They too were settled on a small plot of ground; in return they had to work for nothing one or two days a week on the manor; for the rest they received a wage. Even so, the unequal distribution of farmwork during the course of the year, with slack seasons alternating with periods of feverish activity, would necessitate a temporary reinforcement of these full-time employees. An 'aid' (*auxilium*) would be required from those liable to perform labour services. All Europe was still familiar with forced, unpaid labour, though its economic importance was not everywhere identical.

In the area south of the Loire and Alps, where labour services were worth almost nothing, most holdings had been released from them. Service from the others would be limited to a few days in the year: from thirty-five tenements the cathedral at Mâcon derived no more than two hundred and twenty dayworks a year, or less than had once been due from a single manse on Carolingian manors in the Paris basin. In short, it was primarily a contribution in 'ploughs' (*carrucae*), that is teams of draught animals, that lords in this region expected, gladly dispensing with the services of manual labourers. By way of compensation, technical innovations and the fundamental role played by the work of the plough may have prompted lords to impose new services on ploughmen, whenever they had the power. In this part of Christendom, labour services had probably been light for a long time, though perhaps here and there they were made somewhat heavier in the twelfth century.

In the northern half of the Continent, on the other hand, the Carolingian system of closely associating peasant holdings with demesne farming stayed firmly rooted during this period. Every manorial survey describes plots of land that were cultivated by the tenants (*lots-corvées*), objects made in peasant homes supplied to the manor, and numerous and regular services performed. Even so, this system appears to have undergone a process of slow disintegration after 1100. At the beginning of the twelfth century, for example, the abbot of Marmoutier in Alsace decided to relinquish the *servitium triduanum*, the service of three days a week to which servile tenements in Germany had been subject since the Carolingian period. At the same time, most of the parcels cultivated by forced labour were converted into holdings burdened with rents. By about the middle of the twelfth century, lords in France had finally given up demanding liveries of cloth and woodwork from their subordinates. Rising productivity was making it less necessary to rely on the labour services of the peasants, whose numbers had increased with the population. The availability of money was also enabling lords to acquire better-quality craft products, as well as to hire more efficient workers on a day-to-day basis.

The burden of forced labour in the twelfth century seems to

have been heaviest in the third zone, England, at least to judge by what we can see of the English countryside – the great monastic estates. It did not weigh equally on all tenants. Some, deemed to be free men, were liable solely to 'boonworks' (*precariae*), specific tasks, especially ploughing, subdivided seasonally as on estates in northern France or Germany. Others, the 'villeins' (*villani*) of Domesday Book and later documents, owed, apart from similar occasional services and sometimes the obligatory farming of part of the lord's demesne, what were called 'weekworks' (*opera*): for three days a week the tenement he held placed a man at the lord's beck and call. The villein was a part-time domestic servant, as the Carolingian *servus* had been. Like the *servus*, he joined the household staff for one day in two, working and eating with them. Like the ninth-century slave, he derived from the land granted to him food for his wife and children, and *companagium* for himself. English lords preserved these strict rights during the twelfth century, though without making full use of them. Many elected to 'sell' (*vendere*) them to their dependants for the duration of the year; the peasants purchased the free disposal of their energies and equipment for a few pence. Villeins on one manor belonging to Shaftesbury Abbey had thereby freed themselves from weekworks inside forty years: all were paying a rent of three or four shillings instead.

Thus, in England as on the Continent, similar pressures were prompting lords to exploit the productive capacities of their tenants in a new way. It was wiser to abandon a 'work' which, because of 'the carelessness, uselessness, listlessness and shiftlessness' of those owing labour services, was yielding very little and costing a great deal. Food had to be provided for common labourers, and custom, subtly evolving in favour of the underprivileged, prescribed for them a rising standard of living. It would therefore be preferable to exchange this 'work' for the cash that was falling into peasant hands much more readily than in times past. In this way, without drastically reducing the size of the demesne, the role of forced labour was minimized everywhere. Conversely, the role of wage-earners was extended, so that the monks of Cluny, for example, paid their vineyard workers with money from the taxes offsetting the abolition of certain labour services. The outcome of this development was that most of the manual tasks that the household staff were unable to perform were assigned to hired day-labourers. As for the labour power that compulsory services still provided, it was much less that of people than of draught animals and implements. The village no longer made any contribution to demesne farming except in three ways, the economic value of which had come to outweigh all the others. It supplied ploughs, men seeking supplementary income in casual employment, and the cash for paying these pieceworkers.

Thanks to this contribution, increasingly effective as the countryside was settled by more people, improved its technical equipment and was opened up to monetary circulation, large-scale farming prospered in this period. It provided food for the lords, their servants and any settlers they cared to welcome. Substantial surpluses might be left over which could be sold. In this way, the demesne supplied lords with cash as well.

(*c*) EXPLOITATION OF PEOPLE. All the same, the most substantial cash receipts were not derived from landlordship but from power over men and women. Let us commence with the management of the *familia*. Twelfth-century lords began to see that profits from their 'body-servants' (*homines de corpore*) would be higher to the extent that they left them with greater economic independence. No doubt they recruited most of their household staff from the homes of their dependants, as in former times. Yet they preferred to allow these to settle down and prosper, for the machinery of taxation, which was apparently growing more efficient, enabled them to take a large slice of this new-found wealth. They could 'sell' freedom, as they were selling labour services, which brought in handsome returns. About 1185, for instance, the abbot of Ferrières-en-Gâtinais decided to grant his men certain liberties – the right to come and go, and to dispose freely of their goods and chattels – 'in grateful recognition' of which freedom, 'each head of household shall give to the church five *solidi* rent a year'. To free the *familia* in exchange for a cash rent was the easy solution, but it was certainly not the most profitable. It was preferable to retain the means to make a raid on a dependant's savings. This could be done when he had died: in contemporary Germany, a *Buteil* would leave his lord one-third or one-half of the movable goods; in northern France, the lord would choose the best head of livestock (Latin *melius catallum*, French *meilleur catel*) or, if it were a question of succeeding a woman, the most sumptuous item of clothing. Otherwise, it could be done whenever a dependant infringed custom or committed an offence. Of all seigneurial rights over people, justice was the one that would most readily permit lords to relieve workers of the money they had managed to earn.

Justice usually belonged to the few lords enjoying possession of the *bannum*. French documents, which on this aspect of economic history are perhaps the most informative, permit us to trace the development of banal taxation. During the first half of the eleventh century, while the attributes of royal justice were passing into the hands of local feudatories, records begin to make allusion to various 'customs' (*consuetudines*). References to a right to hospitality (*droit de gîte*) in favour of the territorial lord and his agents, as well as to commandeer hay and oats for castle knights, become particularly common. Later, in the twenty years or so before and after the year 1100, the public carting or ploughing services that the lord reserved for farming his demesnes make their appearance, besides various trading rights that he arrogated to himself: toll, taxes gathered in village market-places, and the monopoly of selling wine at certain times. Approximately 1090 is the date of the earliest traces of the *taille* (*talia, tolta*), a levy effected by the lord on whatever his subjects had put by, as often as he felt need of it. This exaction, the most burdensome by reason of its arbitrary character, underwent two related changes in the mid-twelfth century: it began to be collected in cash, and it was *abonnée* (*abonata*), that is to say, it assumed the form of a fixed annual payment. Such were the principal stages of a sequence of events that coincided with agricultural expansion and the introduction to country districts of commercial exchange. As time went by, banal lords gradually took more from more numerous and less indigent peasants. No document allows us to measure this tapping of wealth, nor to compare it with income from landlordship. It appears to have been far more considerable. By means of the *taille*, a lord in southern Burgundy in the early twelfth century could relieve one peasant of forty *solidi* and a second of one hundred on a single occasion; such cases demonstrate, whatever intervention by family or village community there may have been, the extent of the savings accumulated in cash or livestock in workers' homes. About 1200 another lord could raise the sum of three hundred silver marks from a small section only of the inhabitants of his castellany. To pass judgement was to extract money in still greater quantities: at Lincoln Assizes in 1202 the king of England's justice imposed fines totalling £633 and averaging thirty shillings per offender, at a time when the value of the livestock in moderately well-to-do country houses did not exceed six shillings and when one penny was being paid for a day's work. When in 1187 agents of the count of Flanders undertook to estimate their master's income in the account known as the *Grote Brief*, they classified judicial receipts separately, so disproportionately large had they become.

An enormous share of banal profits served to enrich the *ministeriales*, many of whom belonged to the aristocracy in the twelfth century. In Picardy, for example, every head manor on ecclesiastical estates was held by some local feudatory. The interest shown by knights in these administrative functions proves that they were reaping substantial advantages from them. These advantages enabled non-noble *ministeriales* to climb rapidly up the social scale, notwithstanding all efforts by their masters to delay their ascent. The most dynamic social circle, the only one in which an attempt to enter the seigneurial class was no unusual venture for the lowly-born, comprised lords wielding power to command, sit in judgement and make huge profits as a result. This dynamism, the hope of social advancement that could be pursued far by those endowed with the spirit of enterprise, often took the form of steadily increasing the pressure of banal lordship: the *ministeriales* of princes and great lords themselves arranged the fiscal system from which they were first to benefit. Thus, while stimulating rural production by their growing demands, they showed themselves the most active promoters not only of their own success but also of economic development in general.

For my part, I incline to see the main driving force behind the internal growth of the European economy in the exercise of banal lordship, whether it were entirely concentrated in royal hands as in England, or whether it were dispersed among numerous lords as in France. In effect, holders of the *bannum* had taken upon themselves the duties of former rulers, as well as their prerogatives. The economic function that Charlemagne's court had once fulfilled as the focal point for the concentration and redistribution of wealth, had now to be fulfilled by the court of each 'lord' (*dominus*): that of the duke of Normandy as well as those of minor independent overlords in the Ile de France or the Mâconnais. Such a court was the fountain-head of generosity to churches for the common good of the people, and to knightly vassals as the chief recipients of their lord's gifts in the form of jewellery, entertainment, weapons and horses. These courts were many. One consequence of the establishment of a network of feudal relations was that there were thenceforth hundreds of Carolingians in Europe and hundreds of meeting places for the complex interchange of gifts and return gifts. This devolution of power was itself a potent factor in stimulating the economy. Again, unlike early medieval kings, great lords derived little from waging war unless they were involved in long-distance expeditions against infidels, which admittedly is what nearly every holder of the *bannum* in Christendom did at some stage in the twelfth century. They fought incessantly, and in tournaments their sons played at fighting, though this military activity cost far more than it won. All this made cash flow freely out of the hands of princes, redistributing it among small knights, horse-breeders, weapon-smiths, and the many dealers and entertainers attracted by the rip-roaring fair surrounding each tournament. By a complete about-turn, this was now the main economic function of war: no longer to add to the aristocracy's resources, but to induce its members to spend more. To keep open house, lords had to exploit their rights and take from the subject population all it could give: to strive to expand agricultural production by a conscious policy of clearing land, improving equipment, attracting settlers; to acquire as much money as possible and so to encourage, consciously or otherwise, the development of exchange in a peasant environment. The powers and needs of countless heirs of former kings formed the lynch-pin of the entire economic machinery of the age.

If banal lords were amassing far more money than anyone else, they were also first to run short. Like the abbot of Cluny, they incurred debts. While money loans among small landlords were interchanged between kinsmen and friends, in a mutual round of give and take that is no test of a chronic shortage of cash but was common to all members of this social group, the debts of great lords continued to accumulate. The imbalance between income and expenditure occurred first in the upper ranks of the aristocracy. Once again the phenomenon comes to the surface *c.* 1075 – that decisive turning-point in European economic history. For precious metals or cash, lay magnates had initially turned to the Church. Collected over the generations, her treasures were immense and alms were still available to replenish them. Since the second half of the eleventh century, the desire to protect the patrimony, the briskness of monetary circulation and the gradual mobilization of wealth had prompted the rich to give less land to God's servants and to offer them more money instead. In the monastery of St Trond, for example, one of the monks spent all his time in collecting the coins and silver thread that pilgrims day and night deposited near the shrine of the patron saint. Building projects, the distribution of alms to the poor during famines, the spirit of poverty that moved Cistercians to sell as quickly as possible any articles of jewellery they were offered – to say nothing of the difficulties facing the monastic economy – were not the only factors working to liquidate the Church's reserves. Ecclesiastical dignitaries used Church funds widely in order to act as pawnbrokers. In exchange for an advance of money, the religious community would obtain the usufruct of a piece of property until the debt was settled; the profits represented the interest on the loan and, since the owner was often unable to repay the money, what had been pledged would eventually be incorporated in the estate. Such transactions could certainly be advantageous. After 1075 some of them were on a large scale: Godfrey de Bouillon offered to consign his allodial property to Bishop Otbert of Liège as surety for an enormous loan of 1,300 silver marks and 3,000 of gold. The offer was tempting, for the pledge was substantial, and so they began to remove the gold decorating St Lambert's shrine in the cathedral. The amount of precious metal being insufficient, the bishop did not hesitate to plunder more treasuries in the abbeys of his diocese, despite recriminations from the monks. This source of credit gradually became less plentiful in the course of the twelfth century, not least for moral reasons. The spiritual demands that Gregorian reform was spreading among the religious were giving teeth to reservations about money-lending, a practice officially condemned by the Pope in 1163. But we also know that big religious houses were themselves meeting with financial difficulties. Those of Cluny were shared in the second half of the twelfth century by a large number of abbots and by nearly all bishops, who likewise were living beyond their means. The archbishop of Mainz was so vexed by the need for money that he increased his fiscal demands inordinately, to the point where his subjects rose up in 1160 and murdered him. Great ecclesiastical lords were just as addicted to spending as secular ones. None the less the proportion of bullion and coin in pious gifts was growing, so that they staved off the moment when they ran into debt. But it was necessary to desist from lending themselves and the laity had to turn elsewhere.

During the early Middle Ages, the Jews had accumulated precious metals and cash more or less single-handed. They could lend these to Christians, for the condemnation of usury by the Church was no concern of theirs. The triumph of Christian economic morality therefore promoted their specialization in credit: Jews came to the rescue of the countess of Carcassonne in 957–70, the archbishop of Cologne in the third quarter of the eleventh century, Abbot Peter of Cluny fifty years later. After the middle of the twelfth century the prosperity of Jewish communities is evident in France and in England: countless lords were in their debt, King Henry II of England among them. Two new factors become apparent at this juncture. The first is the presence, among those who lent money and made a profit out of it, of Christians who were neither lay lords nor churchmen, but townsfolk who had done well for themselves in business. The second is a change in the function of borrowing in the internal economy of big aristocratic households: it no longer appears as an occasional expedient, but as a perfectly normal managerial procedure. In less than a century the small world of banal lords became completely accustomed to the use of credit. This fact underlines the vital role played by such facilities in economic growth. These lords were borrowing because they were spending still more than they were getting and, like the abbots of Cluny from the last third of the eleventh century, they were dispensing money lavishly. Further, there were moneyed individuals at their gates who were discovering an interest in placing cash at the disposal of lords. To a great extent the borrowed money equalled that which their own largess and purchases had earlier put into circulation.

III SPENDING

The expenses of princes and castle lords were of the same order as Cluny's in the twelfth century. The monks of Cluny sacrificed money for the glory of God, and spent it to welcome settlers and treat them according to their rank. Their style of lordly living and their anxiety not to dress like the common herd also obliged them to deal with merchants. Every great lord, from a king down to a simple castellan, likewise used the money he collected or borrowed for two ends: sacrifice and adornment. All would have to serve God, for the salvation of themselves and the people under their protection. They would therefore give generously to churches, like kings of former times. In helping to build Notre-Dame de Paris and other cathedrals in the Ile de France, Louis VII was resuming the work of Charlemagne. And there was no banal lord of any standing who did not found a collegiate church or support a monastery where people might pray for himself and his ancestors and members of his line might find a burial place. Pious gifts headed the list of expenses as in the past. Nevertheless they were tending to change their nature in the twelfth century, becoming money offerings or pensions. Thus innovations crept in to acts of religious sacrifice and joined forces with the general process of economic development fostered by the increasing speed of monetary circulation. An offering to God and His servants had in the past simply called for an item of fixed capital to be transferred by passing from one landed estate or treasure-house to another. Henceforth, the donation was such that it would enter straightaway into an expense account, whether serving to build a monument or to feed a religious community. New ways of consecrating riches to the service of God were also spreading. First was the long-distance pilgrimage, an occasion for mobilizing the wealth that quickened the circulation of coins all along the pilgrim routes. Then there was caring for the poor. In the ancient world, with its common penury and its rigid social structure, poverty had possessed hardly any economic significance: in Carolingian usage the word *pauper* indicated submission to authority, and contrasted not with *dives* but with *potens*. Ritualized aid to the needy had been little more than a symbolic gesture in the normal course of liturgical ceremonial. In the early eleventh century, whenever the king of France, Robert the Pious, gave alms to the poor, he played the part of Christ. A fixed number of paupers accompanied him. These were pensioners with walk-on parts, and when one of them died a replacement was swiftly found. The economic thaw of the twelfth century interfered with this routine. The poor man, such as occupied the thoughts of Count Thibaud of Champagne in times of famine, appeared more and more clearly as a victim of economic processes, someone who had to be given assistance for the love of God. This slow change in religious sentiment was the outcome of the new attention that the Gospel commanded from contemporaries, but progress in circulating goods no doubt accelerated it. During the early medieval period no magnate would close his grain-stores to the destitute, with the result that a significant redistribution of wealth took place in rural society. What was new in the twelfth century was that charity was institutionalized: poverty became a value presented to the rich as a salutary model of personal demeanour; and more people came to think that money could best be employed not in supporting expert choristers in monastery or chapter, nor in raising a cathedral, but in sharing it with the poor. In this way, cash became more directly available to the humblest members of contemporary society.

However to be rich in the twelfth century, as in earlier times, meant giving not only to God, but also to friends: to welcome them in large numbers, to make them at home as far as possible, to deck them in finery. Like the big monasteries, seigneurial courts as centres of banal lordship were places where hospitality was normally open to all-comers. The lord's greatest joy would be to dispense pleasures, and his bounteous gifts would scatter the fruits of the earth among his permanent and temporary guests, as well as his servants. The court formed the real terminal point of the consumer economy it nurtured and sustained. For the brilliance of a court was assessed primarily according to its wealth of exotic embellishments for the table, the body and the mind. It was up to the lord to exhibit in himself all the refinements that travels to the East had revealed to Latin knights, and to share them among those in his company. Hence the court was the source of a lively process of popularization, causing new needs to infiltrate an ever larger group of consumers. It was also a place of rivalry where everyone competed in extravagance. Economic growth made twelfth-century social circles increasingly aware of fashion. But the substance of this luxury was strictly speaking 'exterior' (*exterior*), to borrow the term used by monks to describe that which was not produced at home but had to be bought. To be master of the perpetual revels that lay at the heart of the aristocratic way of life therefore necessitated recourse to specialists in supplying unfamiliar and exquisite commodities of distant provenance – the merchants.

The development of commercial activities in twelfth-century Europe was not stimulated by exactly the same pressures as had obtained one hundred or one hundred and fifty years earlier, when on the confines of Christendom adventurers had disposed of booty from warfare without even laying down their arms. In the measure of peace achieved by feudal institutions and gradually consolidated by the strengthening of great regional principalities, commercial trading developed to answer the growing needs of aristocratic households increasingly accustomed to a life of ease and constantly rising incomes made possible by the expansion of rural production. But this development, whose roots went deep down into the countryside, also sparked off an explosion of urban activity. Town growth was closely bound up with the vitality of the greatest seigneurial courts because it depended directly on the higher efficiency of banal taxation.

With the exception of a few crossroads which were not real towns but places where traders met together and stored their wares, the larger settlements of the early Middle Ages had fulfilled two prime functions, religious and military. They had provided shelter for the headquarters of important lordships: those of the bishop, cathedral chapter and monasteries; those of the count whenever he was a town-dweller, as was the case in the entire southern half of Christendom; and those of warrior families guarding the ramparts. Rulers frequently had a palace there. Substantial convoys of agricultural produce from every big country estate converged on the towns: well before the year 1000 it was mainly on the urban market that the fruits of the earth were bought and sold. Whenever the progressive establishment of feudal relations eroded regalian powers, the local lord – the abbot, the count or his deputy, often the bishop by way of royal favour – seized the right to exercise the *bannum*. Hence the towns became the focal points of a widespread network of tax-gathering from the surrounding districts, attracting a higher proportion of surplus rural production than before, which increasingly took the form of money. Those who wielded banal authority could use the proceeds according to personal whim: for building (since the most important ecclesiastical and secular construction sites were gradually concentrated in the towns) or for providing entertainment for their neighbours. Such spending caused a hitherto minor function of the towns to grow – the economic one. Growth itself gave rise to the expansion of those quarters associated with the stronghold and with built-up areas nestling in the shadow of religious houses. These are usually called *burgi*. They extended along the busiest roads leading to the market-place or harbour, or to some improved means of communication: for instance in French towns the foundations of many stone bridges date from the late eleventh century. Growth was all the faster when the town's lord was powerful and rich. The most prosperous towns were those such as Toulouse, Arles or Angers, Orléans or Paris, Winchester or Mainz, where great princes used to make lengthy sojourns: the rise of Vienna began in the second half of the twelfth century, as soon as Duke Henry Jasomirgott chose it as his permanent residence. The connection between seigneurial power and urban vitality is self-evident. When an active court had its seat in the countryside, it would quickly give rise to an urban settlement. Before the year 1000 a *burgus* had formed at the abbey gate of Cluny; by the end of the twelfth century it could probably have mustered some two thousand inhabitants, closely associated for the most part with the economy of the large and extravagant monastic household. In Alsace, Haguenau became a little town shortly after Frederick Barbarossa had founded a palace there in 1164.

The initial role of the *burgi* was to make provision for the lord's court by means of handicrafts and trade. Craft industries appear to have been entirely domestic in origin. They evolved in the form of outgrowths from manorial utilities: bread-oven, forge, tannery and weaving shed. Little by little these workshops offered part of what they produced to outside customers. The man who had charge of a bread-oven at the approaches to the bridge at Mâcon in the late eleventh century first supplied the bishop's household; he also sold bread to travellers, and his business grew as the road became busier, likewise his share of economic independence. The existence of urban craft industries was already conspicuous by the beginning of the eleventh century, as contemporary toll-lists show. One from Arras alludes especially to foodstuffs, and it seems to have been the victualling trades, the bakers' and the butchers', that paved the way to business expansion. This record also mentions woollen cloths, and metal objects sold from market stalls by smiths. Nevertheless, it was apparently in the twelfth century that the phase of rapid growth in the history of urban handicrafts took place, the time when workers broke free from seigneurial domesticity. In 1109 the abbot of Fritzlar gave the men in his *familia* permission to sell in the market-place whatever they manufactured. Regulations issued at Strasbourg in 1170 lay down that 'any member of the church's *familia*, selling in the town articles he has made with his own hands, does not owe tax'. At this stage, the bread, meat, iron and leather trades were working for a local market, which was enlarged by advances in material civilization in the surrounding rural world throughout the twelfth century. Then, to meet the needs of the rich, the number of craftsmen whose clientele was much further removed, began to grow. For they had specialized in manufacturing luxury items, notably those two principal adornments of the noble life: wine and precious fabrics.

Since very early in the Middle Ages town-based magnates,

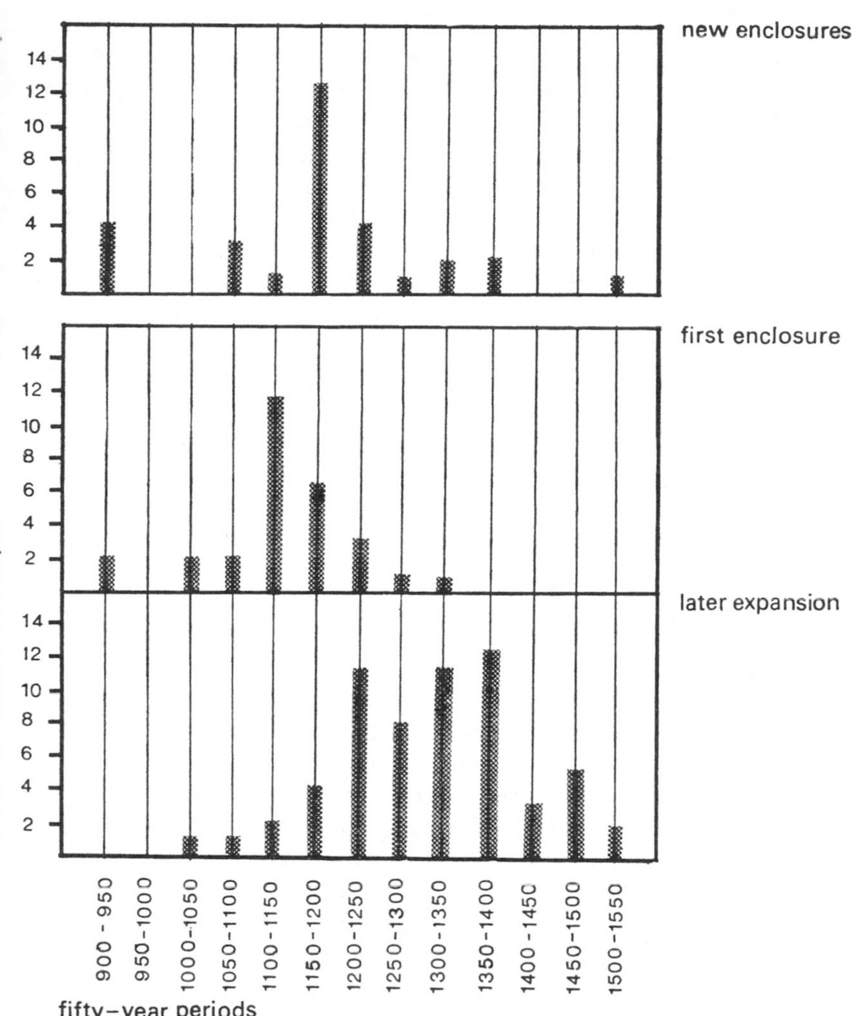

A. Sample of thirteen Italian towns
Bologna, Bréscia, Florence, Genoa, Lucca Mantua, Milan, Parma, Pavia, Piacenza, Pisa, Pistóia and Siena.

B. Sample of twenty-eight northern towns
Aachen, Amiens, Antwerp, Basle, Bruges, Brussels, Cologne, Douai, Étampes, Ghent, Le Mans, Liège, Louvain, Maastricht, Malines, Metz, Middelburg, Namur, Nijmegen, Orléans, Paris, Rouen, Strasbourg, Tournai, Trier, Troyes, Utrecht and Ypres.

Figure 2 Extensions to European Towns

especially bishops, had planned a belt of vineyards round those towns where the climate was not too unfavourable for viticulture. The rise in seigneurial incomes and the popularization of princely habits regularized the use of wine among the whole aristocracy. And the merchant fraternities too acquired the taste for wine in their periodic drinking-bouts. Hence demand was growing for quality as well as for quantity. Great lords would make it a point of honour to serve their guests with the best available liquor, so that the butler's office was one of the most important tasks at the court of the Capetian king. To satisfy these needs, vineyards spread in the regions best suited to the production of quality wine that could easily be exported in bulk; these lay along the middle Seine, the Oise, Loire, Rhine and the Atlantic coastline around La Rochelle. The expansion of wine-production represents a vital aspect of twelfth-century rural growth. One of the most outstanding investments that lords allowed themselves was to create and improve vineyards. They were thinking primarily of the reputation of their tables, but also of the profit promised by the sale of surplus output. They did not hesitate to sacrifice money and land, giving half-shares in their newly developed vineyards to vine-growing pioneers and thereby raising the number of small peasant proprietors. Yet it is essential to stress that viticulture – because of the constant care it demanded, its purely manual techniques, and its permanence on a plot of ground whose quality increased only to the extent that human labour was expended upon it – was very different from work in the fields. Real craftsmen were involved, who in addition remained closely associated with the towns. Everywhere – around Laon, Mainz, Paris, Orléans, later Auxerre, and many a little monastic country town such as Ferrières-en-Gâtinais – it was in the suburbs that viticulture was slowly expanding in a circle so close to the houses that to extend the town would necessitate uprooting vine-stocks and planting others some distance away. The vine-grower was a townsman, a *burgensis* (French *bourgeois*, English 'burgess'), the term used since *c.* 1000. He set up home there and the painstaking tasks of wine-making, the deals he had to carry through to dispose of his harvest, and the money he acquired from them placed him apart from the corn producers and drew him nearer to the cloth merchants or weavers.

Woollen clothing, dyed in unusual colours and woven almost as fine as fabrics brought back from the Orient, was another mark that would distinguish the well-born man from the common people. In the eleventh century there were weavers in every small country town, but their work could not satisfy great lords and their retinues, any more than did the product from the average vineyard, and the yearning for superior finery was responsible for gradual specialization in some workshops. A treatise composed *c.* 1070 in northern France, the *Conflict between Sheep and Flax*, makes it possible for these to be localized. From the Rhineland and Swabia, says this text, come cloths dyed black and red, but they are not of the best quality: 'cloths which appeal to lords [the word *dominus* is used, that is to say, the actual title borne by holders of banal authority], it is you, Flanders, who send them.' The Flemish cloths were green, grey and deep-blue in colour, and were made in centres of craftsmanship in and around the county of Flanders that were not usually linked with a court but focused on the old *portus* whose function had been almost purely economic from the start. They were wholly geared towards exporting, like the great vineyards of the Paris basin and Atlantic coastline. Exports rapidly became long-range. About 1100, in order to join the merchants' association of Novgorod, beyond the Gulf of Finland, it was necessary to offer a piece of cloth from Ypres. This town had then been in existence for no more than fifty years.

Towards the middle of the eleventh century, a major improvement had affected the manufacture of woollen cloth in Flanders (and in Champagne, too, if we can trust a commentary on the Talmud by a Rabbi from Troyes, which is the most explicit written source on this point). Like the whole history of techniques, this change is enshrouded in clouds of obscurity which the ingenuity of researchers may never succeed in dispelling, but we can at least postulate its origins. The vertical loom had been a woman's tool, the instrument used in all the *gynaecea* mentioned by ninth-century manorial surveys and in the hovels of slave tenants, which had supplied broad, short cloths like those *pallia* or so-called Frisian 'capes' (*capae*) which formed the subject of an agreement between Charlemagne and the king of Mercia. This was replaced by the treadle-operated horizontal loom, from which came narrow but very much longer woven strips (the normal length of the new *panni* was from fifteen to twenty metres, whereas that of the older *pallia* did not exceed three). The horizontal loom had been known for a long time, but it was now modified so that when operated by two people it could produce fabrics as wide as the *pallia*. It then became a man's tool, like the plough, a professional tool and, again like the plough, a tool for conquest. The new loom's prime advantage was the capacity to increase the productivity of labour three- or even fivefold; but its product was also far better adapted than its predecessor's to traditional fashions in apparel and wall-hangings, and was as uniform in character as coinage from the mints. Abundance and regularity: the production of this new cloth answered the needs of commerce perfectly. Even so, what was produced would still have to be of very high quality. For this reason, the improvement of weaving was closely associated with that of other processes: cloth had to be fulled to make the material thicker, softer and heavier, so that the fulling mill spread at the same time and at the same pace; it had also to be dyed to relieve the fabric of the greyness of everyday manufactured articles. These complementary dressings, which required care, were consigned to other specialists. Thus in the course of the second half of the eleventh century a handicraft for the first time in Europe took the form of a complex operation where the work of making luxury cloths was shared between several 'crafts' (*misteria*). It was an essential adjustment: upon this sharing depended the value of the product, recognized from one end of Christendom to the other among the wealthiest and most exacting consumers. Such a division of labour demanded close organization and collective discipline. All the weavers, fullers and dyers had to be combined in a veritable commune, where everyone would undertake to respect a set of regulations guaranteeing the reputation and uniformity of the product. Towns alone could offer such a necessary framework: towns like the settlements that had formed at intersections of inland water transport in Flanders and Artois where the power of a lord did not weigh too heavily, and entrepreneurs in long-distance trade were already established. For the keys to success were in the hands of the merchants.

If most craftsmen were selling on the spot, in their workshops or in the market-place, to customers of local provenance, producers of quality wines and manufacturers of luxury fabrics needed middlemen to reach their clientele. The specialists in long-distance trade, the *mercatores*, like the craftsmen, were drifting away from aristocratic households. Their function had been primarily to supply seigneurial courts with foreign wares, some of which, like spices, would come from far afield; to go and search for them; and to offer in exchange money or surplus produce from the manorial demesne. Like the artisan's craft, the commercial function gradually cast off its domestic character, as fast as an expanding consumer economy enabled merchants to present others than their own masters with their wares. Yet trade remained an adventure, both dangerous and profitable, as war had been in times past. In the twelfth century trade was still basically a seasonal expedition mounted in association with others. Merchants established in the same town would form bands as firmly united as groups of warriors about to pillage neighbouring tribes had once been. They constituted among themselves for the duration of the expedition a 'fraternity' or 'brotherhood' (*fraternicia*). Statutes of the fraternity at Valenciennes, whose main features date from the eleventh century, refer to the perpetual danger by land and sea; they mention weapons and forbid anyone to depart from the merchant caravan after it has left the town; they stipulate that mutual assistance shall be given during the journey and that the body of a colleague who has died within less than three days' walk, shall be brought back. Such activity enabled a man to amass money very quickly, but it demanded strength and boldness, and the more resolute would steal a march over the weaker. In the first half of the twelfth century these merchants appear to have comprised a social group large enough for Church intellectuals such as Gerhoh of Reichersberg or Peter the Venerable to classify them as a special *ordo*, in addition to the three orders of traditional sociology.

Just as artisanal and commercial activity in the towns stemmed from the seigneurial courts, so also did the urban population, the 'bourgeoisie' (*burgesia*), have its roots in the *familia*, among the men and women whom the lord protected, used at his pleasure and personally owned. Jews were a case in point. Formerly placed in the king's patronage, their communities were now in that of the banal lord. He levied special taxes on them – very often renders in spices, for they were still trafficking in oriental products – and extracted by all possible means the money they made from usury. This was really the position of craftsmen and traders, too, who were still *ministeriales* in the eleventh century. They formed the backbone of the urban community, and outsiders who sought membership would first have to 'commend' (*commendare*) themselves to the lord of the town, that is to say, to come under his protection. Rather because of the inhabitants who occupied its new quarters than the functions it fulfilled, each town resembled an appendage to the court or seigneurial household. Even so, the strength of their economic activities and the growing role played by craftsmen and commercial exchanges in a society where the standard of living was everywhere rising, filled the towns with people. They attracted immigrants, who managed to find employment and earn a living more readily here than elsewhere. Some would come from far afield, such as 'those migrant settlers [Latin *advenae*, French *aubains*] who are popularly called "dusty folk" [*pulverei*]' and who, still covered with dust from the journey, settled down in the town of Mâcon in the late eleventh century, free to choose bishop or count as their protector. Yet these men of adventure, without roots or ties, were far less common among the newcomers than country-people from the immediate neighbourhood. It was from within a radius of about twenty kilometres that towns recruited the majority of their new inhabitants, who therefore remained bound to their native villages by family connections, rights over land still in their possession, and even the authority exercised over them by a rural lord. The booming twelfth-century countryside had fostered urban growth in two ways: by channelling surplus production towards the towns through the agency of seigneurial taxation, and by feeding their overspill population which the agrarian conquest could not completely reabsorb. The towns grew rich as well: the borough 'farm' of Lincoln, whose yield was proportionate to the taxes paid by the inhabitants, rose from £30 in 1066 to £100 in 1086, £140 in 1130 and £180 at the close of the twelfth century. The construction of a new wall, encompassing recent extensions to the towns and protecting the wealth of their burgesses, marks a decisive stage in this growth and one that can often be dated with a fair degree of certainty. North of the Alps, this stage was distinctly later than in Italy: evidence of frequent fortification-building points in France and Germany to the last third of the twelfth century as the most concentrated phase of growth.

The influx of immigrants and increasing prosperity loosened the population's dependence on the household. Town-dwelling *ministeriales* were no different from country ones, as regards either their legal status or their economic standing. Like village reeves (*prévôts*), certain individuals whose task it was to arrange freshwater supplies moved up the social scale, and doubtless the more rapidly because no environment was more favourable to social mobility than the towns, where money circulated more briskly than elsewhere. Some townspeople were even able to push their way into the knightly class, just like the chief officials of great lords. As far back as the beginning of the eleventh century, documents distinguish from the commonalty of the urban population the *optimi civitatis*, the *primores*, the *meliores*; and these 'best men' were all merchants. Having made their fortunes, they strove to detach themselves from the lord's household. For men whose success was closely dependent on their freedom of action, subordination would be highly inconvenient because of the legal obligations it entailed and the many arbitrary and undefined services a lord could demand. Traders would want to be able to dispose of their own capital, time and means of conveyance without fear of unforeseen requisitions by the lord. On the other hand, when the latter was a powerful figure, membership of his household might also confer distinct advantages. One of these was effective protection: whenever a merchant caravan met with an overdemanding toll-collector, for instance, it would be up to the traders' lord to defend his men. A further privilege was tax-evasion: in the eleventh century the free traders of Arras hastened to enter the abbey of St Vaast's *familia*, whose members did not pay toll; and the count who was responsible for its imposition had to work hard to contain this rush towards servitude, so as not to lose his profits. What big merchants wanted was to obtain their freedom without surrendering the advantages of dependence. To this end they formed associations. First came the bond of lineage, that natural protective partnership whose effectiveness in knightly society was obvious: in the early twelfth century, the urban patriciate emerges as the combination of a few great families, each grouped around a single household. The guild, the sworn fellowship, the artificial brotherhood reinforcing the cohesion of merchant caravans on trading ventures, was another source of refuge. United by the ancient drinking ritual – members of the guild of Saint-Omer, for example, met for two consecutive days every year – a bond would be created as strict and reassuring as that among kinsmen or in the *familia* of the most powerful patron.

> All those who are included in the fellowship [*amicitiam*] of the town [says a charter of association drawn up at Aire-sur-la-Lys in 1188, reproducing an oral agreement of several decades earlier], have confirmed by their fealty and oath that each man shall come to the aid of any other as his brother; . . . If anyone has had his house burned down or if, having fallen into captivity, he has to pay a ransom reducing his means, each of his colleagues shall give one crown [*nummum*] to help the impoverished friend.[1]

[1] *Ordonnances des rois de France*, vol. xii (Paris 1777), pp. 563–4.

This community of interests, based on a sworn association, was spreading to the business world: at Saint-Omer, when a bargain had been struck and the purchaser was preparing to remove the wares at the agreed price, any member of the guild could take away a portion of the goods in question at the same price. Such a 'fellowship' (*amicitia*) was like an organized gang; on its shoulders fell the main struggle waged by the élite of the burgess community (*la société bourgeoise*) to extract privileges from the lord of the town similar to those enjoyed by members of the *ministerialis* class.

What the wealthiest townsmen mainly fought against was personal lordship. They wanted freedom, and the origin of the disturbances at Cologne in 1074 shows the forcefulness of this fundamental claim. The archbishop had ordered a rich trader's boat to be unloaded so that it might be requisitioned *in ministerium archiepiscopi*, meaning, as a domestic service for the needs of the lord's household. The merchant and his son claimed to be free men; in other words they were no longer willing to be regarded as *ministeriales*. They belonged to the guild. They called upon the assistance of their fellow-members, and six hundred merchants set out for the royal court to ask for help against the abuses of arbitrary seigneurial power. Like new farmland created by land clearance, the urban area thus tended to become privileged. There, after a probationary period which custom normally ordained as one year, bonds of servitude were completely undone.

The struggle was also waged against landlordship. The land inside the towns was not lordless; until recently it had been cultivated as vineyards, gardens or for cereals. Plots now built up would still be burdened with dues, often renders in kind, or even labour services. Many burgesses, still tenants, were no longer farmers; they spent valuable time in wrangling with landlords who demanded wine, corn or services from them. With everyone united behind the 'best men', that is to say, the wealthiest, they secured new arrangements. Sometimes, as at Arras, all rents were redeemed by the urban community. More usually it was the rich who came to an understanding with their former lords: by investing in land the cash they earned in trade, they purchased built-up tenements on town sites and rid themselves of the old agrarian-type burdens. They also asked the sitting tenants for a money rent. This is what happened at Ghent, for example, between 1038 and 1120.

Finally, burgesses attempted to relieve the pressure of banal lordship and to secure 'franchises' (*franchisiae*) or exemptions similar to those from which merchants had profited while still the lord's *ministeriales*. They demanded the abolition of the exactions that were most detrimental to business: the easing of toll rates and the suppression of commercial monopolies reserved by the lord. The lords, with varying degrees of reluctance, bargained with the 'communes' (*communia*) or sworn associations which, modelled on the merchant guilds, combined the townsfolk into fighting partnerships. Most of these negotiated settlements are lost to us. History has mainly preserved the exceptional and tragic features of the communal movement that gradually unfolded throughout Europe, from the harbingers of urban revival in Italy and the shores of the North Sea. From the tenth century, these were the areas with the most advanced and active money economies. Often without any violent clash but by slow negotiations and steady tinkering with custom, the *bannum* was adapted to meet the requirements of an urban economy.

Exploitation did not come to an end. Workers already domiciled in the urban district, and those who were arriving in ever greater numbers to settle down, remained subject to twofold economic control. In the first place they came under the new rule arising from municipal authority. Whether or not the commune had been recognized by the lord, the latter had to abandon some of his prerogatives to the community of inhabitants; grant it a certain amount of judicial autonomy; admit that the town could have its own resources, especially for constructing or repairing its ramparts; and consequently relinquish the collection of taxes. Powers conceded in this way to the urban community were exercised by a magistrature. Broadly speaking, the latter was held entirely by the 'best men', those who had conducted the struggle for liberty and whose power was being extended by family or professional partnerships. The commune's leaders, the *échevins*, the *nobiliores civium* who are referred to at Basle in 1118, originated in the upper ranks of the *ministerialis* class. They were either traders grown rich, or knights from the lord's retinue, for participation by the military aristocracy in urban administration was not peculiar to towns of the Midi. In the rising at Laon, as in the *échevinat* of Arras, warriors played a prominent role in the early twelfth century, and manifold connections – of kinship, marriage and mutual interest – linked them with purely burgess pedigrees. These wealthy individuals

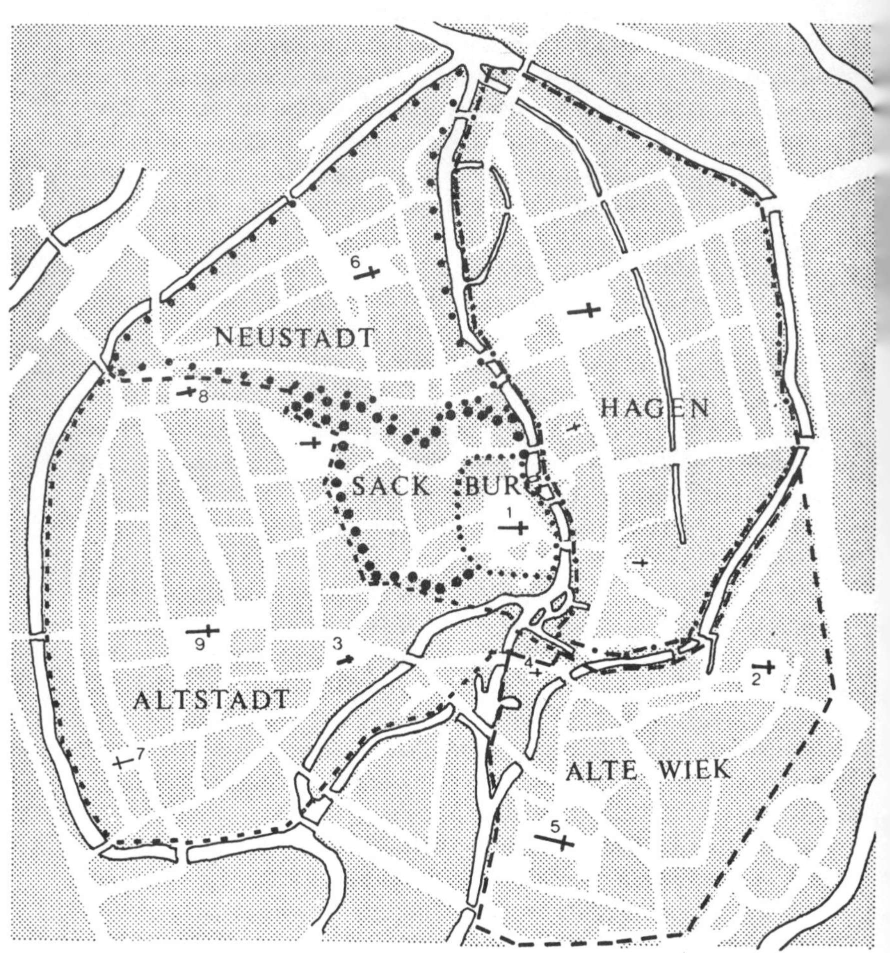

Town quarters

- ...... Dankwarderode enclosure (burgus), tenth century
- — — — Alte Wiek, before 1031
- - - - - Altstadt (old town), after 1100
- —·—·— Hagen, c.1160
- • • • Neustadt (new town), late twelfth century
- ●●●● Sack, 1300

Churches

1. St Blaise's Cathedral, c.1030
2. St Magnus, 1031
3. St Ulric, before 1038
4. St Nicholas, eleventh centur at the latest
5. St Giles, 1115
6. St Andrew, c.1150
7. St Michael, c.1150
8. St Peter, after 1150
9. St Martin, 1180–90

Map 3 Brunswick

owned at least part of the land on which each town stood; its inhabitants were their tenants; and they wielded the judicial, administrative or fiscal powers that the lord had relinquished in the town's favour. The proceeds from the fines they imposed and from the taxes levied in the community's name were utilized for the common good. But urban administrators had a hidden tendency to mistake the funds entrusted to them for the contents of their own coffers, and twist to their own advantage the economic regulations they were empowered to lay down. They were the real beneficiaries of the political conquests and fruits of urban vitality. Hence the community of burgesses began to divide into two classes, of which the dominant one was forging closer links with the lord's court, because of its deeper roots and its origins among the *ministeriales*. This patriciate, always intimately involved in trade yet based on stable family traditions and customs modelled on the nobility's way of life, was the group 'under whose authority the town is governed and in whose hands resides the better part of the law and property', as was said of the *meliores* of Soest in 1165. They had in fact craftily appropriated the lesser attributes of banal lordship. They exploited them less openly than the lord or his *ministeriales* had formerly done, but nevertheless highly profitably and in such a way as to tighten their grip on the urban economy in the second half of the twelfth century.

Most of the powers inherent in the *bannum*, along with its profits, still remained in seigneurial hands. Just as lords of uncultivated tracts had chosen to surrender some of their prerogatives in land-settlement charters so as to attract immigrants and thereby increase the yield from their reduced but regularized fiscal powers, so also did town lords sacrifice some of their rights in the rarely disappointed hope of a marked rise in their incomes. They kept control over the crafts, as well as over the merchant guilds, by the monopolies they conferred on them and the favours they won for them from lords of neighbouring towns. These monopolies and favours were so beneficial to the richest traders that the latter would accede with good grace to requests for loans. By means of *tailles* or *gîtes*, 'at a fixed rate' (*abonati*) but more regularly collected than in the past, and more profitable because immigration was raising the number of households; by means of levies imposed on the movement of goods and coins at bridging-points or in market-places; by means of the higher judicial powers (*haute justice*) they had usually succeeded in retaining; by means of the protection they ensured for Jewish communities and 'migrant settlers' (*advenae*), who as outsiders would pay dearly for their patronage – by all these means the towns were providing such lords with far more money than any country estate. Whatever the scope of the privileges and tax-relief accorded to urban communities, the most powerful twelfth-century lordships were those which were exercising authority over towns. They were also the most prosperous. This explains the eagerness of princes to found new towns – the counts of Flanders, Henry the Lion in Saxony, the Zähringen family in Swabia for example. They were pursuing the same aims as land clearance entrepreneurs: to turn the general movement of growth to their own advantage, to create defensive strongpoints on their estates, to gather together new subjects, and to allow them to get rich in the expectation of taking more from them. And if the burgesses tolerated this exploitation and patricians did not push their claims for autonomy beyond certain limits, this was because each town's lord was the guarantor of peace, and peace was indispensable to business prosperity.

The oaths taken by members of the guild or fellowship were peace oaths. As at Aire-sur-la-Lys, they implied an obligation to 'come to the fray and lend full-hearted support', give chase to trouble-makers in a body, and keep strict order in the town market-place and its approaches – those localities most liable to scuffles and free fights. In fact they assumed the forms and purposes of the collective engagements of the Peace of God. But sworn associations were only an expedient. No man could better enforce security in the town and surrounding district than the lord of the *bannum*, he who had inherited from kings the power to pursue and punish wrong-doers and the duty of instituting justice (in other words, an equitable distribution of wealth); and who undoubtedly was still regarded in the twelfth century, like kings of former times, as master of the magical attributes of fecundity. The mission that Carolingian rulers had once fulfilled of protecting travellers, ensuring peace at markets, maintaining favourable conditions for commercial exchange and upholding that order willed by God which was at the same time the necessary foundation of their mandate to promote fertility – all this was taken over by those, great and small, who were preserving fragments of regalian powers. Thus banal lords contributed to the growth of commercial interchange and monetary circulation not only by their courtly spending, but also by making proper arrangements for protection and control. Here once more is seen the decisive influence of political structures on economic history.

Like the Carolingians, twelfth-century lords were also inclined to concern themselves with commerce for moral reasons. They felt responsible for the well-being of their subjects; they were the guardians of peace and justice. It was to uphold the supernatural order that they intervened, as did the count of Flanders, Charles the Good, in 1126. Commercial life had been disrupted by famine, and its victims were the 'poor' (*pauperes*), those of whom the prince, according to Divine decrees, had to take special care. As Charlemagne might have done in the same circumstances, the count issued prohibitions to re-establish a fair distribution of the fruits of the earth: people were no longer to make beer, but oat-cakes for the needy; costs were to be stabilized; a ceiling was put on wine prices 'so as to discourage merchants from purchasing and stocking wine and, by taking into account the pressing needs of the famine, to encourage them to choose different commodities for their trading, better suited to feeding the poor.'[1] And a careful watch was to be kept over weights and measures, regarding money in particular.

Pre-eminently a royal attribute, the right of mintage had been dissipated at a very early date. Any lord who exercised control of mintage would deduct a portion of the silver brought to his mint for conversion into coins. This tax, the *seignuragium*, became all the more profitable with the growing use of currency. Let us not forget that in the feudal age money was primarily a tool which, like a mill or an oven, the lord placed at the users' disposal while charging a fee. More mints answered the same needs as more flour-mills. Dispersion of the right to strike coins varied from place to place in Europe. It was less marked in the north, where political power was less fragmented and territorial princes such as the dukes of Normandy preserved their monopoly of coinage. This dispersion was less too in the south, no doubt because the velocity of monetary circulation was greater and the coins issued readily became current over a wide area. (Down to the close of the twelfth century, only foreign coins were used throughout Provence.) It was nowhere pushed further than in the kingdom of France. In Berry there were no less than twelve mints, operated by an abbot,

[1] Galbert of Bruges in J. P. Migne (ed.), *Patrologia Latina*, vol. clxvi (Paris 1854), col. 947.

a count, a viscount and various castle lords. An awareness of the currency and exchange value of different coins was first aroused in France. Yet more than the dissemination of mints, a continual depreciation of coins characterized the monetary history of the feudal age. This can be explained initially by the fact that the stock of precious metals remained the same: the exhaustion of the silver mines, particularly at Rammelsberg, caused a fall in output, which by the early twelfth century could scarcely make up for wear and tear on the very thin and consequently fragile coins of this period. The underlying reason for such constant depreciation was the growing need for specie. To meet this need as much as to increase profits from their right to *seignuragium* (the more coins they struck the greater their gain; the lighter these were, the more they struck) lords able to mint money steadily reduced the weight and degree of fineness of the *denarii* they put into circulation. Those of Lucca and Pisa in the second half of the twelfth century weighed three times less than Charlemagne's. In Germany the thickness of coins was so attenuated that they had to be struck on one side only. Those issued by the kings of France were falling in weight – 1·53 grams at the end of the eleventh century, 1·25 grams thirty years later and 1·22 grams *c.* 1200 – at the same time as the silver content of the alloy was falling in quantity. Yet, baser and baser and thinner and thinner, these coins were becoming more and more flexible media of exchange as their increasing speed of circulation caused their value as legal tender to decline. Hereafter money could be used by the poorest people and for the humblest needs. When they were truly desirous of performing the mission with which God had entrusted them, lords would consciously promote greater flexibility of this kind: during the 1125–6 famine, Charles the Good had half-*denarii* issued in Flanders 'for the poor'. Occasionally prompted by concern for the common weal, more often by greed – for in their hands mintage was the most profitable industrial monopoly – these holders of public authority after *c.* 1075 adjusted the currency to the functions it could fulfil in a go-ahead rural world. At the right moment, debasement was a powerful stimulant of economic vitality. None the less, after the middle of the twelfth century, the extension of commercial horizons and the expansion of business interests created a need for means of payment at once less fluctuating and less absurdly small. Rather than use piles of *denarii*, of unequal value because they wore out at different rates and came from different mints, great merchants whose activities reached beyond the confines of a small region had recourse to other measures. For evaluating their wares they would refer to the weight of certain rare commodities, sometimes pepper, more often silver bullion. Hence the mark became the standard unit of value for estimating gross payments. To the extent therefore that money was becoming better adapted to the requirements of the *rural* economy, it was ceasing to cater for advanced sectors of the *urban* one. In the towns a growing proportion of commercial life was evolving without the intervention of cash. This process conflicted with the interests of lords who owned mints, and the most powerful of them took action. They set about issuing a stable, genuine coinage that could be of use to long-range traders. This is what King Henry II of England did when he decided to strike sterling, the strongest currency in Western Europe during the last quarter of the twelfth century.

For the most far-sighted of lords, it was after *c.* 1150 no longer simply a question of keeping up their estate, but of encouraging progress. A prince like Philip of Alsace, who held the county of Flanders from 1168 to 1191, pursued a policy of genuine economic development. His actions were inspired less by the hope of gain than by the desire to fulfil in every way an office that was by nature fundamentally religious and vaguely magical. In a spirit akin to that which moved him to distribute alms and found churches, Count Philip gave military support to merchants from the county in their struggle against taxes imposed on them by the counts of Holland along the road to Cologne; had canals cut across maritime Flanders for linking the Scheldt valley to the coast; and created new ports – Gravelines, Nieuwpoort, Damme – capable of receiving ships of greater tonnage. He wished to be the dispenser of plenty. The same intention motivated the archbishops of Bremen–Hamburg when they organized the agrarian colonization of marshy tracts in their principality, and the Hohenstaufen when they interested themselves in populating and equipping their estates. This was also what prompted Count Thibaut the Great of Champagne to extend beyond the boundaries of his lordship the 'safe-conduct' (*conductus*) or protection he accorded merchants who frequented the fairs in his county.

Indeed, it was probably by the strengthening of security along commercial highways and their essential meeting points, the fairs, – that is to say, by the steady enlargement of the peacemaking function of princes – that the impact of holders of public authority on the development of an exchange economy was most deeply felt. The reconstruction of strong territorial principalities – itself based on the enrichment of princes, the growth of towns and the acceleration of monetary circulation – favoured the evolution of a coherent cycle of mercantile activity in north-western Europe. The wool trade, which led to the appearance of cloth-producing workshops in Artois and Flanders, was organized round a double network of fairs: Winchester, Boston, Northampton, St Ives and Stamford in England; Ypres, Lille, Bruges, Messines and Torhout in Flanders. At the same time markets for horses and cattle that had long been held in certain small country towns of Champagne were changing in nature. They too attracted buyers and sellers of cloth. By 1137 traders from Arras and Flanders were staying in Provins for the duration of the fair; in 1148 money-changers from Vézelay arrived there; and comital authority was used to extend guarantees to visitors to these markets, to make better security arrangements, and to build up an effective jurisdiction, capable of maintaining peace wherever transactions were carried out and on all access routes. Soon merchants from Italy chose these fairs as the most convenient location for meeting Flemish cloth dealers: in 1172 businessmen from Milan came to purchase textiles. In this way there gradually took shape, through the conscious action of a powerful lord who wanted to increase his cash resources, yet who in the first instance knew himself to have been commissioned by God to uphold the peace, what was to become the hub of commercial and financial activity in the West during the thirteenth century.

Central to the revitalized principalities, towns now held the key position in the political order that slowly emerged from the tangle of feudal relations. Towns were the seats of restored authority, military strongpoints of prime importance. With their walls, their permanent garrisons of knights, and their inhabitants who were more familiar with weapons and much better accoutred for fighting than peasants, towns were also the places where the original foundations of princely administration had been laid down around a palace. During the last years of the twelfth century we can see another group rising within the fabric of urban society, barely distinguishable from the upper ranks of the burgess class, and closely related both to them and the prince's court: the body of controlling agents. As a far more flexible and open class of *ministeriales*, it brought together in the prince's service not only men from the higher 'orders' of traditional society, clerics and knights, but also merchants as members of the new *ordo* that had steadily detached itself from the working masses. Merchants had a common culture and a certain common attitude towards worldly values. They could read and write; above all, they were numerate. For them wealth was expressed by means of figures and precise references to monetary units. They were accustomed to reckon their master's power in *denarii*, and in those abstract units of account which were the *solidus* and the *libra*. Money had become the most potent instrument of power by the second half of the twelfth century. It was primarily through the use of money that the prince bound these faithful assistants to himself. They were no longer paid, as they had been until recently, by a landed endowment that had made them irremovable, nor were they retained by ties of personal dependence: they were wage-earners. Through the use of money the prince, exploiting the financial difficulties of the 'barons' (*barones*), recovered regalian rights piecemeal and gradually took back into his own hands the full complement of higher powers, the basis of more oppressive taxation. Through the use of money the prince began to domesticate the knightly class, marshal it in his own service, and recruit mercenary fighters as specialists in effective warfare. For some lords the function of treasure was still of capital importance, just as it had been in the early Middle Ages; yet there was a difference. The reserve of precious metals was no longer an adornment but a tool. It consisted mainly of coins that could be counted and used to acquire more. The prince left the burgesses to amass *denarii* little by little. He then extracted from them as much as he could, by taxation and – even more perhaps – by borrowing.

The principal source of this monetary reserve was to be found inside the towns themselves. The lord of a large town would be very rich, but rich in rights and lands, that is to say, in immovable wealth. If he wanted to mobilize it, he had to ask his burgesses to open up their coffers. Greater financial flexibility, enabling principalities to grow stronger, rested on credit from the townspeople. But the lord would not be the sole debtor of the merchants. From the town came the increasingly rapid and widespread flow of money steadily percolating through the entire rural economy. The towns also provided most of the *denarii* for commuting labour services, defraying transfer charges, and paying for harvest-time purchases in every village.

Townsmen in the late twelfth century, even the wealthiest, were still more than halfway to being peasants. They owned all the land in the immediate neighbourhood and in the districts where their ancestors were born. They farmed these themselves. They drew their supplies from them, and even a fair proportion of the commodities which they sold to travellers or which artisans utilized in their workshops. The provisioning of the urban market depended much less on abstract commerce than on this intimate connection between the towns and surrounding villages, maintained through the rural background of the burgess community and the territorial power retained by every town-based lord. Not all the livestock, leather, wool, wine, corn and dye-plants that traders exported far afield could be derived from their own resources, nor from those of lords whose property interests they managed. They had therefore to buy from country producers. And while the volume of business steadily expanded, while townsmen specialized still more in their chosen occupations and gradually detached themselves from the land, we can sense the growing influence on the countryside of both money and trade. In this way, staging posts were interposed between large towns and peasant producers. These were substantial villages favoured by the far-sightedness of a lord who made up his mind to grant franchises and to provide special protection for a market. All these features were powerful stimulants of dynamic growth. Among the farmworkers, those who lived in these privileged villages would be first to plunge resolutely into an exchange economy. Clauses inserted by such lords in charters of liberties reveal the interest they were taking in trade and money. There is an example in the mid-twelfth-century customary of one small town, La Chapelaude, founded in Berry close by a monastic priory. There the lord still held effective commercial monopolies: no one could sell wine before the lord had disposed of his own vintage, and he had the right to purchase on credit in the town. The inhabitants were permitted to keep weights and measures at home; they sold bread and meat on the spot to passers-by; individuals might carry wine some distance on a donkey or cart to obtain a better price for it; fairs were held during which seigneurial monopolies were void. But the lord was expected to maintain price levels, prevent exorbitant rises that might encourage foreign buyers to take their custom elsewhere, and issue a currency 'useful to himself and to the inhabitants of the *burgus*' that would circulate in the surrounding villages. The economic arrangements that this record illuminates had been exposed to pressures of urban origin. These demands heightened the effects of seigneurial exactions and breathed fresh life into rural production. In these arrangements we can see the spread of what was properly speaking an external sector, in the sense that it did not serve to support the producer and his family and was no longer absorbed by the levies imposed by the lord. It was geared towards selling, that is towards the town. This sector was marginal in relation to the village arable, still devoted principally to feeding people, in other words, to cereal growing. It operated in the enclosed plots for gardening, whence came dye-plants and grapes, and in tracts of land as yet untamed where meat- and wool-producing animals grazed. In the household economy of peasants, it was the field for a little adventure. It was for private gain, the narrow breach by which the profit motive was seeping into peasant consciences. It was for money, indispensable not for making purchases (except iron for tools and beasts for the plough-team) but for delivering to lords what was their due from the land and its occupants. Nevertheless this sector remained very limited in the twelfth century – too much so to satisfy contemporary needs for specie. By means of credit more than commerce, the cash that lords took from the peasantry and spent in the towns found its way back to the countryside from the burgesses' coffers. Despite ecclesiastical prohibitions, traders from the towns, like the Jews, lent at interest to country-folk of all ranks the money they lacked. They lent to the landlord who had to dower his daughter or dub his son a knight, to the squireen preparing for a tournament where the whole district would see him show off and where he might spend in one day, even if he were to win at his sport, a hundred times the amount of money he had, as well as to the humble tenant forced to replace a sick ox or hounded by *taille* collectors. Churchmen denounced these 'usurers' (*usurarii*), these 'grinders of the poor' (*pauperum corrosoribus*), as Guibert of Nogent says, who filled their purses with 'ill-gotten gains' (*turpibus lucris*) and piled up 'mountains of precious metals' (*metallorum plurium montibus*). But in their prime of life, and as long as approaching death did not arouse their fear of sinning, business venturers had few qualms about putting back into circulation as credit the money they had made and not used. Coins were not valuables to which people could become personally attached. They were not usually regarded as reserves of wealth. They were made for circulating. The more they circulated, the greater the returns. The most perceptive of burgesses began to feel that all economic activity, and consequently the very success of their own enterprises, depended on the liveliness of such channels of circulation.

Here we touch upon the factors that moulded the character of the twelfth century. In a civilization that was still basically rural and whose development was inspired by peasant conquests, money came to occupy an unequivocal position, central to every aspect of growth. The part it played was being enlarged and *c.* 1180 that part became dominant. Then opened a new phase, in which the circulation of money was to sustain the whole march of progress through the length and breadth of the European Continent, just as it had in those peripheral borderlands which warfare had brought to life two centuries earlier.

9 Take-off

Still rare remained those for whom money represented anything but a unit of measurement, to be employed in circumstances that were exceptional, almost abnormal, and in any case highly tangential to economic realities. One of the most effective curbs on development lay in the tenacious resistance of certain mental attitudes and of the cultural models reinforcing them. The most solid and fascinating of these had been constructed to serve the dominant 'order' of feudal society – chivalry. It exemplified as the sole outlook worthy of the perfect man characteristic forms of behaviour with regard to wealth: not to produce but to destroy; to live in lordly fashion from the ownership of land and authority over people, the only sources of income not to be held ignoble; and to spend on entertainment without thought for the cost. When in the second half of the twelfth century the financial difficulties of the upper ranks of the lay aristocracy worsened, when the debts of great lords to townsmen accumulated, when the art of governing with money inclined princes to choose their best servants no longer from the nobility but from mercenary warriors and numerate merchants, this model or cult of cavalierish indolence and extravagance became even more entrenched in feudal Europe. It formed the sinews of class consciousness in a social group whose members could see for the first time living examples of preferment from the hitherto completely downtrodden rank and file. They therefore began to feel their economic superiority threatened. One of the themes to become increasingly popular in the late twelfth century in a literature composed for knightly audiences is that of the upstart villein, the man of rustic origins who has climbed up the rungs of the social ladder, taken the place of well-born men in the exercise of seigneurial authority by paying cash for it, and endeavoured to ape their manners while succeeding only in making himself ridiculous and hated. What was shocking about the *nouveau riche* was that he was not unselfish, generous, or immersed in debt like the nobleman. As the advance of a money economy gathered pace, the moral outlook of gentlemen condemned more insistently than ever the profit motive and taste for increasing personal wealth. In the middle of the thirteenth century the treatises on practical husbandry written for England's lay aristocracy – a social class that was supremely anxious to run its landed estates properly, since the strength of the monarchy left it but little authority over the populace – still propose to organize the household economy in terms of spending, place a ceiling on output for that purpose, and take care only that it should be maintained at that level. 'Inspecting the accounts', according to Walter of Henley, 'is done in order to find out how matters stand', not in order to determine what could be invested. And if there happened to be a surplus, his advice was to put it aside for a rainy day, to use it for making the home more comfortable, but not for expanding profits.

The consequences of the noble way of life were all the more profound to the extent, on the one hand, that economic processes were still orientated towards lordship and, on the other, that entrepreneurs in the most dynamic social circles – those who appear as the real pace-makers of growth – pursued no other aim than to enter the nobility and behave like gentlefolk. The fascination of aristocratic cultural models kept up the pressure for social advancement. The most grasping (it seems) put all their effort into making money simply in order to sacrifice these riches one day as free gifts, with regal munificence. The 'upstart villein' of the secular poems is no mythical figure. All *ministeriales* dreamt of forcing their way into the nobility, of living without turning a finger, surrounded by their underlings and receiving the income from a lordship. Townsmen who made their fortunes hastened to acquire rights over land, settle annuities on one another, reject contact with money except indirectly, and make knights of their sons. This is what happened to Hucquedieu of Arras at the beginning of the twelfth century. It also accounts for the education received by Francis of Assisi from his father, a merchant, three-quarters of a century later, which directed him firmly towards military adventure, lyrical singing and boundless generosity. Businessmen were driven more insistently than anyone else to give with both hands, for they knew their souls to be in peril. Through almsgiving they might be saved. The sacrificial gestures performed by early medieval kings, then members of the 'order of fighters' (*ordo bellatorum*) in the eleventh century, gradually became the concern of townsmen in the twelfth. These were the pious gifts collected in towns that made it possible to build Gothic cathedrals, found hospitals at the approaches to suburbs, and launch charitable institutions such as the Order of Trinitarians and confraternities of the Holy Spirit (all of them urban undertakings). The *Gesta* of the bishops of Cambrai tells the story of one Werimbold, who died *c.* 1150. He was extremely rich, probably from usury, and the owner of a spacious stone and timber house flanked by baths, storerooms and stables. His wife used to feed the poor and finally retired to a monastery, as did their four children. After giving twenty-five 'settlers' (*hospites*) to the abbey of St Hubert, providing for the upkeep of a bridge, and enriching the hospital of the Holy Cross by his gifts, he ended his days, stripped bare like a monk, in the service of the destitute. He anticipated by twenty years Peter Waldo, the merchant of Lyons who distributed all his goods to the poor and wanted to share their way of life; and Francis of Assisi by fifty. Of most individual careers it can be said that anything bordering on a profit-making economy was ultimately subsumed in a gift economy, triumphant once again.

The prevailing ideology was thus still nourished by the spirit of largess bequeathed by the early Middle Ages, whose strength was in no way affected by the headlong course of economic change. The Church expressed and propagated this ideology. Although countless canons and monks were busy promoting land clearance, seeking sound investments for money derived from alms, and selling goods for the best possible price, the Church continued to condemn profit and forbade monasteries to practise lending against security. It maintained that work was a curse; to indulge in it could only be an ascetic experience for a well-born man. At Cîteaux, manual tasks were exercises in mortification and, in order to be truly poor, Waldensians refused to work with their hands. The Church set before the rich an ideal of perfection: poverty, renunciation of worldly goods, and contempt for money, which twelfth-century heresiarchs and orthodox preachers, like the monks of the first millennium, deemed a blemish on the soul. For the men of this age as for their more distant forebears, and all the more readily because their material circumstances kept them secure from want, economic realities were of secondary consideration. They were epiphenomena; the real world was of the spirit, on a supernatural plane. It alone merited attention. Subordination of the economic to the ethical was total, and applicable for a long time to come. On 5 December 1360 a decree by the king of France echoed the monetary provisions made by the count of Flanders in 1126, still proclaiming money to be essentially a means of being charitable: 'We ought to make good and strong gold and silver coinage, besides alloyed currency, *whereby the poor can freely be given alms*.' The strength of these moral representations constituted the chief obstacle to lasting capital accumulation. Savings that were not impounded by the fiscal machinery ultimately became immobilized in real estate, or were dispersed as gifts of all kinds. Patrician dynasties did exist in the towns of France, England and Germany in the late twelfth century, but for the most part they had withdrawn from business, concerned as they were with founding chaplaincies and marrying their sons into families belonging to the traditional aristocracy. What boosted economic progress in this period was not the accumulation of money capital, but the accumulation of power over land and people: power to exploit the expansion of rural production, the profits from which served to support an ever more flamboyant style of living; power which for that reason was the motive force behind increasing expenditure and commercial vitality.

There were places in Latin Christendom, however, where mental attitudes were markedly different, namely, the cities of Italy. Here the moral outlook was the same and the fascination of aristocratic models just as lively, as the story of Francis of Assisi proves strikingly. But for two main reasons the general atmosphere presented a contrast. It was not *ministeriales* who had kindled the renewal of an urban economy, but free citizens, owners of landed estates who had used money precociously for managing their resources. To reckon up and earn cash were not practices that anyone would feel obliged to offload on to his household staff because he was anxious about his dignity. Amongst aristocrats who were for the most part urbanized, the sense of profit was accommodating itself to a moral philosophy of good citizenship. In maritime cities such as Venice, Pisa or Genoa it remained difficult longer than elsewhere to distinguish trade and profit-making from pillage, that is to say, from an essentially aristocratic preoccupation. Yet, unlike the Vikings, seafaring adventurers from twelfth-century

Italy did not devote the precious metals they brought back from their expeditions to the adornment of their graves; they used them in business. When the Genoese fleet took possession of Caesarea, a few items were set aside from the spoils for the cathedral treasury and to reward the naval captains, but from what was left one-sixth was assigned to the ships' owners and each of the eight thousand sailors received forty-eight *solidi* in silver and two pounds of pepper; in other words, a small capital sum that might enable them to launch out into commerce. Money was not simply a unit of measurement in Italian towns: it was a living value, capable of bearing economic fruit. Let us have no hesitation in describing such an attitude towards money as 'capitalist'.

This money would be invested prudently in small amounts and in various partnerships. The names of these *societates* differ from one town to another but everywhere one man provided the capital and another used it abroad to realize a profit. They entered into a mutual dependency for a specified, short-term commercial operation.

> I, Giovanni Lissado da Luprio, and my heirs have received in *colleganza* [Latin *collegancia*] from you, Sevasto Orefice, son of Master Tridimundo, and your heirs two hundred *librae* of *denarii*; I for my part have invested one hundred *librae* of *denarii*. Of these, we are to hold two-thirds in a ship whose captain is Gosmiro da Molino. I am to take everything with me in the said ship to Thebes. . . . The profit shall be divided between us half and half.[1]

The document is Venetian and very early, dating from 1073. Countless similar agreements were concluded at Genoa and Pisa. Starting from the middle of the twelfth century, notarial registers provide plenty of such records. When stakes were high, these agreements promised speedy enrichment. Let us take the case of the Genoese, Ansaldo Baialardo, which has been carefully investigated. In 1156, as quite a young man and freed from his father's control (commercial ventures were private concerns), he fell in with a big merchant who put up two hundred *librae*. He himself had nothing. He embarked on a voyage to the ports of Provence, Languedoc and Catalonia. On his return he received his minimal share of the proceeds – eighteen *librae*. Or rather, he did not take physical possession of them, for he and his partner reinvested the whole capital sum, 254 *librae*, in a second voyage that same year.

[1] R. Morozzo della Rocca and A. Lombardo (eds.), *Documenti del commercio veneziano nei secoli XI–XIII* (Turin 1940), vol. i, no. 13, p. 12.

This time the profit was 244 *librae*, or almost 100 per cent; fifty-six *librae* reverted to Ansaldo, besides his personal contribution. Having set out with nothing, he had accumulated a capital sum of seventy-four Genoese *librae* in a few weeks. Two years later, still with the same partner, he mounted a more complex operation. For a voyage to Egypt, Palestine and Syria, they got together a principal of nearly five hundred *librae*, half of which was advanced by various investors; Ansaldo himself risked sixty-four *librae*. On the expedition's return and after sharing the proceeds, he found himself in possession of the sum of 142 *librae*. This was the reward for his trouble and his courage, his due for having braved the perils of the sea, disease and piracy from those who had enriched themselves without stirring an inch and who, like his senior partner, had trebled their outlay in three years. The example is illuminating but in no way exceptional. It affirms the qualitative contrast in economic activity between the coastal cities of the south and the rest of Europe.

Riches thus won on trading expeditions usually finished up immobilized in land-based property interests. We know about those of Sebastiano Ziani, who was doge of Venice in 1172; they consisted of estates in the lagoon district, the Po delta and the country around Padua. When Bishop Otto of Freising set eyes on the towns of Italy in the mid-twelfth century, he was scandalized to see so many sons of artisans and traders attaining knighthood. In Italy, as elsewhere, rich men's sons would aspire to the idle life of the nobility. Yet they dealt with the administration of their country possessions as a business proposition, where money had to bring in a return. They demanded from their tenants not money rents but corn and wine, which they intended to sell themselves. They formed 'companies' (*societates*) with rural workers, operating on the same principle as commercial partnerships: they provided the capital, the peasant his labour and trouble, and the proceeds were shared. In this way, *soccida* and *mezzadria* contracts poured money into plantation, stockraising and farming schemes. This hastened the process of providing rural households with equipment, gave birth to a new and highly productive agrarian landscape around the villages, and stimulated a sharp rise in the growth-rate (except along the coastal plains infested with malaria), from which the urban economy benefited more directly than it did beyond the Alps because of these close monetary connections.

From the last quarter of the eleventh century, traders from Italy were crossing over the Alps in ever greater numbers in search of easier profits. They brought with them to the exits from the Mont Cenis and other passes money, a bag of coins accumulated in the ports and towns of the Po valley, but still rare and precious in this new environment. They also brought techniques which, in the rustic economic system over the mountains, would confer on them that superiority to which Jews had long held a preferential right: practical experience of writing, figures and those contracts of joint capital association which were in use along the whole Mediterranean coastline from Constantinople to Bougie. They also brought another economic outlook, an attitude towards specie, value and profit that was very different from that of peasants and lords. Of the repercussions of this unfamiliar mode of behaviour, of the way in which it could be manipulated and diffused, of the success of Italian ventures and the stir they created, the records reveal almost nothing before the last years of the twelfth century. At that point we enter a fast-changing world.

In the complete absence of statistical data, it is very hard to distinguish particular phases within the broad movement of growth and to mark off dividing lines between them when the pace was altered. Nevertheless it is tempting to recognize signs of an important qualitative change in the 1180s, and there to fix one of the main turning-points in European economic history. This seems to have been the moment when urban vitality came definitely to prevail over that of the countryside everywhere, and no longer just in Italy. Hereafter rural areas would always lag behind in economic development: the peasant yields to the townsman the role of prime mover and, in progressive circles, mental blockages soon give way universally. Two features are revealed: an acceleration of the growth-rate; and the formation across Latin Christendom of a single entity out of three geographical areas hitherto separated by profound economic disparities and now brought together by the multifarious links of trade. This new-found unity had slowly been anticipated by advances in monetary circulation and commercial exchange. It proceeded from the achievements of mercantile adventure.

It is not in Mediterranean Europe that we should look for signs of this change. Here facilities that were then being adopted in other parts of the West had long since been established. Thus in the late twelfth century, while profitable warfare continued uninterrupted in Castile, despoiling Islam of her riches and inducing the Christian ruler to strike a gold currency in 1173, so did the expansion of Italian business activity and the perfecting of various legal forms of *societas* or capitalist partnership. Colonies founded at important points of commercial interchange in Islamic and Byzantine countries by traders from the maritime cities went on growing. Some had already become so intrusive that their presence sparked off outbursts of xenophobic hostility among the local populace, as at Constantinople in 1176 and 1182. The crusading spirit, an initial springboard of overseas adventures and a justification for profit-making and accumulation of monetary capital, waned in the ports of the Adriatic and Tyrrhenian Seas. It seemed clear to every would-be trader that freebooting, weapon in hand, was less rewarding than commercial operations conducted peacefully with the infidel. Not by chance was Francis of Assisi, who wanted to substitute missionary work for the crusade, the son of a merchant who frequented the Champagne fairs. In the coastal cities crusaders were now almost always from beyond the mountains. They were treated as clients; they were willingly advanced cash for their passage, but everyone strove to extract the maximum profit from these simple-minded debtors. For ships' captains, money-changers, traders of all sorts and notaries drawing up contracts, the expedition to the Holy Land was a business proposition. It seemed appropriate to exploit it as such. When Italian traders made their way into England at the close of the twelfth century, their purpose was to recover debts from crusaders. They were paid off in sacks of wool; they intended to sell these in Flanders to cloth manufacturers and, for permission to stay and negotiate the deal, they offered to lend the king money. This is how the business network with its nerve-centres in the big Italian towns, which had developed over a large stretch of the coastlines of Byzantium, the Levant and Barbary and which had lately been extended as far as the Champagne fairs, expanded suddenly and forged a direct link between the Mediterranean world and the North Sea. Here commercial contacts with the far side of the Baltic were imparting renewed vigour to mercantile activities.

In the closing decades of the twelfth century, change was more noticeable on the northern and eastern fringes of Latin Christendom, in the former barbarian part of Europe whose original characteristics had dissolved as it became less underdeveloped. Here, none the less, change came slowly. It took place over a long time as an integral feature of the onset of agrarian expansion. Throughout the twelfth century princes from the eastern plains, eager to increase the yield from their land so as to live as sumptuously as their western neighbours, had attracted and welcomed peasants from Flanders and Germany. They knew them to be masters of more effective techniques, capable of turning to account soils neglected by native farmers. Enlisted by their priests and guided by entrepreneurs who were bent on making a quick fortune out of the organization of land clearance in the prince's name, tens of thousands of pioneers settled east of the Elbe and Danube. They introduced the appropriate type of plough, marked out long, deep furrows in the heavy soils, pushed back marshland and scrub, and extended the corn-growing area. Following their example, independent peasants colonized the margins of their arable plots and little by little replaced shifting tillage by the practice of regular crop-rotation in permanent fields. The influx of immigrants, endowed with lightly burdened holdings, exempt from labour services, and yet making a good return for the landowner, brought about a gradual dissolution of big, slave-based estates and a general improvement in peasant circumstances. By means of tithes and rents, surpluses from cereal production poured into the grain-stores of princes and *locatores*, the men in charge of colonization. By the mid-twelfth century, the agricultural achievement had been far enough advanced to give rise to the flowering of towns.

After *c.* 1150 many changes can be seen in the nature of the old *castra*, the fortifications sheltering princely palaces and cathedrals. They were gradually emptied of their military inhabitants. The warrior retinues disbanded and the knights went off to settle down on country estates, as they did farther west. During the same period, handicraft production in Bohemia ceased to be scattered among villages of specialized servants; it was progressively concentrated in the suburbs of towns. At some distance from the *gród* or fortified enclosure, a cluster of houses would develop round the *rynek* or market-place; here foreigners specializing in trade would set up shop – as at Györ, for instance, in the district known as the *vicus Latinorum*, the 'Latin quarter'. Thus, in former *civitates* economic functions imperceptibly stole a march over others. As in Western Europe, a network of large villages was established, acting as intermediaries between the big urban market and peasant producers. And new towns were founded. The most decisive of these foundations was Lübeck, which arose directly out of the economic preoccupations of a prince who, like his contemporary the count of Flanders, wanted to increase his cash income by taking advantage of commercial activities. By 1138 German traders had settled in the old emporium of Hedeby, a fine location for trading in the Baltic and for supplanting local Scandinavian merchants. When the site was destroyed in 1156–7, the duke of Saxony, Henry the Lion, welcomed the merchant colony. He installed it in a town which had been built a few years before by the count of Holstein, but which the duke founded virtually afresh. Here he instituted a coinage, market-place and toll; 'he sent messengers into the northern realms' offering peace to Russian and Scandinavian princes so that their merchants 'might have freedom of travel and access to his town of Lübeck'; and he promised any traders from the Rhineland and Westphalia willing to live there a set of privileges as favourable as those of Cologne. Baltic commerce was then dominated by peasants from the island of Gotland who found complementary resources in overseas trade. Here too adventurers from Germany had settled by 1133–6, founding a colony at Visby, the island's main port. In 1161 Henry the Lion took under his protection 'the community of merchants from the Roman Empire who frequent the island of Gotland' and helped them secure, in concert with the Gotlanders, an advantageous position on the Novgorod market. In the 1180s capacious ships of considerable tonnage, or 'cogs' (*coggae*), were bringing to Lübeck honey, furs, pitch and tar from the eastern arms of the Baltic. Carried overland as far as the North Sea and transferred to similar ships, these commodities were destined for Flanders and England; meanwhile, boats from the north were already venturing towards the Atlantic. New harbours were prepared for them on the Flemish coast and at La Rochelle, provided with wharves capable of receiving vessels with a large draught. These would set sail again, loaded with salt and wine. Their entry into the Atlantic afforded opportunities to salt-makers from the Bay of Bourgneuf and gave rise to a new and extensive wine-exporting region on Oléron and around La Rochelle. In this way a new meeting-point was established: a crucial one, for it ignited a blaze of rapid growth from east to west of Europe's economic orbit.

In the heart of the West, in England and the old Frankish lands of Gaul and Germania, the turning-point of the late twelfth century stands out most clearly. Here it assumes the aspect of a veritable take-off (*démarrage*). We have already seen many tell-tale signs of its appearance in the course of this essay. The time has come to gather the various strands together.

First, the history of techniques is one whose chronology is in the highest degree uncertain. Yet it is tempting to place the culmination of an early phase of technological development in the last quarter of the twelfth century. At this point in time, while the process of increasing the amount of farmland in Picardy seems to have come to a standstill and signs of mounting demographic pressure multiply, do we not also observe the equipment of working households in the final stages of improvement? Were not mills, forges and plough-horses becoming common? Was not triennial rotation being put into practice? An initial leap forward had enabled output from agricultural endeavour to rise appreciably within a few decades, through the conquest of virgin lands and the refinement of tools. Cereal cultivation had apparently reached some kind of ceiling, and the most distinct advances in rural production were hereafter recorded not in the arable fields, but in the grasslands and forests to meet the more urgent demands from an urban economy. Towns were growing again at this precise moment because of a series of technical improvements. It was now, for example, that the spinning-wheel and the stamp mill (as applied to fulling cloth, treating hemp and forging iron) made possible rapid strides in handicraft production, while ships of greater tonnage facilitated the carriage of heavy merchandise. Further, the discovery of the Freiberg silver mines in Saxony dates from *c.* 1170; and this not only inaugurated the first great period of European mining history, but also supplied the exchange economy with what it needed most – the means to increase the number of coins in circulation.

Second, the impetus of commercial expansion became far more powerful. Whilst Italian traders were trying their luck in England and, conversely, the presence of merchants from Arras is attested at Genoa, traders from this city won from the duke of Burgundy in 1190 privileges that those from Asti already enjoyed; after crossing the Jura and Alps they were allowed to pass through the Burgundian towns at minimal expense when on their way to the Champagne fairs. *Denarii* from Provins began to vie with those of Paris for pre-eminence among the currencies circulating in northern France. Machinery for merchants to meet and make financial settlements started to function regularly at Troyes, Lagny, Bar-sur-Aube and Provins; these towns served for a century as the springboard of long-distance trade throughout Europe. At the same time urban growth became clearly more intensive: the main period of town development in Westphalia commenced *c.* 1180, continuing until about the middle of the fourteenth century.[1] Contemporary with this widespread economic boom, we can detect a relative shrinking of the urban market in regard to handicraft production. This was an effect of growth, determined as it was by competition from other towns, the proliferation of small rural townships, and a return to the countryside of certain operations such as those of the smith. It made necessary a stricter organization of production and so led to greater emphasis on craft regulations. Lords of towns had scarcely given recognition to artisans till now, except to levy taxes on them as on former household servants; at Paris, London and Toulouse they began to give their attention to grouping them into more rigorously constituted craft guilds. Then, as proof of the greater briskness of trade, prices rose, and quickly too. The earliest series of manorial accounts, which come from England, show the evolution of the price of corn. In comparison with the period 1160–79 inclusive, it was 40 per cent higher between 1180 and 1199, and 130 per cent higher between 1200 and 1219 – an increase of 25 per cent in terms of the number of pennies and 50 per cent when taking into consideration the silver content of the coins. These figures indicate simultaneously a progressive depreciation of the coinage and a sharp rise in prices, both caused by the build-up of exchange.

Third, in the last quarter of the twelfth century, an initial erosion of primitive economic attitudes can be discerned in rural society. At a time when a renewal of the lesser aristocracy began to manifest itself clearly by the entrance of individuals of humble birth into the knightly class (hence the formulation of the theme of the parvenu that was spreading in chivalric literature) and when the propensity for more lavish spending began to introduce into the finances of small country squires an embarrassment comparable to that experienced by princes and prelates for the last hundred years or so, knights could no longer find among their kinsmen or noble neighbours adequate credit facilities. They too had to borrow from townsmen and sell them fragments of their estates. No longer able to bear the costs of entertaining, some refrained from dubbing their

[1] C. Haase, *Die Entstehung der westfälischen Städte* (Münster 1960), pp. 39–74, 285–6.

sons as knights and clung to their privileges as nobles all the more tenaciously. In England we can see new methods of farm management being practised: great Benedictine abbeys ceased to put their manors to farm *c.* 1180 and resumed direct exploitation of them. The desire of lords to make their land yield more led to various innovations in the English countryside. This accounts for their anxiety to bring the status of villeins close to that of former slaves, so as to exploit them more harshly, and to have the administration of farm bailiffs strictly controlled by accountants who knew how to reckon up exactly. To resume direct exploitation was a decision of supreme importance for economic history: the series of manorial accounts in England starts in the last quarter of the twelfth century, making possible the first statistical approach to economic phenomena (the movement of corn prices can be traced from this point onwards) and marks the dawn of quantitative history in Europe. The appearance of these book-keeping documents reveals above all a change in outlook: the desire to find out with precision how matters stood, to draw up a balance-sheet, and to estimate profitability – representing a further advance of the profit motive. The financial experts whom princes took into their service, such as those who calculated the revenues of the count of Flanders in 1181, were conveyors of this spirit. They brought to rural areas the practices of town merchants; they diffused them by slow degrees among small-scale entrepreneurs like the *ministeriales*, 'farmers', and overseers of sites where land was being cleared; they whetted their appetites for profit and drove them to play a still more active role in the pursuit of economic development. The spirit of the urban economy was instilled deep into the countryside by these men.

I have chosen the 1180s as the chronological limit to this exploratory essay because this seems to me to correspond to a major turning-point in European economic history. The same applies to our initial point of departure, the seventh century, though less definitely because the documents are scarcer. In this earlier period a movement of growth had commenced. Progress in agricultural production had sustained it and met the requirements of a military aristocracy who owned the land, terrorized those who laboured on it, and had as their prime concern to make their munificence ever more ostentatious. Before the first millennium output from farmwork had remained low; growth had been mainly that of a war economy, with slavery and pillage forming its twin foundations. In the feudal peace that had then been established, the determining conquests had gradually become those of the peasantry, goaded by seigneurial constraints to keep on producing more, increasingly numerous and therefore increasingly free to manage their labour in their own way and to sell its fruits. The change attributed to the end of the twelfth century did not affect the rate of agricultural progress: its pace did not slacken, but was to be maintained for several decades longer. What changed radically was its function: until now, agriculture had been the main driving force behind all development; henceforth it became an auxiliary. During the late twelfth century we can discern the first symptoms of landhunger, which before long was to bring about a lasting deterioration in peasant circumstances. The rural economy, hereafter in a subordinate position, was destined to experience the pressures of domination by the urban economy. About the year 1180, throughout Europe, the age of the businessman was at hand. After 1180 the profit motive steadily undermined the spirit of largess. Nostalgia for this virtue still lingered, yet it adorned none but mythical heroes, at once symbols and guardians of values that medieval people had long extolled as living and supreme. Such had been the early Middle Ages: an age of peasants who worked the land; an age of warriors who were their lords.

Bibliographical Guide

Here I have chosen the most accessible and illuminating works. Further references can be found in the bibliographies of these books.

I. GENERAL WORKS

M. Bloch, *La société féodale*, 2 vols (Paris 1939–40); trans. L. A. Manyon, *Feudal Society*, 2nd edn (London 1962).

R. Boutruche, *Seigneurie et féodalité*, vol. i, *Le premier âge des liens d'homme à homme*, 2nd edn (Paris 1968); vol. ii, *L'apogée (XIe–XIIIe siècles)* (Paris 1970).

Caratteri del secolo VII in Occidente, 2 vols (Settimane di studio del Centro italiano di studi sull'alto medioevo, 5) (Spoleto 1958).

C. M. Cipolla (ed.), *Storia dell'economia italiana*, vol. i, *Secoli settimo-diciassettesimo* (Turin 1959).

C. M. Cipolla (ed.), *The Fontana Economic History of Europe*, vol. i, *The Middle Ages* (London and Glasgow 1972).

R. Doehaerd, *Le haut moyen âge occidental: économies et sociétés* (Paris 1971).

W. Hensel, *La naissance de la Pologne* (Wroclaw 1966); English trans. of the original Polish by H. Andrews and K. Klinger, *The Beginnings of the Polish State* (Warsaw 1960).

I problemi comuni dell'Europea post-carolingia (Settimane di studio del Centro italiano di studi sull'alto medioevo, 2) (Spoleto 1955).

I. M. Kulisher, *Allgemeine Wirtschaftsgeschichte des Mittelalters und der Neuzeit*, vol. i, *Das Mittelalter*, 2nd edn (Berlin 1958).

É. Lesne, *Histoire de la propriété ecclésiastique en France*, 6 vols (Paris 1910–43).

R. S. Lopez, *The Commercial Revolution of the Middle Ages, 950–1350* (Englewood Cliffs 1971).

G. Luzzatto, *Storia economica d'Italia*, vol. i, *L'antichità e il medioevo* (Rome 1949).

L. Musset, *Les peuples scandinaves au moyen âge* (Paris 1951).

H. Pirenne, *Histoire économique et sociale du moyen âge*, revised edn by H. van Werveke (Paris 1963); English trans. of the 1933 edn by I. E. Clegg, *Economic and Social History of Medieval Europe* (London 1936).

É. Salin, *La civilisation mérovingienne, d'après les sépultures, les textes et le laboratoire*, 4 vols (Paris 1949–59).

Second International Conference of Economic History, Aix-en-Provence, 1962, vol. ii, *Middle Ages and Modern Times* (Paris 1965).

J. Vicens Vives, *Manual de historia económica de España*, 5th edn (Barcelona 1967); trans. F. M. López-Morillas, *An Economic History of Spain* (Princeton 1969).

P. Wolff and F. Mauro, *Histoire générale du travail*, vol. ii, *L'âge de l'artisanat, Ve–XVIIIe siècle* (Paris 1960).

2. ECOLOGY, DEMOGRAPHY AND TECHNOLOGY

A. M. Bautier, 'Les plus anciennes mentions de moulins hydrauliques, industriels et de moulins a vent', *Bulletin philologique et historique* for 1960, vol. ii, pp. 567–626.

M. Bloch, 'Les "inventions" médiévales', *Annales d'histoire économique et sociale*, vii (1935), pp. 634–43; trans. J. E. Anderson, 'Mediaeval "inventions"' in *Land and Work in Mediaeval Europe: Selected Papers by Marc Bloch* (London 1967), pp. 169–85.

H. C. Darby (ed.), *An Historical Geography of England before AD 1800* (Cambridge 1936).

T. K. Derry and T. I. Williams, *A Short History of Technology from the Earliest Times to AD 1900* (Oxford 1960).

G. Fournier, *Le peuplement rural en Basse Auvergne durant le haut moyen âge* (Paris 1962).

B. Gille, 'L'industrie métallurgique champenoise au moyen âge', *Revue d'histoire de la sidérurgie*, i (1960), pp. 13–20.

B. Gille, *Histoire générale des techniques*, vol. i, *Les origines de la civilisation technique* (Paris 1962).

H. Jankuhn, 'Die Entstehung der mittelalterlichen Agrarlandschaft in Angeln', *Geografiska annaler*, xliii (1961), pp. 151–64.

E. Le Roy Ladurie, *Histoire du climat depuis l'an mil* (Paris 1967);

trans. B. Bray, *Times of Feast, Times of Famine: a History of Climate since the Year 1000* (New York 1971).

J. C. Russell, *British Medieval Population* (Albuquerque 1948).

J. C. Russell, *Late Ancient and Medieval Population* (Philadelphia 1958).

J. Schneider, 'Fer et sidérurgie dans l'économie européenne du XIe au XVIIe siècles' in *Actes du colloque international: le fer à travers les âges, hommes et techniques* (Nancy 1956), pp. 111–41.

C. Singer, E. J. Holmyard, A. R. Hall and T. I. Williams (eds), *A History of Technology*, vol. ii, *The Mediterranean Civilizations and the Middle Ages c. 700 BC to c. AD 1500* (Oxford 1956).

R. Sprandel, *Das Eisengewerbe im Mittelalter* (Stuttgart 1968).

A. E. Verhulst, *Histoire du paysage rural en Flandre de l'époque romaine au XVIIIe siècle* (Brussels 1966).

L. White, jr, *Medieval Technology and Social Change* (Oxford 1962).

3. RURAL ECONOMY

(*a*) *General Works*

W. Abel, *Deutsche Agrargeschichte*, vol. ii, *Geschichte der deutschen Landwirtschaft vom frühen Mittelalter bis zum 19. Jahrhundert*, 2nd edn (Stuttgart 1967).

Agricoltura e mondo rurale in Occidente nell'alto medioevo (Settimane di studio del Centro italiano di studi sull'alto medioevo, 13) (Spoleto 1966).

H. Aubin and W. Zorn (eds), *Handbuch der deutschen Wirtschafts und Sozialgeschichte* (Stuttgart 1971).

M. Bloch, *Les caractères originaux de l'histoire rurale française*, 2 vols, 3rd edn (Paris 1968); English trans. of the 2nd edn by J. Sondheimer, *French Rural History: an Essay on its Basic Characteristics* (London 1966).

G. Duby, *L'économie rurale et la vie des campagnes dans l'Occident médiéval*, 2 vols (Paris 1962); trans. C. Postan, *Rural Economy and Country Life in the Medieval West* (London 1968).

G. Franz, *Deutsche Agrargeschichte*, vol. iv, *Geschichte des deutschen Bauernstandes vom frühen Mittelalter bis zum 19. Jahrhundert* (Stuttgart 1970).

P. J. Jones, 'Per la storia agraria italiana nel medioevo: lineamenti e problemi', *Rivista storica italiana*, lxxvi (1964), pp. 287–348.

F. Lütge, *Deutsche Agrargeschichte*, vol. iii, *Geschichte der deutschen Agrarverfassung vom frühen Mittelalter bis zum 19. Jahrhundert*, 2nd edn (Stuttgart 1968).

M. M. Postan (ed.), *The Cambridge Economic History of Europe*, vol. i, *The Agrarian Life of the Middle Ages*, 2nd edn (Cambridge 1966).

B. H. Slicher van Bath, *The Agrarian History of Western Europe AD 500–1850*, trans. O. Ordish (London 1963).

(*b*) *Special Studies*

A. Déléage, *La vie rurale en Bourgogne jusqu'au début du XIe siècle*, 3 vols (Paris 1940).

G. Despy, 'Villes et campagnes aux IXe et Xe siècles: l'exemple du pays mosan', *Revue du Nord*, l (1968), pp. 145–68.

R. Dion, *Histoire de la vigne et du vin en France, des origines au XIXe siècle* (Paris 1959).

P. Dollinger, *L'évolution des classes rurales en Bavière depuis la fin de l'époque carolingienne jusqu'au milieu du XIIIe siècle* (Paris 1949).

F. R. H. du Boulay, *The Lordship of Canterbury: an Essay on Medieval Society* (London 1966).

G. Duby, *La société aux XIe et XIIe siècles dans la région mâconnaise* (Paris 1953).

H. P. R. Finberg, *Tavistock Abbey: a Study in the Social and Economic History of Devon*, 2nd edn (Newton Abbot 1969).

R. Fossier, *La terre et les hommes en Picardie, jusqu'à la fin du XIIIe siècle*, 2 vols (Paris and Louvain 1968).

D. Herlihy, 'The agrarian revolution in southern France and Italy 801–1150', *Speculum*, xxxiii (1958), pp. 23–41.

R. Lennard, *Rural England 1086–1135: a Study of Social and Agrarian Conditions* (Oxford 1959).

W. Metz, 'Die Agrarwirtschaft im karolingischen Reiche' in H. Beumann (ed.), *Karl der Grosse: Lebenswerk und Nachleben*, vol. i, *Persönlichkeit und Geschichte* (Düsseldorf 1965), pp. 489–500.

E. Miller, *The Abbey and Bishopric of Ely: the Social History of an Ecclesiastical Estate from the Tenth Century to the Early Fourteenth Century* (Cambridge 1951).

C. E. Perrin, *Recherches sur la seigneurie rurale en Lorraine d'après les plus anciens censiers, IXe–XIIe siècle* (Paris 1935).

C. E. Perrin, 'Observations sur le manse dans la région parisienne au début du IXe siècle', *Annales d'histoire sociale*, iv (1945), part 2, pp. 39–52.

M. M. Postan, *The Famulus: the Estate Labourer in the Twelfth and Thirteenth Centuries* (Cambridge 1954).

J. A. Raftis, *The Estates of Ramsey Abbey: a Study in Economic Growth and Organization* (Toronto 1957).

A. E. Verhulst, *De Sint-Baafsabdij te Gent en haar grondbezit, VIIe–XIVe eeuw* (Brussels 1958).

C. Verlinden, *L'esclavage dans l'Europe médiévale*, vol. i, *Péninsule ibérique, France* (Bruges 1955).

4. MONEY, TOWNS AND MERCHANTS

(*a*) *Money*

M. Bloch, 'Le problème de l'or au moyen âge', *Annales d'histoire économique et sociale*, v (1933), pp. 1–34; trans. J. E. Anderson, 'The problem of gold in the Middle Ages' in *Land and Work in Mediaeval Europe: Selected Papers by Marc Bloch* (London 1967), pp. 186–229.

M. Bloch, *Esquisse d'une histoire monétaire de l'Europe* (Paris 1954).

C. M. Cipolla, *Money, Prices and Civilization in the Mediterranean World, Fifth to Seventeenth Century* (Princeton 1956).

C. M. Cipolla, *Le avventure della lira* (Milan 1958).

R. Doehaerd, 'Les réformes monétaires carolingiennes', *Annales – économies, sociétés, civilisations*, vii (1952), pp. 13–20.

G. Duby, 'Économie domaniale et économie monétaire: le budget de l'abbaye de Cluny entre 1080 et 1155', *Annales – économies, sociétés, civilisations*, vii (1952), pp. 155–71.

R. Kiersnowski, 'Coins in the economic and political structure of states between the ninth and the eleventh centuries' in T. Manteuffel and A. Gieysztor (eds), *L'Europe aux IXe–XIe siècles: aux origines des états nationaux* (Warsaw 1968), pp. 453–60.

T. Lalik, 'La circulation des métaux précieux en Pologne du Xe au XIIe siècle', *Acta Poloniae Historica*, xviii (1968), pp. 131–54.

R. S. Lopez, 'An aristocracy of money in the early Middle Ages', *Speculum*, xxviii (1953), pp. 1–43.

Moneta e scambi nell'alto medioevo (Settimane di studio del Centro italiano di studi sull'alto medioevo, 8) (Spoleto 1961).

P. H. Sawyer, 'The wealth of England in the eleventh century', *Transactions of the Royal Historical Society*, 5th series, xv (1965), pp. 145–64.

H. van Werveke, 'Monnaies, lingots ou marchandises? Les instruments d'échange aux XIe et XIIe siècles', *Annales d'histoire économique et sociale*, iv (1932), pp. 452–68.

(*b*) *Towns and Urban Society*

J. B. Akkerman, 'Het koopmansgilde van Tiel omstreeks het jaar 1000', *Tijdschrift voor rechtsgeschiedenis*, xxx (1962), pp. 409–71.

P. Bonnassie, 'Une famille de la campagne barcelonaise et ses activités économiques aux alentours de l'an mil', *Annales du Midi*, lxxvi (1964), pp. 261–303.

É. Coornaert, 'Des confréries carolingiennes aux gildes marchandes', *Mélanges d'histoire sociale*, ii (1942), pp. 5–21.

P. Dollinger, *La Hanse, XIIe–XVIIe siècles* (Paris 1964); trans. D. S. Ault and S. H. Steinberg, *The German Hansa* (London and Basingstoke 1970).

E. Ennen, *Frühgeschichte der europäischen Stadt* (Bonn 1953).

La città nell'alto medioevo (Settimane di studio del Centro italiano di studi sull'alto medioevo, 6) (Spoleto 1959).

'L'artisanat et la vie urbaine en Pologne médiévale', *Kwartalnik historii kultury materialnej*, x (1962), pp. 279–571.

P. S. Leicht, *Operai, artigiani, agricoltori in Italia dal secolo VI al XVI* (Milan 1946).

Les origines des villes polonaises (Congrès et colloques de la VIe section de l'École pratique des hautes études, 2) (Paris and The Hague 1960).

J. Lestocquoy, *Aux origines de la bourgeoisie: les villes de Flandre et d'Italie sous le gouvernement des patriciens, XIe–XVe siècles* (Paris 1952).

J. H. Mundy and P. Riesenberg, *The Medieval Town* (Princeton 1958).

H. Planitz, *Die deutsche Stadt im Mittelalter, von der Römerzeit bis zu den Zunftkämpfen* (Graz and Cologne 1954).

J. L. Romero, *La revolución burguesa en el mundo feudal* (Buenos Aires 1967).

C. Sánchez-Albornoz, *Estampas de la vida en León durante el siglo X*, 3rd edn (Madrid 1934).

F. Vercauteren, *Étude sur les 'civitates' de la Belgique seconde* (Brussels 1934).

C. Violante, *La società milanese nell'età precomunale* (Bari 1953).

(*c*) *Trade*

J. Dhondt, 'Les problèmes de Quentovic' in *Studi in onore di Amintore Fanfani*, vol. i, *Antichità e alto medioevo* (Milan 1962), pp. 181–248.

R. Doehaerd, 'Au temps de Charlemagne et des Normands: ce qu'on vendait et comment on le vendait dans le bassin parisien', *Annales – économies, sociétés, civilisations*, ii (1947), pp. 266–80.

T. Endemann, *Markturkunde und Markt in Frankreich und Burgund vom 9. bis 11. Jahrhundert* (Constance 1964).

J. le Goff, *Marchands et banquiers du moyen âge*, 3rd edn (Paris 1966).

P. Grierson, 'Commerce in the Dark Ages: a critique of the evidence', *Transactions of the Royal Historical Society*, 5th series, ix (1959), pp. 123–40.

H. Jankuhn, 'Die frühmittelalterlichen Seehandelsplätze im Nord- und Ostseeraum' in T. Mayer (ed.), *Studien zu den Anfängen des europäischen Städtewesens* (Constance 1958), pp. 451–98.

A. R. Lewis, *Naval Power and Trade in the Mediterranean, AD 500–1100* (Princeton 1951).

A. R. Lewis, 'Le commerce et la navigation sur les côtes atlantiques de la Gaule du Ve au VIIIe siècle', *Le moyen âge*, lx (1953), pp. 249–98.

R. S. Lopez and I. W. Raymond, *Medieval Trade in the Mediterranean World* (London 1955).

M. M. Postan (ed.), *The Cambridge Economic History of Europe*, vol. ii, *Trade and Industry in the Middle Ages* (Cambridge 1952).

M. M. Postan, E. E. Rich and E. Miller (eds), *The Cambridge Economic History of Europe*, vol. iii, *Economic Organization and Policies in the Middle Ages* (Cambridge 1963).

Recueils de la Société Jean Bodin, vol. v, *La foire* (Brussels 1953).

Y. Renouard, *Les hommes d'affaires italiens du moyen âge*, 2 vols (Paris 1949).

C. Warnke, *Die Anfänge des Fernhandels in Polen* (Würzburg 1964).

Index